Home Inspector's Handbook

Phil Parnham
MRICS

and

Chris Rispin
FRICS

Acknowledgements

The authors and publishers wish to thank the following for permission to reproduce copyright material:

The 'Home Inspectors Inspection and Reporting Requirements' (formerly known as the Reporting Requirements and Guidance Notes) and the format of the 'Home Condition Report' are reproduced with the kind permission of the Office of the Deputy Prime Minister.

Note: The Home Inspectors Inspection and Reporting Requirements and Home Condition Report format are under constant review. The content of this publication is based upon the draft of Home Inspectors Inspection and Reporting Requirements available at the time of going to press (April 2005) and will be the subject of further and regular revision as is found necessary.

No responsibility for loss occasioned to any person acting or refraining from action as a result of the material included in this publication can be accepted by the authors or the publisher.

BRE material reproduced by permission of BRE Bookshop.

The diagram in Figure 1.1 is reproduced from RICS Safe As…steps to becoming a Home Inspector

The definitions in Table 3.1 are reproduced by permission of NHS Estates.

Dedications

General

Many thanks to Stephen O'Hara and Stuart Fairlie of Elmhurst Energy Systems Limited for their help and assistance with Chapter Five of the Handbook.

Personal

To Joan and Chris, the other two women in my life.

Phil Parnham

The list of those who gave me the space to contribute to this book is huge and very distinguished, thanks.

Chris Rispin

Published by RICS Business Services Limited
a wholly owned subsidiary of
The Royal Institution of Chartered Surveyors
under the RICS Books imprint
Surveyor Court
Westwood Business Park
Coventry CV4 8JE
UK
www.ricsbooks.com

No responsibility for loss occasioned to any person acting from or refraining from action as a result of the material included in this publication can be accepted by the authors or publisher.

ISBN 1 84219 203 5

Reprinted 2005

Typeset by Columns Design Ltd, Reading, RG4 7DH. UK
Printed by Cromwell Press Ltd, Trowbridge, Wiltshire

Contents

2 THE HOME CONDITION INSPECTION

4   WRITING THE HOME CONDITION REPORT

Preface

A revolution is about to take place in the residential property sector. The *Housing Act* 2004 will radically change the way homes are bought and sold in England and Wales to an unprecedented extent. Established practices and interests will be turned on their heads as new competitors challenge the dominance of traditional stakeholders. The market will be split wide open allowing a range of new entrants to operate in a sector usually closed to them as the Home Inspector is born. The Internet and other new technologies will ensure that working practices and customer relationships will be changed forever.

The *Housing Act* 2004 allows for the introduction of the Home Information Pack, which will include a Home Condition Report. This is an entirely new product, which will challenge existing practitioners to produce an objective assessment on the condition of residential property that can be clearly understood by the layperson. The purpose of this book is to provide guidance on how this can be achieved.

The preparations for the Home Information Pack are approaching the point where many commentators are confident that the sector will be ready for the 2007 target date. As this book goes to the printer, the first batch of Home Inspectors will be getting their licence and the Home Condition Report is developing a robustness that promises to make it a successful and popular product. It is against this background of change that we have written this book, focusing on just one aspect of the new system – the Home Condition Report and the role of the Home Inspector. This is not another variation on a familiar survey format, or a fad or fashion that will soon be revised or even abolished; it is an entirely new way of assessing the condition of buildings. Anyone that underestimates the scale of the difference and fails to respond will risk being left behind in a fast moving market. If the residential sector provides you with a living then we think you need to read this book.

It has been written principally for those people who want to qualify as a Home Inspector and are already following the assessment process, or those who are thinking of registering soon. It will also be of interest and use to those who do not intend to become Home Inspectors, but are involved in the process of buying and selling residential properties. This may include:

- estate agents;
- legal advisors;
- lenders;
- associated specialists such as structural engineers and service engineers, and
- sellers and buyers!

The Handbook has been written to complement two important documents:

- The National Occupational Standards for Home Inspectors; and
- Home Inspectors Inspection and Reporting Requirements.

Where relevant, a short summary has been included at the start of each chapter, identifying which parts of the National Occupational Standards the particular chapter relates to. This will enable those progressing towards their Diploma in Home Inspection to acquire the necessary underpinning knowledge.

The Handbook will be of most use to residential practitioners who have some practical experience of assessing the condition of properties, since most chapters assume a certain level of background knowledge. However, we hope the book is accessible to a wide range of readers; it will be of increasing use to new entrants to the sector as they progress through the qualification.

The Home Inspector's Handbook has been written during a time of vast change for the initiative. We have already seen four different versions of the Home Inspectors Inspection and Reporting Requirements, and this is not the only change! New methodologies relating to the collection of data for the SAP energy report have yet to be finalised and many other issues are still being refined. For example, the Home Inspectors Adjudication Service is still in its infancy, while a lot of detail still needs to be added to important areas such as conflicts of interest and insurance arrangements. Despite this, in partnership with the publishers, we decided that an early publication that is still able to offer valuable guidance on some unresolved issues will be more useful to the residential sector than a 'definitive guide' published much later. Hundreds of practitioners from all backgrounds have registered an interest in becoming a Home Inspector and if we are going to meet the government target of being ready to go live in 2007, then training must begin now.

The information, techniques, and procedures in this book have been tried and tested in our technical training courses for Home Inspectors, where they have proved to be durable and robust. Consequently, we are confident that you will find this a useful reference that complements the formally issued guidance.

Phil Parnham & Chris Rispin, April 2005

Foreword

Everyone knows that the process of buying and selling homes can be fraught with difficulty, often resulting in stress and frustration. Too often transactions fail and people's time and money is wasted. For an individual family this is frustrating – for the nation it is profligate.

Providing essential information about the home 'up front' through the Home Information Pack will help make the process more transparent and efficient, addressing the underlying problems that cause delay and failure. We intend that Home Condition Reports will be an essential part of the Home Information Pack, to ensure that buyers and sellers have a sound basis on which to agree the terms of the deal.

To complete the new Home Condition Report competently, even the most experienced surveyor will need to acquire new skills. The Home Condition Report will be an objective report on the condition of the property that will be in a standard format prepared in accordance with National Occupational Standards. It will cover matters of importance to a buyer – such as the condition of the interior and exterior of the property, how energy efficient it is, as well as identifying any defects or other matters requiring attention.

The Home Condition Report can be relied upon by the buyer, seller and the buyer's mortgage lender.

Relying on the report, the seller can decide whether to obtain estimates or repair any defects identified in the report. The buyer can confidently agree a price for the home with the benefit of reliable information on its condition and lenders can rely on the report to help decide whether the property offers adequate security for a loan.

RICS has been a strong supporter of Home Information Packs since 1997 and has been giving impartial advice on the home buying reforms through the government's advisory groups. RICS has been actively involved in the development of the Home Condition Report as well as the standards that Home Inspectors will be required to meet through the Diploma in Home Inspection.

The *Home Inspector's Handbook* will be a valuable tool for all those wishing to take up the challenge and aspire to become Home Inspectors. I hope that many will seize the opportunity, and get in early.

Rt Hon Keith Hill MP
Minister of State for Housing and Planning

1 How to become a Home Inspector

INTRODUCTION

The government first introduced legislation to reform the house buying process in 1997. This failed in the last few minutes of that parliament and the new Housing Bill was reintroduced into parliament on 8th December 2003 after a period of public consultation and pre-legislative scrutiny. This successfully passed through parliament, and the *Housing Act* received Royal Assent in November 2004.

The main effect will be the creation of the Home Information Pack, which will have to be assembled before a property can be marketed. The content of the Home Information Pack is prescribed in the legislation and includes:

- terms of sale;
- evidence of title;
- replies to standard preliminary enquiries made on behalf of buyers;
- copies of any planning, listed building and building regulations consents and approvals;
- copies of warranties and guarantees for new properties;
- guarantees for any work carried out on the property;
- replies to local searches; and
- a Home Condition Report based on a professional inspection of the property, including an energy efficiency assessment.

Additionally, a Home Information Pack for leasehold properties includes:

- a copy of the lease;
- most recent service charge accounts and receipts;
- building insurance policy details and payment receipts;
- regulations made by the landlord or management company; and
- memorandum and articles of the landlord or management company.

An important part of the Home Information Pack is the Home Condition Report – an impartial report on the condition (not the value) of the property. Only a licensed Home Inspector can produce a Home Condition Report. The licensing scheme has been established and will be administered by the Home Inspector Certification Board (HICB). The government hopes that the scheme will become effective in 2007, with voluntary schemes beginning as early as June 2006.

THE DIPLOMA IN HOME INSPECTION

The process of becoming a Home Inspector is well defined and described in this section. We have tried to simplify the explanation, but a number of acronyms do occur. To help you, we have included a glossary in Appendix A.

Before Home Inspectors can practice, they will have to get a licence by obtaining a Vocationally Related Qualification (VRQ) called the Diploma in Home Inspection. This has been established and administered by the Awarding Body for the Built Environment (ABBE), based at the University of Central England.

A VRQ is a competency-based framework within which candidates must demonstrate their competence at carrying out specified roles, and this is where a VRQ differs from traditional qualifications such as HNDs and degrees. The VRQ assesses your ability to do something competently rather than the ability to pass exams that are focused on testing knowledge and understanding, not performance.

THE NATIONAL OCCUPATIONAL STANDARDS FOR HOME INSPECTORS

The VRQ is based on the National Occupational Standards (NOS) for Home Inspectors. This describes the skills and knowledge required to be a Home Inspector, and identifies best practice and competence. The NOS were produced by a working party on behalf of the Office of the Deputy Prime Minister and break down the role of the Home Inspector into component parts, called **units**. These units are further broken down into two or more **elements** relating to an activity that a Home Inspector must be competent to carry out. Each element carries the following information:

- performance criteria that a competent Home Inspector must be able to do;
- related knowledge and understanding that a Home Inspector must have; and

- the range (or scope) of different situations that a Home Inspector must be competent to deal with.

To show that you are competent in any particular element or across a whole unit, you will have to demonstrate that you can cope with a variety of different situations and possess the appropriate knowledge and understanding.

Every qualification that is listed in the National Qualification Framework (NQF) is usually given an educational 'level'. The VRQ in Home Inspection has been set at level four, putting it on the same level as a pass degree (not including Honours) or a HND. The Qualifications and Curriculum Authority define this as:

'Competence which involves the application of knowledge and skills in a broad range of complex, technical or professional work activities performed in a wide variety of contexts and with a substantial degree of personal responsibility and autonomy. Responsibility for the work of others and the allocation of resources is often present.'

The NOS in Home Inspection is a large document and a summary of the different units and elements has been included in Appendix B. A complete copy can be downloaded from www.assetskills.org.

Assessment centres

The Diploma in Home Inspection can only be taken at assessment centres approved by ABBE to assess candidates against the competencies stipulated in the NOS. Assessment centres will typically include further and higher education establishments, professional bodies and private sector organisations, including property sector companies or commercial training organisations.

The following organisations are either approved assessment centres or currently seeking approval:

- Royal Institution of Chartered Surveyors (RICS);
- Association of Building Engineers (ABE);
- Institute of Management and Building Maintenance (IMBM);
- Surveyors and Valuers Accreditation (SAVA); and
- ABBE's own assessment centre.

As the scheme progresses, it is anticipated that more assessment centres will gain approval. Registering with an assessment centre is the only route to qualification. The only choice you will have is which assessment centre you choose.

HOW TO QUALIFY AS A HOME INSPECTOR

There are two routes to becoming a Home Inspector. These are the Experienced Practitioner Route (EPR) and the New Entrant Route (NER).

The Experienced Practitioner Route carries two routes within its remit, for practitioners with:

- relevant experience and qualifications (EPR1); or
- relevant experience but no qualifications (EPR2).

Similarly, the New Entrant Route (NER) has two routes within its remit, for people entering the sector for the first time with:

- relevant qualifications but no experience (NER1); or
- little or no residential experience and no qualifications (NER2).

To help you assess how your profile matches the NOS, we have included a self-assessment profiling schedule in Appendix C, showing the different units with their respective elements. The schedule does not include underpinning knowledge, range of experience and other more sophisticated techniques that assessment centres will normally use. However, it will help put you in the right ballpark in terms of the gaps that you may need to fill and what additional training you may need to undertake.

The remainder of this chapter will describe the various qualification routes in more detail, but we'll first establish exactly what constitutes **relevant residential experience** and **relevant qualifications** within the context of gaining a Diploma in Home Inspection.

Relevant residential experience

A period of three years is considered a minimum by most commentators, but with all of this working in a role with a reasonable level of responsibility and autonomy. This experience should be in the residential environment and should not include your training period. It does not have to be directly associated with the buying or selling of property, but does have to involve assessing the condition of property in its broadest sense. Experience solely with commercial or industrial buildings will not satisfy the requirements.

Relevant qualifications or professional membership

One of the underlying principles of the VRQ is that it is open to anyone whatever their background. It does not matter which precise qualification or professional association the candidate holds as long as it matches the required standard and that they are able to display their ability to do the job. This represents a change from the previously restrictive nature of the residential sector. In terms of qualifications, assessment centres should favourably consider holders of HNCs, foundation degrees, HNDs, degrees, and relevant NVQs. The content and emphasis of the course is very important and ABBE has given a listing of topic areas that should cover most of the background knowledge for the Home Inspector qualification. This has been included in Appendix D.

EPR1 (Relevant experience and qualifications)

The timescale for getting enough Home Inspectors qualified will be short, but with so many professionals already working within the residential sector, it is hoped that they will make up the bulk of the first 'wave' of inspectors. Therefore, ABBE has established a route that will suit experienced practitioners and take account of their existing knowledge, experience and professional membership. The full criteria for qualification routes are still to be finalised and with reference to professional membership, no prescriptive list has been produced. However, members of the following organisations should be considered suitable:

Table 1.1: Organisations suitable for assessment centre accreditation

• Royal Institution of Chartered Surveyors (RICS)	• Chartered Institute Of Building (CIOB)
• Association of Building Engineers (ABE)	• Institute of Structural Engineers (IStructE)
• Institute of Management and Building Maintenance (IMBM)	• Independent Surveyors Association (ISA)
• British Institute of Architectural Technologists (BIAT)	• Royal Institute of British Architects (RIBA)

This is not an exhaustive list and other professional organisations will put themselves forward in due course. Several organisations have already obtained 'credit tariff' directly from the ABBE, enabling their members to gain varying levels of recognition for their qualifications from the assessment centres. However, applicants will be considered on their own merits. There are no exemptions and everyone will have to show that they properly match the National Occupational Standards. For example, although the profile and experience of a chartered surveyor who has been successfully carrying out mortgage valuations and homebuyer surveys for over thirty years will be very beneficial, they will not automatically be awarded the Diploma. They will still need to provide enough evidence to show the assessor that they meet the National Occupational Standards. Some professions will have less work to do than others, but all will have to submit to the process.

If a candidate has the appropriate experience and qualifications, they will have to progress through a number of distinct steps. These are summarised in Figure 1.1, a flow chart produced by RICS' Safe As… assessment centre. Although it is not exactly the same as the more generic process described in this chapter, it does help to present a specific approach to the assessment process.

Step one – registering with an assessment centre

You will have to register with an appropriate assessment centre and provide all the appropriate information needed for step two. A fee will usually be payable and the level of this fee will vary, as the process will be market-driven. Some assessment centres may initially charge a registration fee, with subsequent phased payments as you progress through the assessment process.

Step two – skills analysis and profiling

Candidates will have their skills and knowledge 'profiled' at this point, which may be done online, through a face-to-face interview or by an application form. The assessment centre will be interested in a range of issues, including:

- CPD records and training;
- employment history, job role, types of surveys/inspections carried out;
- qualifications, including any surveying or other relevant NVQs; and
- professional membership.

Assessment centres will be able to produce an overall profile for each candidate, properly matched against the NOS. After the profiling has been completed, advice will be given on the further training that may be needed to fill any gaps, as it is anticipated that few candidates will immediately satisfy all parts of the NOS.

Step three – additional Home Inspector training or qualifications

Depending on the skills profiling, requirements for extra training will vary. Virtually all candidates will have to take a training course on the Home Condition Report itself. External training providers will usually provide these, but some assessment centres may include this as part of their commercial package.

When taking courses or attending training events to enhance your profile, it is important to make sure the events are of the right quality and meet the necessary requirements. Gone are the days where you could attend a seminar, collect the CPD certificate, put it in your files and forget all about it. To make the event more meaningful, all sessions should clearly state the objectives or learning outcomes, and be relevant to Home Inspectors by meeting individuals' training needs and those of the NOS. Finally, there should be some provision of evidence of the learning that occurred. This could be through formal/informal assessment or you could produce a reflective personal statement demonstrating how you intend to use your new knowledge and skills in your daily work. Whatever the method, the value of the training event should be clearly demonstrated. Your assessment centre will be able to advise you further on this matter.

Step four – produce a portfolio of performance evidence
This step involves collating a portfolio of performance evidence for submission to the assessment centre. For most experienced candidates, this will include ten residential reports that have been carried out within the last three years. At least three of these reports must follow the latest Home Condition Report format and the assessment centres will usually want at least one of these to be done under supervised conditions. With regard to ABBE, a report under supervised conditions means a report accompanied by a witness testimony stating the report to be *'…bona fide and a fair reflection of the property concerned'*. The witness could be an assessor from the assessment centre, a representative from the training provider or an experienced and occupationally competent member of staff at the candidate's employment practice.

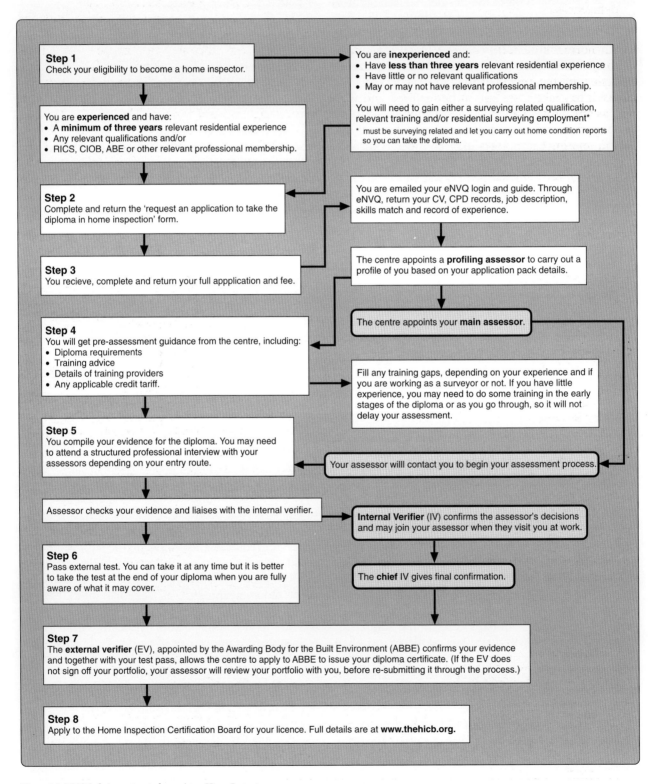

Figure 1.1: RICS Safe As… steps to becoming a Home Inspector

Assessment centres will require more than just standalone reports, which must be accompanied by supporting evidence, including:

- a complete set of original site notes, with plans of all floors and quick sketches of parts of the property that may help to illustrate its condition; and
- photographs of the property, covering at least all of the principle elevations, main defects and deficiencies.

This provision of information is beyond what would normally be required for a Home Condition Report, but necessary to show that the report is a fair reflection of the property that was inspected. Our advice is to make sure that you provide the assessors with as much information as possible because they are looking for evidence of your competence. If you submit minimal site notes and a report with little explanation, the submission is likely to be sent back requesting more information or worse still, be failed.

The remaining seven reports can follow a variety of different formats. ABBE has suggested that those included in the top half of Table 1.2 may closely match the NOS. The reports identified in the lower half of Table 1.2, although relevant, may not satisfy all the requirements.

ABBE has also produced guidance on the components that the reports should include. The components are divided into mandatory and secondary requirements, which are summarised in Table 1.3.

Not all reports will mirror the criteria outlined in Table 1.3. Where they are not entirely suitable, candidates can increase the number of Home Condition Reports they submit. In fact, there are advantages with this approach because the reports can be mapped exactly against the NOS, making them more straightforward to assess. The submitted reports should cover a variety of property types. You will need to submit reports for detached, semi-detached and terraced properties for each of the following time frames:

Table 1.2: Report formats and the NOS for Home Inspection

Report formats that assessment centres may find acceptable

Generic name of practitioner	Professional organisation	Name of product
Building Surveyor	ABE	Building Survey
Technologist	BIAT	Building Survey
Building Manager	CIOB	Building Survey
Building Surveyor	CIOB/ASI	ASI Buyer Report
Environment Officer	CIEH	Building Survey
Valuation Surveyor	ISA	HSV Report
Maintenance Surveyor	IMBM	Structural Report
Engineer	IstructE	Structural Report
Architect	RIBA	Building Survey
Valuation Surveyor	RICS GP Faculty	HSV Report
Building Surveyor	RICS BS Faculty	Building Survey

Report formats that may not meet all the requirements of the NOS

Generic name of practitioner	Profession/Organisation	Name of product
Asbestos Surveyor	Asbestos Surveyor	Specialist Report
Housing Manager	CIOH	Building Survey
Tradesmen/Manager	Builder/Foreman	General Report
Services Engineer	CIBSE	Building Survey
Clerk of Works	ICW	Building Report
Estate Agent	NAEA	Sales Particulars
Woodworm/Damp Surveyor	IRTS – RDS	Specialist Report

Table 1.3: Evidence that should be included in reports submitted to assessment centres

Mandatory elements or primary evidence that should be included in all ten submitted reports	Secondary evidence that should be included in at least fifty per cent of the submitted reports
• health and safety guidance notes; • external condition of the building; • internal visual condition; • a summary of findings and recommendations; • site notes; and • plain English.	• terms of engagement; • building services including electric, gas, water and drains; • grounds of the building; • handling of further enquiries; and • estimation of reinstatement costs.

- pre 1914;
- between 1915 and 1939; and
- post 1949.

There should be an even spread between all the different property ages, types and conditions. Inspecting properties in a similar condition and type will not test your skills and is unlikely to be accepted by the assessment centres. The sample should also include furnished as well as some vacant properties.

Step five – the structured professional interview (SPI)

To ensure that the candidate has a suitable profile and appropriate competencies, ABBE has insisted that those following the Experienced Practitioner Route should attend a structured professional interview (SPI) with a qualified assessor, either at the assessment centre or the candidate's place of work. This approach has been adopted to enable experienced practitioners to progress quickly through the assessment process.

The SPI will usually last for 1.5 to 2 hours and focus on the individual profile of the candidate, with the assessor looking for evidence that the candidate has the full range of competencies. The SPI will be rigorous and probing. Candidates may be asked to take along supporting evidence to their SPI if it is not in their place of work. However, this will be much less than the level of information submitted with the portfolio of performance evidence.

The SPI will allow the candidate to demonstrate that they have:

- acquired and kept up to date the theory needed for all five units;
- the practical ability needed for units one, two and three; and
- demonstrated they possess the performance ability for units four and five.

A proper record of the interview will be made and the assessor will usually make an audio or video recording of the event to complement written notes.

The SPI is more than a straightforward discussion. Candidates should take it seriously and prepare for it accordingly. Before the SPI, you should review your profile, focus and improve upon any gaps in your knowledge and experience, and make sure you have the right blend of supporting evidence to reassure the assessor of your competence. Although you will not be 'failed', the assessor may refer you for a further period, which will delay your progress and may incur an additional fee.

Step six – the Home Inspector's external test

The final step in the assessment process is the external test, which is independent of the assessment centres, and directly created and administered by ABBE. This is ABBE's method to ensure that all candidates, whatever their background, take one final and consistent form of assessment before the

licence is awarded. The test will be taken online and candidates will get instant feedback on how they have performed, although the formal results will be confirmed later.

It is likely the test will be administered by specially appointed invigilators and will be undertaken in full examination conditions at a computer facility in one of several locations around the country. It will take 1.5 hours and unique test papers will be generated by ABBE for every group taking it. The test will be multiple-choice, where a statement or a problem will be given, with candidates expected to select the correct answer from a choice of four options.

The test paper will be split into three different sections:

- Section one will include a fixed number (usually twenty) of multiple-choice questions. The subject matter will be drawn from a range of topics including Code of Conduct, Guidance Notes and general underpinning knowledge designed to test currency of knowledge.
- Section two will test the theory behind the practice. Questions will include sketches or photographs, with candidates expected to identify a range of building components and other technical features.
- Section three will present a number of detailed photographic case studies and text-based information. These will test candidates' analytical skills and their ability to make specific judgments.

The pass mark for the external test is currently seventy per cent, although ABBE may adjust this from time to time depending on candidate performance.

Step seven – the award of the Home Inspector Diploma

Once the assessment centre is fully satisfied that a candidate has met the requirements of the VRQ, the Diploma will be awarded. An application can then be made to the HICB for a Home Inspector's licence.

Time period of qualification

As long as each step progresses normally, ABBE estimates that the qualification process will take three to six months.

EPR2 (Relevant experience but no qualifications)

This route will suit those people who have extensive relevant residential experience, but no relevant qualifications or professional membership. They might have carried out a variety of relevant duties, but never obtained formal qualifications or joined an appropriate professional organisation. The steps to qualification will be similar to those described for EPR1. Where there are differences, these have been described in detail.

Step one and two

These steps are the same as in EPR1.

Step Three – Obtain relevant accredited training/qualification or part-time qualification

Candidates following this route will usually lack underpinning knowledge and theory in crucial areas of the NOS. As the Home Inspector initiative develops, more courses will be offered by a variety of providers and these will include free standing courses (HNC or HND in an appropriate discipline) or an approved series of modules that cover the required elements of the NOS. It is important that candidates work closely with assessment centres to ensure they take approved courses that will provide the necessary underpinning knowledge and experience they need.

Step four to seven

These steps are the same as in EPR1.

Time period of qualification

As long as each step progresses normally, ABBE estimates that the qualification process will take between twelve and twenty-four months.

NER1 (Relevant qualifications but no experience)

This route will suit those who have relevant qualifications (such as new or existing graduates), but no residential experience, and might suit practitioners from other non-residential sectors. Examples could include construction managers, site engineers, clerk of works, etc.

The steps to qualification will be similar in many respects to those described previously and have been briefly outlined below, with the main differences emphasised.

Step one – obtain relevant employment in the residential sector

If a candidate has no experience in the residential sector, it is important that they get a suitable job as soon as possible. It is unlikely that an assessment centre will approve a candidate's profile unless they play an active role in the sector. A Home Inspector Licence cannot be obtained just by taking a few relevant training courses. Competence is based on candidates taking a professional and active role in the residential sector, carrying out real work for real clients.

Step two to four

These steps are the same as in EPR1.

Step five – develop a portfolio of performance evidence

A candidate following this route will have to construct a more conventional portfolio of performance evidence by adopting an incremental approach to assembling the evidence over a longer period of time.

It will still include the ten reports, but all of these will be in the Home Condition Report format.

Step six – Assessment centre monitoring

This will take the place of the structured professional interview. The assessment centre will monitor the development of the candidate's portfolio at regular intervals through a combination of meetings and reviews of submitted material.

Step seven and eight

These are the same as in EPR1.

Time period of qualification

As long as each step progresses normally, ABBE estimates that the qualification process will take between eighteen and twenty-four months.

NER2 (Little or no residential experience and no qualifications)

This route will suit candidates with little knowledge about the residential sector and very few qualifications at an appropriate level. This is the longest route and would usually begin with formal academic courses or NVQs offered by one of the many providers. As previously discussed, while the initiative develops, courses that are more relevant will be offered by training providers. In the meantime, various HNCs, HNDs and degrees will be appropriate.

Step one

Obtain accredited qualification (HNC/foundation degree/degree) or relevant training.

Step two

Obtain relevant residential employment (see NER1).

Step three

Register with an assessment centre (see EPR1).

Step four

Develop a portfolio of performance evidence (see NER1).

Step five

Assessment centre monitoring (see NER1).

Step six

Sit ABBE Home Inspector external test (see EPR1).

Step seven

The award of the Home Inspector Diploma (see EPR1).

Time period of qualification

As long as each step progresses normally, ABBE estimates that the qualification process will take between thirty-six and forty-eight months.

CONCLUSIONS

Based on anecdotal experience in relation to the qualification process, we believe that many experienced practitioners may be surprised at the amount of work they have to do to get their Home Inspector Licence. This is usually based on misconceptions about their own knowledge and skill levels, as well as the nature of the assessment process. The more open qualification process will allow a broader range of candidates from different professional backgrounds to enter the residential sector and in time, this may increase competition for jobs in the sector.

2 The home condition inspection

The content of this chapter will help you to understand and meet the requirements of the following elements of the National Occupational Standards for Home Inspectors:

- **Element 2.1 – Contribute to the maintenance of health and safety at work**
- **Element 2.2 – Contribute to the security of self, colleagues and others**
- **Element 2.3 – Contribute to the security of property**
- **Element 3.2 – Investigate relevant matters relating to the property**
- **Element 4.1 – Inspect property for condition**
- **Element 4.2 – Make complete and comprehensive records of findings**

(A summary of the different units and elements that make up the NOS in Home Inspection has been included in Appendix B. A complete copy can be downloaded from www.assetskills.org.)

THE INSPECTION PHILOSOPHY – COMPARISONS WITH OTHER INSPECTIONS AND SURVEYS

In chapter three, the nature of the Home Condition Report is discussed and we conclude that it is a condition report that has no relationship with value. It should give an objective description of the property at the time of inspection, identify any defects or deficiencies, and give an indication of what type of action is required. One way of identifying the unique nature of this new format is to compare and contrast it to other, more familiar surveys and inspection types. The three most common types of product currently used in the residential sector include:

- **The mortgage valuation** – RICS state this is a valuation, not a survey. It is a limited check carried out on behalf of a mortgage lender to detect anything that might affect the security of the loan. The lender wants to know if the property is worth the amount of mortgage being asked for.
- **The homebuyer survey and valuation (HSV)** – RICS state that this is not a detailed survey of every aspect of the property and focuses only on major and urgent matters. It is not suitable for properties that are more than 150 years old, properties in need of renovation or those that are going to be altered or extended.
- **The building survey** – A building survey is a comprehensive inspection suitable for all properties. It is particularly suitable for all listed buildings and older properties, properties that are to be renovated or altered, or any property constructed in an unusual way regardless of its age. A building survey is a detailed examination of all accessible parts of a property and can be **tailored** to suit individual needs and concerns.

The methodology for the home condition inspection is discussed in detail later in this chapter, though at this stage we thought it would be useful to place the level of inspection in context with other products. We think the home condition inspection will sit somewhere between the HSV and the building survey, as shown in Figure 2.1. Based on descriptions in various drafts of HICB Home Inspectors Inspection Reporting Requirements and Guidance Notes, (from now on referred to as the Guidance Notes), it is clear that the inspection routine exceeds those laid down for the HSV, but stops short of the building survey methodology.

The courts have always been active in defining what a surveyor should or should not inspect. For example, in *Cormack v Washbourne* (1996) EGCS 196, CA, the surveyor undertaking a building survey was expected to have looked at the geological survey map for the area to establish whether the property was built on clay and therefore susceptible to movement.

The Home Inspector will not be expected to completely lift carpets or move furniture, but will be expected to seek or undertake further investigations if there is a trail of suspicion. This was held in the case of *Roberts v J Hampson & Co.* (1989) 2 EGLR 181, (1989) 2 All ER 504 and clarified in *Lloyd v Butler* (1990) 2 EGLR 155. Similarly, in *Hipkins v Jack Cotton Partnership* (1989) 2 EGLR 157, during a building survey it was held that the cracks in the render plus the

	Mortgage Valuation	Typical Homebuyer Survey	Home Condition Inspection	Building Survey
	1	2		3

Brief inspection based on a visual inspection of visible elements without any tests, checks or moving of furniture, etc. Average time for a three bedroom house in satisfactory condition is between 30 to 40 minutes.	Longer inspection based on a visual inspection of visible elements with only basic checks of services that are easy to operate. Only small/light furniture is moved, corners of carpet lifted, etc. Average time for a three bedroom house is between 90 to120 minutes.	Detailed survey of all accessible areas and elements, including checks and some tests. Small/light furniture is moved, corners of carpet lifted and some opening up of works where appropriate, etc. Average time for a three bedroom house is between 4 to 5 hours.

Figure 2.1: Comparison of different types of inspection and survey

slope of the land should have alerted the surveyor to a more serious issue. Even before this case, in *Hingorani v Blower* (1976) 1 EGLR 104, the Court thought recent redecoration and modernisation should have alerted the surveyor to look more carefully to establish whether the seller had concealed anything.

Inspections, evidence and legal claims

The use of seller's questionnaires (see Appendix F) might be a useful method of dealing with any legal implications that might occur after an inspection. In one disputed survey, the seller had not identified that there was a cellar in the property. Although the presence of a cellar is clearly visible in Figure 2.2, at the time of inspection the trap door was covered by an item of furniture.

After the seller had moved out, the new owner noticed problems with the flooring around the cellar access – the cracking to the floor tiles, visible in Figure 2.2 had been caused by a defect in the cellar. An inspection in the cellar revealed the cause of the cracked tiles. Dry rot had weakened the joists and the temporary timber props suggest that the former owner knew about the problem.

Since this defect was not mentioned in the survey report, the new owner made a claim against the surveyor. However, as a result of the surveyor using good site notes (see Figure 2.4), he was able to show that access to the cellar was concealed beneath a piece of furniture at the time of inspection and that he was unlikely to have missed the cracking around the floor as a result of rotten floor joists. The extensive and detailed floor plan clearly shows the restriction on the inspection. We have outlined the conservatory (CNSV) and identified the precise position of the cellar trap door, which was hidden by an item of furniture. Recording these sort of details can provide evidence to help avoid expensive claims. As we suggested, other evidence that may be useful in avoiding claims is the seller's questionnaire. Figure 2.5 shows an extract from the seller's questionnaire for this property inspection and shows that the seller did not reveal the presence of the trap door

However, provision of supporting evidence does not *always* work and in the case of *Hacker v Thomas Deal & Co.* (1991) 2 EGLR 161, the surveyor failed to identify dry rot. The judge stated that it has a distinctive smell, which even a surveyor of limited experience should be able to detect. So, part of your equipment needs to be a good nose and if you have no sense of smell, then this may be a limiting factor noted in the circumstances of the inspection!

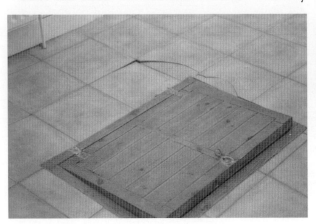

Figure 2.2: Cellar trap door (concealed during inspection)

Figure 2.3: Weakened joists in the cellar

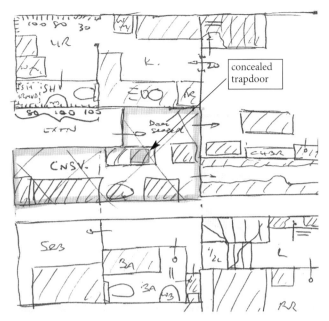

Figure 2.4: Extract from surveyor's site notes

The legal context for the inspection

It is not the purpose of this section to provide you with a concise guide to the law in respect of surveys, valuations and inspections. Instead, we want to try and set the legal context for the home condition inspection and report. For a comprehensive guide to the law in respect of valuations and surveys, see Murdoch, J., *Negligence in Valuations & Surveys*, RICS Books, 2002.

In essence, the Home Inspector will have a contract with the seller of the property and/or their agent. This contract will set down the terms upon which the Home Inspector must operate. Any failure to meet those terms will be a contractual matter and subject to acts of parliament such as the *Supply of Goods and Services Act* 1982. Amongst other things, this sets down criteria in respect of 'reasonable care and skill' and even 'timeliness'.

At the time of writing, there is no case law applicable to the production of the Home Condition Report, so what follows is conjecture. The case of *Shankie-Williams v Heavey* (1986) 2 EGLR 139, CA is in a similar area. In this case, a seller undertook some works on a house that had been converted into three flats and commissioned a report from a surveyor who knew that the report would be shown to prospective buyers. The surveyor was shown to have missed dry rot and had a liability to the buyer. This of course will be no different for the Home Inspector, therefore many of the current principles will apply if not in contract, then in tort.

Basis of law

An important principle was established in *Hedley Byrne & Co. Ltd v Heller & Partners Ltd* (1964) AC 465. It was held that a person who provides advice may owe a duty of care to someone with who he or she does not have a contract, provided the parties are in a 'special relationship'.

There have been many cases that have shown that the surveyor acting for a lender owes a duty of care to a buyer. For example, in *Smith v Eric S Bush* (1989) 1 EGLR 169, (1990) 1 AC 831, HL, it was found that the buyers were more likely to rely on the surveyor's report for a lender, which was not commissioned specifically for them. This was because the house in question was 'modest'. If they were buying a larger house or commercial property, the court would have expected them to buy their own report.

The Home Condition Report is prepared for the seller and the buyer, and can be relied upon by either party's professional advisers, which would include the lender. There can be little doubt about this because it clearly states this in the Terms of Engagement within the Guidance Notes.

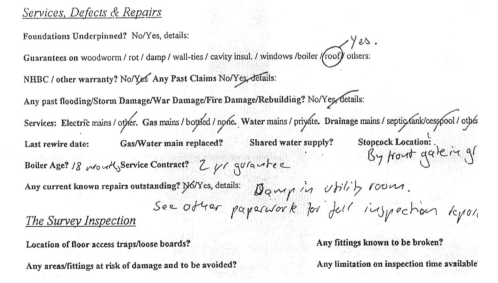

Figure 2.5: Extract from the seller's questionnaire

There will be the obvious contractual obligation created between the Home Inspector and whoever has agreed the terms and paid the fee. This could become complex if commercial bodies such as lenders, estate agents, financial intermediaries, conveyancers, utility companies and other Home Information Pack providers subsidise or pay the whole fee. In these cases, you should ensure that you have a formal service agreement to cover the contractual liability of the provision of the service.

Compensation

A duty of care will apply to the seller, buyer and lender. Consequently, should the actions of the Home Inspector result in a foreseeable loss, this may well attract an allegation of negligence. The forms of losses could be more extensive with the Home Condition Report than with other surveys because they were limited to liability to the buyer and lender. Table 2.1 identifies some possibilities.

PREPARING FOR THE INSPECTION

Knowing your limitations

The Guidance Notes state that before you accept an instruction to carry out a home condition inspection, you must be sure that you are competent to look at that particular property. No Home Inspector can be completely familiar with every type of domestic residential property. We have listed a number of property types that can cause problems for Home Inspectors.

System-built properties

Since the end of World War One, local authorities and building contractors have experimented with new ways of building residential properties. Thanks to recent initiatives such as the Egan Report (Department of Trade and Industry, *Rethinking Construction*, 1998), this trend carries on today. The result is that hundreds of different varieties of 'system-built' or prefabricated properties exist in the residential sector. Some types are widely recognised and have good supporting technical advice from government agencies, including Cornish Unit, BISF and Unity dwellings, while other types are so restricted in distribution and number that very few Home Inspectors know of their existence, let alone their condition (e.g. 'Malton' types that are found in specific neighbourhoods in Sheffield).

The Guidance Notes state that Home Inspectors must be able to:

* recognise and identify the types of system buildings that can be found in their area;

Table 2.1: Nature of Home Inspection liabilities

Client	Potential loss situation	Incidental losses
Seller	• Recommendation for the provision of reports (e.g. structural engineer) where there was no good reason • Recommendation for the provision of reports/ information that are not provided by the seller (e.g. warranties, test certificates, etc.), but cause some buyers to be deterred (must be proven) • Incorrect rating that deters buyers	Loss of sale, expenses to date
Buyer	Situations where a buyer has unforeseen loss after buying the property, which are proven to be a result of the negligence of the Home Inspector	Apart from the loss in value, distress, fees for both legal and technical advice
Lender	Situations where failure to correctly diagnose condition or other matters such as environmental considerations leads to loss of value in the lender's security (usually limited to the amount of the advance)	Fees and expenses

* recognise whether they are designated under the *Housing Defects Act* 1984;
* identify the potential problems that apply to each system;
* be familiar with the type of approved repair systems and their general acceptance for mortgage purposes; and
* note the implications and risks in connection with the mutual support between adjoining or adjacent properties.

You are not expected to carry all this information around in your head. Even the most knowledgeable Home Inspector will have to check a few facts and details from time to time, but if you are answering 'no' more than 'yes' to these questions, then you should consider whether to go ahead with the Home Inspection without taking additional training.

Historic buildings

This covers the range of property types that are generally older than the average dwelling. The important feature about this type of property is that they are constructed using traditional materials and techniques that are now considered as 'specialist'. Traditional materials perform differently to modern materials and this characteristic has to be accounted for when inspecting the property. Applying the same performance criteria to both a 16th century timber-framed property and a 1960s semi would obviously be inappropriate, while dampness at low level in lime-plastered rubble-filled wall stone would have a different diagnosis to a similar defect in a modern masonry wall. Thatched roofs provide another example – one of the authors lives in an area where they are common, whereas the other author has only seen them on picture postcards – a side effect of working exclusively in an urban environment!

Regional constructional techniques

In some areas of the country, building practices have evolved in an insular way so that they are geographically restricted to small areas of the country. Examples include Mundic concrete in Cornwall, 'Bungaroosh' cob construction along the south coast and black ash mortar in Yorkshire. Building techniques like this can be very difficult to assess unless you are familiar with local conditions, so care must be taken if you work outside your normal area.

TOOLS AND EQUIPMENT

The Guidance Notes list the mandatory and optional tools that Home Inspectors should take with them on every inspection. It is important that you have all of these tools or you will contravene the Terms and Conditions of the Home Condition Report. If you miss a defect because you did not have a particular tool then you will have little defence if challenged in court. For example, in *Fryer v Bunney* (1982) 2 EGLR 130, a surveyor was negligent for not using a damp meter properly. However, in *Hacker v Thomas Deal & Co.* (1991) 2 EGLR 161, the surveyor was **not** negligent for not using a torch and a mirror because RICS Guidance at the time did not specify these items as essential.

Tools for the inspection

The mandatory section of the Guidance Notes state that Home Inspectors must have the essential tools to undertake the inspection. We have listed these below, with commentary added where appropriate. Some are self-evident, but our experience has shown that many inspections are carried out with inadequate equipment, so we think it is best to be explicit.

Binoculars

These can either be standard size or compact binoculars (the ones that fit in your pocket), as long as they are 10x magnification. These are essential for the roof, chimney and other upper building elements that may be viewed from a distance.

Ladder

This will prove to be a controversial issue. The Guidance Notes state that the ladder must be sufficient to '…*gain safe access to building elements which are three metres or less above the surface on which it rests.*' Traditionally, surveyors have used three metre sectional ladders and most manufacturers have catered for this demand by providing ladders between 3 – 3.5 metres long. However, reviewing recommended health and safety advice, ladders should extend at least one metre above the level that they are giving access to. To safely inspect at a height of three metres, you will need a ladder that is four metres long. Finding one will be quite a challenge as not many manufacturers make them this long!

Measuring tape

We think a 5 – 7.5 metre retractable steel tape is suitable for most inspections. Some rooms will often have one dimension that is greater than five metres, making the additional length useful. Many inspections are carried out using handheld laser distance meters and practitioners claim that these can speed up the measuring process. However, there will be occasions when there is no opposing wall to 'bounce' the laser off, so you will always need a measuring tape as a back up. Externally, you may need to take longer measurements to check the relative positions of boundaries, etc., for which a 20 – 30 metre fabric tape will be required.

Electronic moisture meter

We recommend that a conductivity moisture meter be used (the one with steel pins), as these are generally more reliable than the 'flat plate' varieties. You should always carry spare batteries and the meter should be calibrated in accordance to manufacturer instructions.

Torch

The Guidance Notes are not prescriptive about the size of the torch. A powerful 'mini' flashlight is acceptable, but we prefer a 'professional' sized torch (the type that takes two or three D-type batteries). These are more robust and give a more reliable light source. You should always carry spare batteries and bulb.

Lifting equipment/crow bar

The main purpose of this equipment is for lifting inspection chamber covers. A 'crow bar' (minimum length of 450mm) is sensible because chamber cover lifting 'keys' rarely work because the lifting holes are always rusted or full of debris. To make the lifting of covers easier, we think that a few other tools are useful:

- a robust claw hammer or small (2kg) club hammer;
- a large flat head screw driver – for levering up the cover; and
- a bolster or cold chisel – for loosening up the most difficult of covers!

These additional tools can also be used for other, simple 'opening up' tasks such as lifting loose floorboards.

The remainder of the list of tools in the Guidance Notes includes those that can be very helpful when you are 'following the trail' of a defect. In our view, some of the tools are beneficial, but others are less effective:

- Some tools are related to health and safety issues and will not contribute to the quality of the home condition inspection. We have described these in detail in the later section on *Health and safety equipment*.
- Some of the other tools can be useful, but the information they provide must be interpreted with care – they could be misleading rather than helpful.

Despite these reservations, we have listed all those that are in the Guidance Notes, together with accompanying commentary and some suggestions of our own.

Spirit level

The size and type is not specified, but two spirit levels are useful:

- A small handheld level (sometimes called a 'boat level') is useful for checking alignment of doorframes, windowsills, etc.
- A 1 – 1.5 metre 'bricklayer's level' will be essential to check the levels on floors and the verticality of walls. The longer, the better.

Marble or golf ball

Some inspectors use these for assessing whether the floors of a property are sloping. The drawback is that they do not work very well on carpeted floors. Even if they do reveal a slope, it is difficult to assess how seriously the floors are sloping. The best way of measuring the slope of a floor is to use your longer spirit level. This can be levelled up by inserting 'shims' (e.g. pieces of thick cardboard) under one end until it is level. The gap between the floor surface and the underside of the level can then be measured and a simple calculation will give the precise slope.

Pocket mirror

This is a very useful instrument to have. They can be used to look under floors, within ducts and other voids. A large and small sized 'search' mirror that can be mounted on a telescopic arm is particularly useful.

Plumb bob

This can provide a quick and effective way of checking the verticality of walls, especially when dropped out of a convenient window. A one metre spirit level gives some indication of whether a wall is vertical, but a plumb line is much better. The problem is that unless you can take precise measurements between the line and the wall (hard to do when you are on your own), it can only give you a general indication. Therefore, be careful what conclusions you draw when using it.

Compass

This is a really important tool. A compass can give an indication of which part of the building is affected by the prevailing weather – important information when looking for dampness.

Measuring rod or ruler

We think this should be added to the list as a two metre folding 'boxwood' rule is excellent for measuring heights of rooms and other features.

Digital camera

Although photographs are not a formal part of the Home Condition Report (it is not possible to upload them to the national database), they are very useful for helping to keep track of records. The digital revolution has produced cameras that are able to take and store a large number of images, which can be very useful when you are writing your justification clauses, reviewing your report or responding to an enquiry or a challenge. However, it is important to remember that images are no substitute to adequate and clear site notes. If you do take photographs, it is important to store them securely where they can be easily retrieved.

Health and safety equipment

On an inspection, you will need other items to protect your own health and safety. Some of these have been identified in the Guidance Notes, but we have put together a more comprehensive list of what we think you will need:

- A personal attack alarm (just in case of emergencies) and spare battery.
- A mobile phone so that you can call for help and advice if there is a problem.
- A first aid kit that suits your particular professional role.
- A safety helmet – not required for most normal inspections, but where you are looking at a partially complete, renovated property or one in poor condition, then a helmet should be worn.
- A facemask with disposable filters for loft inspections and other dusty environments. It should be suitable for general use and does not have to have 'asbestos' grade filters because you should not go into spaces that contain asbestos products. If you think there is a strong possibility of asbestos dust then you need to leave the area immediately.
- Protective gloves for lifting inspection chamber covers, etc. Many organisations are now recommending disposable latex gloves because if reusable gloves have been used to lift an inspection chamber cover and then put back in your toolkit box, they could contaminate your other tools.
- Safety shoes that have appropriate toe and sole protection when inspecting partially renovated properties or those in a poor condition. Wellington

boots (with similar sole and toe protection) are also recommended for very muddy gardens and grounds.

- Disinfectant hand wipes to clean your hands after an inspection (and especially before you eat your sandwiches)!

SELLER ENQUIRIES

Before the inspection

Before carrying out a home inspection, you should get as much information from the seller as possible. The exact process and timing of this will depend on the circumstances, but the more you get, the better informed you will be. Some of the information will help you decide whether you can carry out the home inspection, while the rest will improve the quality of your inspection. A full list of questions has been included in Appendix F.

The responses you get will have to be taken at face value. Sellers and Home Information Pack assemblers may not understand or be able to answer all the questions that you ask and there is a chance that some may even be economical with the truth! Whatever the circumstances, you will occasionally turn up at a property that you are unable to inspect because you do not have the specialist knowledge or experience. In this case, you have two options:

- phone up the seller and inform them that you are unable to carry out the home inspection, giving your reasons; or
- carry out a very thorough inspection with detailed site notes and clear photographs so that you can seek further information on the property type back at the office.

Some of the questions in the seller's questionnaire are similar to those asked by legal representatives. Nevertheless, this information is so useful because it can give you an 'agenda' for the inspection and establish clear trails of potential problems before you even turn up on site. You must substantiate the information provided by third parties through your own observations and assumptions. The Guidance Notes recommend that the source of all provided information should be recorded in your site notes. Ideally, you should ask for the questionnaire to be returned by post before the inspection. If not, ask for it to be available at the start of the inspection and go through the questions in person with the seller.

On arrival

A positive relationship with the seller can reveal a lot of useful information about the property. It is surprising how forthcoming a proud owner can be, even about the problems in their homes. Conversely, an over attentive seller can get in the way of a home inspection, making it difficult to approach the task in a methodical and systematic way. Here are a few tips:

- arrive on time with proof of identity – the person who gives you access might not be the person who you originally talked to.

After arriving:

- explain the purpose of the home inspection – not all sellers understand the complexities of house sale and purchase procedures;
- outline your approach to the inspection – how long it will take, what rooms and spaces you will need to inspect, etc.;
- ask them for the seller's questionnaire if you have not received it and if it is still uncompleted, sit down and complete it with them face-to-face;
- ask the seller to show you around the property (maximum five minutes) – this introduces you to the property, allows you to ask gentle but probing questions, and make arrangements for inspecting occupied areas i.e. bedrooms with sleeping occupants;
- ask the seller if there are any defective elements that may be damaged if operated or checked, such as windows that do not shut, taps that cannot be operated; and
- once the initial and brief walkabout is complete, politely inform the seller that you want to carry out the rest of the inspection on your own.

During the inspection

During the inspection, take great care not to damage the property in any way. It is guaranteed to harm your relationship with the seller. Typical problems have included:

- marking wall and ceiling surfaces when assembling ladders for loft inspections or similar;
- soiling carpets with muddy boots or a ladder that has previously been used outside;
- disturbing decorations when unscrewing access hatches or using moisture meters; and
- knocking ornaments from mantelpieces, shelves, etc.

It is important to remember that you are in someone's home and it needs to be treated with due respect and consideration.

Dealing with seller enquiries

Many sellers will be confused about the role of the Home Inspector and find the concept of objectivity difficult to understand, so some may not fully appreciate your professional role. Most will be very interested in what you thought of their home and what you might include in your report, which is understandable as this might affect both the appeal and value of their dwelling.

You may be asked to give an instant judgment based on your opinion and you should approach this situation carefully. It is unreasonable not to offer any comments when faced with direct questioning, but this should be limited to factual issues including general descriptions of the property and any obvious defects. You should not mention anything about the ratings or what you are likely to include in your Home Condition Report because you should allow yourself time and space to reflect fully on the longer-term implications of any defects that have been revealed during the inspection. This can only be done away from the property when you have had time to review your site notes and take into account all the relevant issues. Instant feedback will usually be inaccurate and can often lead to more serious misunderstandings and possible future disputes.

After the Home Condition Report has been produced and submitted, a Home Inspector must be prepared to explain any sections or terms to the seller. To do this, you must be completely familiar with the format, Terms of Engagement and explanatory text of the Home Condition Report.

Unaccompanied and unattended inspections

Although many inspectors would prefer to carry out property inspections without anyone else around, it does present a number of difficulties, discussed below.

Access arrangements

You need to clarify how you are going to gain access to the property. Getting the answers to the following questions may help:

- Where can keys be obtained from and for how long?
- Are there any security alarms and who has the codes?
- Are the services activated and if not, will anyone be able to activate them?
- Do you have permission to open windows, access hatches, etc?
- Who will answer all the pre-inspection enquiries that you usually ask?

Problems during the home inspection

During the Home Inspection, you might encounter a number of other problems that will need reporting immediately to the person in charge of the property:

- The Guidance Notes state that where unaccompanied inspections are undertaken, it may be appropriate to mention when confirming the arrangements, that you will only operate water installations required for the inspection and will not take responsibility for any hidden faults that emerge.

- If the property is unsecure when you arrive or you are unable to secure it at the end of the inspection. This could include an external door that cannot be shut once opened or a casement window that binds against the frame.
- If the property is damaged through vandalism or there is evidence of unauthorised occupation or use. In many areas, empty property can attract squatters, drug users, thieves, and vandals. Not only can these compromise the security and condition of the property, but they can also be a risk to the Home Inspector. If you find yourself in this situation, it is advisable to leave the property immediately and phone the person in charge from the relative safety of the your car.

HEALTH AND SAFETY AND THE HOME INSPECTION

Problems posed by the building

Each property has to be taken on its own merits, but the development of an inspection routine will help you recognise and minimise risks. Safety awareness has to be a top priority when entering any form of property. RICS state that the surveyor should be aware of the ordinary risks of the job and

'... *obvious signs of a need for extra care, shown for example by the disrepair or age of the building, should heighten the surveyor's awareness of his own safety.*' (Reville, J., *Surveying Safely – Rights and Responsibilities*, Structural Survey, 16 (4), 1998, p. 175).

Table 2.2 outlines some examples of potentially dangerous situations that you need to be aware of for an inspection. It provides a selection of some potential risks that you might encounter during an inspection. Experience will result in many of these checks becoming automatic, but unless safety is seen as an essential consideration from the earliest stages, then a lack of awareness could lead to increased risk. Trade bodies may also have their own health and safety literature and this should also be referred to. *Surveying Safely – Your guide to personal safety at work* is available from www.rics.org.

Travel and general vehicle safety

Most inspectors spend a considerable amount of time in the car travelling between the office and the properties to be inspected. You should take care to ensure that the car is well maintained and road-worthy. In addition to the formal servicing, read the car maintenance manual and maintain routine checks.

It is also important to carry an emergency car kit in case of a breakdown, as well as a map to reduce the need of having to stop and ask for directions.

Table 2.2: Health and safety risks – the building itself

Source of potential risk	Considerations for the inspection
Walls and flooring	● Is the building structurally stable – are walls or ceilings likely to collapse? ● Does the flooring in the building seem in good condition or is it likely to collapse due to rot or beetle infestation? ● Are there any floorboards missing or other openings in the floor? *The essential indicator here would be the general condition of the building.*
Utility services	● Are the electrical installations safe? ● Are there any exposed wires? ● Do the heating appliances appear in good condition or do scorch marks or flue stains suggest that combustion products could threaten health? ● Is there a smell of gas or combustion products?

Roof and loft areas	● Will a terrace over a flat roof take the weight of a person?
	● Will the roof covering come loose and fall on to people below?
	Look out for uneven surfaces, ponding of water, and any other signs that may suggest poor condition. Special care should be taken in situations made worse by bad weather – strong winds, high snow loads or heavy rain.
	● Is it safe to enter the loft space?
	  ○ Are the ceiling joists strong enough to support a person? *(Suggested minimum: 38 × 72mm at 600mm centres).*
	  ○ Are the joists overloaded by stored items?
	  ○ Is the loft space boarding properly secured or just a haphazard collection of different timber panels that are likely to collapse or tip up when stood on?
	  ○ Will it be safe to walk across the back of the ceiling joists or are they covered in insulation?
	  ○ Are the roofing members close enough to walk steadily on?

Health hazards	● Is the building contaminated with material that could affect your health? *Examples include used and unprotected syringes that are often found in squatted properties, surfaces that may be contaminated with chemicals or other hazardous substances and where there is a threat of disease and illness due to the presence of rats, pigeons, cockroaches, fleas, etc.* **Particular care should be taken when soft asbestos products are discovered. Sprayed asbestos, thermal insulation, and pipe lagging are rare in domestic situations, but are highly dangerous. If you suspect an area is contaminated with asbestos fibres, you should end your inspection immediately and inform the seller as soon as possible. Only complete the inspection once a specialist contractor has removed the material.** *The correct use of protective clothing and equipment can help reduce health risks. For example, a facemask is essential when in a space infested by pigeons, and a handy can of flea spray will save hours of embarrassing scratching!*
Exterior	● Are the outbuildings safe to go in? ● Are the gardens safe to walk around? *The main dangers could include debris or vegetation covering various holes, excavations, inspection chambers, cesspools, etc.* ● Are there any dangerous animals loose? Is there any fast moving or deep water?
Location	● Is the property in an area that has a higher than average risk? *These might include building sites, farms, areas subject to landslip and subsidence, some inner city areas, and workshops where semi-industrial processes are undertaken. Risk assessment in these locations must be carried out more carefully.*

The journeys should be planned so that you do not get tired. Take regular breaks on long journeys and follow the highway code. Accident statistics show that younger males are at greater risk during this part of the inspection, so kill your speed!

Inspections in occupied property

Health and safety rules and regulations are usually associated with working environments where the dangers are more obvious. Building sites, under-ground mining and many industrial processes present a range of tangible health and safety risks that have to be identified, assessed and minimised. Inspecting residential properties using nothing more dangerous than a moisture meter is usually considered low risk. However, lone working in other people's property does have its own particular challenges that occasionally result in serious injury and even death. Organisations such as the Suzy Lamplugh Trust (www.suzylamplugh.org) and the Health and Safety Executive (www.hse.gov.uk) have produced excellent guidance for people whose work involves visiting people in their homes. Based on this information, the Guidance Notes, and our own experience, we have outlined what we feel is a framework for a safe working environment for Home Inspectors.

Personal safety

When you are in someone's property, it is important to remember that it is their home and you are imposing upon their territory. Before you do the inspection, consider whether you have to go alone. This may be difficult when resources are scarce and workloads are heavy, but two people will be much safer than someone working alone. In many cases, accompanied inspections can be part of a new entrant's training programme or justified by formal quality assurance requirements. If it presents difficulties, two person inspections could be restricted to areas where the risk is considered to be the greatest.

Before leaving your workplace, make sure somebody knows where you are going and what your plans are, what time you expect to finish the inspection and return to work or arrive home. Arrange to check in with someone in the office to confirm you have finished the inspection even if you go straight home. A call from the safety of your armchair may stop your colleagues worrying about your whereabouts.

Always carry a fully charged mobile phone and your personal attack alarm. Go to the inspection in daylight wherever possible and organise your day so that you are travelling in darkness rather than inspecting buildings in a fading light. During winter months, this may mean completing the inspection by mid-afternoon.

Before arriving at the property, think about its location (whether it is in a high-rise block, down a country lane or on a one way street) and if there are any associated dangers. Upon arrival, park in a position where it will be easy to leave quickly. Always lock your car and do not leave valuables in full view.

When gaining access to the property, state who you are, why you are there and show them your ID or business card. Check who you are talking to and make sure it is the same person that you arranged access with and if this is not the case, consider carefully whether you should go in. If the property is occupied by children or juveniles, you should postpone your inspection until an adult can be present. Wait to be invited into the property – be assertive, but remember you are in someone else's property.

Inform the occupants how long you estimate the inspection to take and where in the house you will need to go. When carrying out the inspection, do not let the occupier lock the doors behind you. A night latch that can be easily opened is not a problem, but a mortice lock that can only be opened with a key will restrict your ability to leave the property. Try to familiarise yourself with the layout of the property so you can get out quickly if necessary and do not leave possessions in several different rooms across the

property as this may delay your departure if you need to leave in a hurry.

Do not take documents into the property that you do not want the occupant to see and be careful when using a personal recorder to dictate notes. Owners may be offended by even the most objective assessments of their home. Different people live in different ways. Try not to react to the condition of the property even if it is very untidy, smelly, or plain dirty. Do not judge and if you do, try not to let your feelings show.

If dogs or other animals appear threatening, politely ask them to be kept out of the way. It is surprising how many inspectors have been badly bitten by dogs who 'wouldn't hurt a fly'. It is important to ask whether there are animals outside before you inspect the garden/grounds.

If you slip, fall, injure or cut yourself, consider postponing the inspection until you have recovered. The smallest of cuts or bumps can get worse if they are not properly treated. Also, carefully evaluate any offer of first aid assistance from the seller. Although it might be offered with the best of intentions, unless they are properly qualified they could make matters worse.

If you accidentally enter bedrooms, bathrooms and WCs where occupants are sleeping or changing, apologise and leave the room quickly. If you notice that valuables have been left around the property, you should consider asking the seller to remove them. If any of the occupants appear to be drunk, aggressive or overly attentive, then say that you have an urgent appointment and leave immediately.

Keeping it in context

It is not the intention to fuel the anxieties of newly qualified Home Inspectors. The fear of crime and dangerous incidents is usually out of all proportion to the likelihood of the events actually occurring. However, unless you are aware of the dangers and plan accordingly, you could be vulnerable. The potential for violence may depend on a whole range of factors which could be nothing to do with you. The reason for the property being sold might be marriage break-up, bankruptcy or bereavement and the seller might be very worried about the effect that a negative set of condition ratings might have on the value. Therefore, you must always remain alert to the possible dangers. The Suzy Lamplugh Trust advises that you should do what is necessary to protect yourself, trust your instincts and act accordingly. If you follow these suggestions, they will become a habitual part of your normal inspection process.

LIMITATIONS DURING THE INSPECTION

Moving furniture, panels and floor coverings

The furnishings in most occupied dwellings will limit the extent of an inspection. The Terms of Engagement attached to the Home Condition Report itself state that it is a non-invasive inspection where floor coverings are not taken up, furniture not moved and the contents of cupboards not removed. Neither should floorboards be lifted or electrical fittings undone. From a buyer's perspective, most people would be disappointed if an inspector refused to move small and easily movable items, and we think it is reasonable to move the following:

- easy chairs, sofas, beds, etc. where there is enough space, and if they are on castors, making it easy for one person to push aside;
- small coffee tables, magazine racks, dining room chairs, standard lamps, waste baskets, etc.;
- a few ornaments and other possessions (say three or four items) to enable furniture to be moved; and
- corners of carpets that are loose and would be easy to put back down.

In all cases, the owner's permission must be obtained before anything is moved. This can be requested when you get to the property or in a standard letter sent prior to inspection. Part Two of the Guidance Notes state '*It may be appropriate to inform the seller that it is not necessary for them to clear cupboards, move furniture or roll back carpets in preparation for the inspection.*' This seems to limit seller preparations prior to inspection, but we think it is a matter of finding the right balance. One of the positive aspects of the Home Condition Report is that the seller has an interest in helping the Home Inspector carry out a full and effective inspection. This obviously stops short of lifting the floor coverings and shifting all the furniture to the middle of the room, but minimal preparations will allow a more complete inspection to be carried out. This is different to previous arrangements where there was no contractual relationship between the surveyor and the seller, and a level of 'unhelpfulness' was almost seen as 'normal'.

Whatever the seller does to help the inspection, larger items such as sideboards, dressing tables, wardrobes, fridges, freezers, washing machines, televisions, etc. would be too heavy to move, so should be left in place. It is difficult to be more precise as each case must be judged on its own merits, but you should always apply the test of reasonableness. If the Home Inspector cannot carry out a complete inspection, reservations will be expressed in the report itself and this may delay a possible sale. However, if you think the seller has deliberately concealed potential problems by putting stored possessions or heavy furniture in the way, you should politely ask them to move the item. If they refuse or are unable to do so, the Guidance Notes state that you should note this restriction in the Home Condition Report.

What to do with the services – tests versus checks

The Guidance Notes mention services in a number of different sections. We think it is important that you get a clear view of what should be done with services in relation to home condition inspections and the text appearing in *italics* is what is stated in the Guidance Notes.

Before moving on, it's worth establishing what constitutes a test and a check in the context of Home Condition Reports. A test is defined as involving activity that goes beyond the level of a check, while a check is defined as a purely visual, non-destructive inspection or observation, or an exercise that is part of normal inspection.

Part one – Mandatory requirements

The Guidance Notes state that '*If the services are found to be turned 'off' during the inspection, this must be reported in the HCR.*'

Part two – Producing Home Condition Reports (guidance)

In respect of unaccompanied inspections ' *... the Home Inspector will only operate water installations such as taps and toilets, and electric lights required for the inspection and will not take responsibility for any hidden faults emerging from any such operation.*'

Additionally, '*Home Inspectors are not required to turn mains services on or off. If the services are 'off' at the time of the inspection, the seller should be asked to turn them on if it is appropriate, to see them in operation. In the event that such a request is refused, this should be recorded in the site notes with the explanation.*'

In relation to health and safety risks to the Home Inspector, the following cautions are given:

- ' *... Home Inspectors should satisfy themselves that they are sufficiently fit and agile to carry out the task e.g. ...lifting drainage inspection covers*'; and
- '*If unsafe electrics are detected, do not touch any part of the electrical installations.*'

The Terms of Engagement attached to the actual Home Condition Report

This section briefly considers a Home Inspector's Terms of Engagement in relation to inspecting and reporting on a property's services. At the beginning of Section F (Services) of the Home Condition Report, the following statement is included:

'*Services are difficult to inspect as these are generally hidden within the construction of the property, for example, pipes beneath the floors and wiring within the walls. Only the visible parts of the available services have been inspected. Specialist tests have not been carried out. The visual inspection did not assess the efficiency, operational effectiveness or compliance with modern standards.*'

The Guidance Notes state that a Home Inspector is not required to hold the qualifications of a 'services engineer' and is therefore not expected to give a comprehensive test report on any of the services. The Home Inspector reports on those parts of the services that can be seen, without undertaking formal tests. If services such as the boiler or mains water are turned off, the Home Inspector will state that in the report, but not be expected to turn them on. Otherwise, Home Inspectors should turn on a selection of water taps to sanitary appliances, and lift covers on the drainage inspection chambers where it is safe and practical to do so.

Finally, the Home Inspector reports only on the services expressly covered in Section F (Electricity, Gas, Water, Heating and Drainage). All other services and appliances are excluded from the report, such as security and door answering systems, television, cable, wireless and satellite communication systems, cookers, hobs, washing machines and fridges (even where built-in).

What a Home Inspector should do

This section outlines the remit of a Home Inspector in relation to inspecting for both occupied and unoccupied properties.

In an occupied property

Electrics

- Switch the lights on and off and operate any extractor fans or other fixed appliances, etc.
- Do not switch the mains supply switch on if it is turned off.

Water

- Operate all hot and cold water taps and mixers, switch on showers and flush all toilets
- Do not turn the main stopcock on and off.

Heating

- Ask the owner to switch on the main heating systems and all the individual room heaters.
- Do not switch the heating on if the owner has not, and do not operate the main gas/oil switch to the property.

Drainage

- Lift inspection chamber covers and observe water running through the inspection chamber (e.g. leave a tap running or get the owner to flush a toilet).
- Lift inspection chamber covers over septic tanks and cesspits.

In an unoccupied property

Make sure you have the owner's agreement to operate ' ... *water installations such as taps and toilets, and electric lights required for the inspection.*' However, a Home Inspector '*will not take responsibility for any hidden faults emerging from any such operation.*' Do not turn on any of the services at the mains if they are turned off. This might be because:

- the electrical system is dangerous;
- there is a leak on the gas system;

- the heating system is defective; or
- the plumbing is leaking.

If the services are turned on and apparently operational, carry out the normal checks, but make a note of what you did on your site notes and report any problems to the person responsible for the property.

Vantage points

You will not be able to see all parts of a property and should use vantage points with due consideration to practicality and safety. These match previous standard practice and are identified and discussed below, based on the advice in the Guidance Notes (which appears in **bold**) and our own explanatory commentary:

- **The inspection should be conducted only from the property itself and any adjoining public space** – This is usual practice for most practitioners. Looking at the property from within the boundaries, the main street, public open spaces and pathways can help complete the inspection and reveal the condition of those 'hard to see' details around the back of chimneys, along valley gutters, etc.

- **Home Inspectors must not trespass on neighbouring property, except by express invitation from the adjoining owner him/ herself. Utilising such permission should be recorded in the site notes** – This is self-explanatory and you should avoid the temptation to 'nip over the fence' to get a better look. This applies even with properties that have more open, shared rear gardens and yards. One owner may have a right to pass through another's property to access their back door, but this does not give a Home Inspector the right to wander around as they choose. If viewing a property from a neighbouring property is important, ask the seller to go and request permission so you do not waste your time knocking on doors.

- **Home Inspectors must use all suitable vantage points to view as much of the property as possible, without danger or undue inconvenience to themselves. You are not required to balance precariously on garden walls, but should cross the road, if, for example, the opposite pavement gives the best view of the roof** – Many injuries occur because inspectors simply do not take enough care. Rather than go out to their car and get a ladder, some practitioners would prefer to balance rickety chairs on top of tables so they can get into the loft. If you fall and your insurance company finds out you were being irresponsible, then you could lose your compensation. Younger inspectors are often the most at risk.

Other vantage points are noted below and discussed in other parts of this chapter. Additional vantage points include the use of a ladder to inspect a flat roof, viewing a lower roof from a higher window, and looking at the condition of similar properties nearby.

INSPECTION METHODOLOGY

Systematic inspection

Most experienced inspectors will have their own approach to carrying out an inspection. We have described our preferred method previously (Parnham, P. and Rispin, C., *Residential Property Appraisal*, Spon Press, 2001) and consider that it is just as suitable for Home Condition Reports as any other type of survey. The main rule is that your approach must be methodical and systematic, following the same routine in every inspection. This can help create an impression of competence if challenged in court. Table 2.3 outlines a typical systematic procedure for internal and external inspection of a property.

This systematic approach is fine in theory, but some defects may show signs in more than just one space. Therefore, you will have to inspect some areas a number of times to properly follow a particular 'trail'. Once the inspection has been completed, always inform the owner that you are leaving and make sure you have collected all your equipment.

This method of inspecting a property does not match the layout of the Home Condition Report form, so you have two options:

- create site notes that match the way you inspect the property, or;
- use site notes that match the layout of the final Home Condition Report form and accept that you will have to keep flicking back and forwards through the form during the inspection.

This is discussed in more detail in the *Home Condition Report site notes* section later in this chapter.

Time requirements for a home condition inspection

On average, an inspection for a typical 1960s three-bedroom semi-detached house should take between 1.5 and 2 hours to carry out and is similar to previous survey types. However, most inspections will vary depending on the particular circumstances, which we will briefly consider.

Property condition

Older properties in a poor condition will take longer to inspect because it will take longer to complete your site notes, take longer to take additional measurements and photos, and take longer to follow defect trails to reflect on the cause of problems. Legal precedents have clearly established that an inspector should follow the 'trail of a defect' to the point where appropriate advice can be given. This does not mean that you have to pursue the problem until it is fully exposed, but just to the point where it becomes clear what action needs to be taken. The link between condition and time does not automatically mean shorter inspection times for newer dwellings, as these often need careful consideration because the signs of defects will be less apparent.

Property size

The bigger the property, the more time it will take to look around it. Smaller flats will be inspected very quickly.

Accessibility

Fully furnished properties will take longer than those that are empty. Properties that are fully occupied will take longer as you work around the occupants.

Level of experience

If you are newly qualified or new to Home Condition Reports, you should plan to take a little longer for inspections until you are familiar with the range of information that you need to collect. More experienced Home Inspectors will have a practiced, almost intuitive 'feel' for what is required and will often proceed at a quicker pace.

It can be helpful if the seller is in the property at the time. They can be asked to do all sorts of useful jobs that will help speed up the inspection process, including:

Table 2.3: Inspection routine for a residential property

Internal	External
<ul><li>inspect the loft space first (if there is one)</li><li>inspect the rooms on the uppermost floor by working around the entire floor in a clockwise direction</li><li>finish on the landing and inspect the stairs down to the next floor</li><li>follow the same process on each floor down to the lowest one</li><li>inspect any cellar or sub-floor void if accessible</li><li>in each room, inspect the various elements in the following sequence: ceilings, walls (including skirtings), floors, windows, doors, heating, electricity, plumbing, other amenities (e.g. toilets, basins, sinks, etc.), fittings and fixtures (e.g. cupboards, fitted wardrobes, fireplaces, etc.) and any unusual or special features</li></ul>*The external inspection is carried out last to avoid tramping muddy boots through the house.*	<ul><li>inspect the main elevations (including secondary elements such as doors and windows, etc.)</li><li>inspect observable roof surfaces including chimneys stacks</li></ul>*On flat roofs three metres or lower, this should include a ladder if the roof cannot be inspected from the windows of upper rooms. Rainwater goods should be assessed at this point.*<ul><li>inspect any significant garden features such as retaining walls</li><li>inspect all outbuildings</li><li>inspect boundaries, fences and gates</li><li>inspect any special features such as rights of way</li><li>inspect drainage facilities</li></ul>

- opening access hatches to concealed areas (e.g. roof spaces, underfloor areas, etc.);
- opening a selection of windows;
- clearing aside personal belongings that would otherwise clutter understair cupboards, roof spaces and basements; and
- identifying the positions of services, including meters, rising main, heating controls, etc.

The guiding principle is being prepared to be flexible. If you are taking between an 1 and 2.5 hours, you are probably in the right ballpark. If you are outside of this margin, then you need to reflect on your approach to the inspection. If you take too little time, you may be missing important features and if you take too long, you will be undermining your fee income and probably going beyond the Terms of Engagement.

Home Condition Report site notes

Making a record of your inspection is an integral part of the process. The National Occupational Standards (Asset Skills 2003) clearly state that you should:

'*make complete and accurate records of your inspection findings. You must record information using appropriate methods (e.g. written, photographic) and ensure that records are legible and complete.*'

The courts have expressed opinions on the importance of site notes. In the case of *Watts v Morrow* (1991) 2 EGLR 152, (1991) 4 All ER, 937, CA, the court was critical of a surveyor who dictated the full report whilst on site. This was contrary to the relevant guidance given by RICS, which stated that the notes needed to be transposed. The judge considered the report unnecessarily long and lacking reflective thought.

It is for this reason that we have not focused on this method of recording information. We believe best practice is to put the information either on paper or record it electronically on a handheld computer. If the latter, then you should be capable of reviewing the content substantially and for this reason, we have some concerns about the palmtop type model as only limited information is available on screen. We have used our own paper based site notes, but acknowledge the introduction of handheld 'tablet' computers. The same principles apply, however, as if you were recording the information on paper.

Our site notes (see Appendix G) are loosely based upon those produced for the Building Research Establishment (BRE) pilot exercises. Since that time, the Home Condition Report has changed and so the site notes have been modified. We have also made some of our own changes to reflect our method of operation and included where information is required by the new Reduced Data Standard Assessment

Procedure (RDSAP) methodologies (see Chapter Five). These changes highlight some essential points:

- Site notes are there to record what you see on site, but with the purpose of feeding that information into a report. Therefore, the site notes need to provide the answers to the questions in that report.
- Site notes must reflect a logical inspection of the property and form a basis for the final report, although the format of the report may not follow the same logic. For example, the report summary can only be written after the property has been fully inspected.
- If you are experienced in producing site notes and reports, you may have adopted a pattern that works well for you. Therefore, the suggested model may need to be adapted to suit your own style.

Whatever your level of experience, you should review the adequacy of the site notes you produce because the quality and focus of site notes form part of the assessment procedure for Home Inspectors. You will not be awarded your Licence if they do not conform to the required standards.

The importance of site notes

We hope that from the previous sections you are in no doubt that failure to adopt a robust technique to inspect a property could lead to expensive claims. Satisfactory inspection techniques must be supported by good quality notes.

Most people reading this book will be aiming to qualify as a Home Inspector and it is likely that the basic site notes that we have provided will not be sufficient to show your assessor that you have the necessary underpinning knowledge to qualify. However, there are a number of reasons why they are important:

- they help to record everything that you see on site and in the vicinity;
- they act as a checklist to ensure that you have not forgotten anything;
- they provide a basis upon which you can produce the report; and
- they provide an indication of competence to anyone needing to review your work that you have undertaken the inspection in a logical and thorough manner.

Site notes can also help you to save time in certain situations. For example, if you use a secretary to type finished reports, it saves dictation time if the secretary can copy some of the information directly from the notes, such as the accommodation details.

Site notes included in Appendix G

We referred previously to 'good' site notes, but what do good site notes look like? Let's consider what is prescribed for in the site notes provided in this book.

The first two pages include information collected at the outset of the inspection and includes:

- the address of the property;
- information about the Home Inspector who inspected the property;
- appointment details;
- circumstances of the inspection, such as whether the property was furnished;
- date of construction;
- tenure;
- property type and construction;
- accommodation;
- services;
- general information about the outside of the property;
- information needed for flats and maisonettes; and
- general sections that will help you collectively record legal, environmental, health and safety issues.

Page three provides space to include a plan of the site and to record measurements relating to pieces of information that you would collect whilst outside the property, e.g. information for features such as the garden, outbuildings, orientation, nearby roads and other location characteristics.

Similarly, pages four and five provide space to include internal floor plans. These are important because sketching a plan can help you establish how the property is put together. You should also make a note of any obstructions and get a feel for any issues that can be followed up later on. If there are more than two floors, you should include supplementary sheets.

Page six relates specifically to movement, dampness, and timber defects. As you go around a property, you can note movement and dampness problems under the features they principally affect but also include them here. This means that when you draw the final report together, it will be easier to locate and reflect upon very serious defects. Although this might create some repetition, it helps to ensure that important factors are addressed accordingly and not overlooked in the final report.

Pages seven to sixteen relate to individual elements of the property, both exterior and interior. Each element has a number of different sections:

- an inspection checklist in the left-hand column, based on a range of external and internal features which we will cover later in this chapter; and
- a box for free text entry and additional comments such as descriptions, condition justifications, etc.

The condition rating for an element does not have to be entered immediately. In many cases, you will have to finish the whole of your inspection before you can properly reflect on your decision. These sections also include all the information that will be needed to produce the reduced data standard assessment procedure (RDSAP) rating, in relation to the

property's services. RDSAP is discussed further in Chapter Five.

The latest version of the Home Condition Report and Guidance Notes allow the sub-division of each individual element up to five times. We think this is a beneficial feature because different types of building elements can be fully accounted for. For example, the case study property in Chapter Seven has four different types of roof:

- the main pitched roof;
- the flat roof over the lounge extension;
- the flat roof over the rear entrance extensions; and
- the flat roof over the front porch.

On the site notes for the case study property in Chapter Seven, we have sub-divided the roof covering element into three, as follows:

- the main pitched roof because it is unique in terms of its construction and condition;
- the flat roofs over the lounge and rear entrance extension have been combined because they are similarly constructed and have the same condition rating; and
- the flat roof over the porch is in a different condition and has been kept separate. We eventually decided and to report on this under 'Other', but included it in the site notes under 'Roof coverings'.

To sub-divide elements in the site notes, simply draw a line horizontally across the element's box. In some cases you may not have enough space if there are a number of sub-divisions and so should carry over your description to a continuation sheet at the end.

Pages seventeen and eighteen cover those elements within the grounds of a property, including boundary walls, outbuildings and common facilities.

Page nineteen includes a risk assessment schedule for the inspection itself. You should fill this out as you arrive at the property and after you have completed your first precautionary walk around. This will allow you to plan for your own safety more effectively and give more evidence to your assessor that you have accounted for health and safety issues.

Page twenty includes a schedule of photographs that will assist you in relating an image to respective parts of the building. Often, when a complaint is received, it is impossible to trace which part of the building an image relates to. Although it might take a little time at this stage to compile the schedule of photographs, it will save you hours in the future and also help present clear and well structured information to your assessor.

It is important that site notes are legible and this can be difficult when it is pouring with rain and your fingers are cold, so the use of tick boxes can be particularly helpful. We believe that splitting the notes into different sections can help with the production of the report at a later stage, and provides a logical sequence for how you conduct your inspection on site. We are not so bold as to suggest that this is the only format, but it does meet the requirements of the National Occupational Standards and they will assist in producing a logical framework for inspections.

Techniques with site notes to help you complete the portfolio

Thorough site notes can be a very useful indicator of competence. However, if they are incomplete or incomprehensive, they can also be a very useful indicator of incompetence. All aspiring Home Inspectors are required to complete ten reports, three of which must be in the Home Condition Report format. In this instance, you are not producing for your own benefit, but to convince an assessor that you are competent.

The process is a difficult challenge for any assessor given that they will only have the evidence that you produce. It is worth trying this yourself by asking a colleague to give you a copy of their site notes and corresponding report for a property. See if you can properly assess competence from the information they have provided. An important consideration is that you cannot see the property, so have no idea whether anything important has been missed. Even if something has been mentioned, is the diagnosis correct? Here are a few tips that will help the assessor review your site notes and reports:

- provide photographs of front and rear elevations (together with shots of any defects) and complete the photograph schedule that has been included at the end of the site notes;
- provide a rationale on the site notes for some of the decisions made, similar to the case study property in Chapter Seven;
- as you produce the report, tick the checklists in the left-hand column of the site notes so that you can show you have been systematic and that you have not omitted anything;
- ensure that everything included in the report is mentioned in the site notes, otherwise the assessor will question the source of the information;
- if information has been provided by the agent, seller or buyer, ensure this has been emphasised in the site notes;
- attach any letters, emails and records of other correspondences and telephone conversations connected with the property;
- it is not sufficient to make statements such as 'Environmental Issues: NONE'. There will need to be a justification to show you have knowledge of the subject, so refer to information in the public domain and where it came from. For example, 'No radon – outside the significant areas as noted in the Radon Atlas of England and Wales'.

- it is also useful to reference comparable properties that have similar problems, such as a damaged chimney stack and its known repair costs;
- use the BCIS Housing Repair Cost Guide and quote the costs from there; and
- ensure information is complete and site notes are legible.

Although it is not a formal part of the Home Condition Report process, it is useful to the assessor if you include a Health and Safety Risk Assessment in the site notes (see page nineteen of the site notes in Appendix G). This will show that you are fully aware of health and safety issues in your daily routines. While some of these recommendations may seem unnecessarily bureaucratic, remember that the Home Inspector Diploma is evidence-based, so your route through the qualification will be much smoother if you can provide the required evidence.

THE INSPECTION – ELEMENT BY ELEMENT

Part Two of the Guidance Notes finishes with a description of each building element and the extent of the inspection that a Home Inspector should carry out. The indicative defects commonly found with all elements are provided by way of examples in Part Three of the Guidance Notes. There is no explanation for what causes these defects or how to identify them and it is this pre-existing, underpinning knowledge that Home Inspectors will have to acquire elsewhere.

We have adopted a similar approach to the Guidance Notes for each building element, but combined Parts Two and Three for convenience. There is also additional advice of our own, with each element split down into a number of sections:

- **The specific parts of the building that should be included under that element** – In most cases this will help you include the right part of the building in the right section of the report. These lists can then be built up into a rudimentary checklist (we have used them on the site notes, for example). This approach is based on advisory notes produced by the Building Research Establishment (BRE) for the earlier technical trials, the latest Guidance Notes, and our own additional input.
- **The extent of normal inspection that is expected** – Two levels of information have been included in this section:
  ○ **The formal advice that is described in the Guidance Notes** – This has been reproduced word for word and appears in **bold**.
  ○ **Own commentary** – This is our own interpretation of the Guidance Notes and has no formal status. We have included it for two reasons:
  1. Our experience with other forms of standard surveys, especially the Homebuyer Survey and

Valuation (HSV), revealed that surveyors often developed their own approach to the inspection of properties. A main reason for this was that official guidance was often vague and inconclusive, allowing people to fill these gaps with definitions of their own. We found a great deal of variation between how surveyors carried out the inspection for what should have been a well-defined nationwide product.

2. Although the Guidance Notes include a considerable amount of detail for some elements, others have brief and superficial advice – we hope that our additional information will help to provide a more consistent approach for Home Inspectors.

● **Typical examples of defects commonly associated with each element** – The Guidance Notes have identified defects that can be typically associated with each element. We have included them because they act as a good checklist and help define the extent of inspection for each element.

● **The information that you will have to collect for the RDSAP assessment.**

Specific elements

Now that we have established the scope of the inspection and the range of information associated with it, we will look at all elements individually while considering the nature and scope of information outlined above. We have named and numbered the sections to exactly match that of the Home Condition Report.

SECTION D – EXTERNAL CONDITION

D1 (Chimney stacks)

Parts of the building to be included in this element	Stacks, pots, flaunching, pointing to stack, support to stacks, condition of the chimney breast within the roof space, flashings between stack and roof covering.
Normal inspection	**Inspect from ground level using binoculars** – you should use those with at least 10x magnification. **Inspect all sides provided there are sufficient and reasonably practical Vantage points** – see the section on *Vantage points* for further information. **Note construction/materials, including flashings, pots and flaunchings, party stacks, etc.** **Also check for support, damp penetration, etc. inside the roof void** – it is important to check in the roof space for any related defects, especially if the external inspection reveals several defects. To do this properly, you will have to carry out more than a 'head and shoulders' inspection. Be prepared to walk over and closely inspect the chimney breast within the roof void (as long as it is safe to do so).
Typical defects	● Unsafe height (too tall or too short); ● Leaning chimney stacks in danger of toppling over; ● Evidence of sulphate attack; ● Unsafe pots and crumbling flaunching; ● Deteriorated mortar joints; ● No flashings or flashings that have come loose; ● Condition of back gutters; and ● Inadequate support for TV aerials.

D2 (Roof coverings)

Parts of the building to be included in this element	Slates, tiles, thatch, etc.; battens, sarking felt, sheet coverings (flat roofs), flashings to neighbouring buildings, parapets and other features (not chimney stacks); valley gutters, dormers, roof windows and lights, etc.; condition of ventilators through the covering (but not the overall ventilation to the roof space).
Normal inspection	**Inspect from ground level using binoculars** – see the section on *Vantage points* for further information. **Inspect from all sides, provided suitable Vantage points** – see the section on *Vantage points* for further information. **View surrounding properties for comparison** – this can give a useful insight into the performance of similar local roof coverings and can usually be done during the course of the normal external inspection or simply by taking a short walk up and down the street. **Flat roofs (use ladder if not unsafe or impractical)** – if you are unable to see the flat roof from a suitable vantage point within the property, then you should inspect the covering from your ladder. You should be able to put this up safely without having to move garden furniture or other heavy items. **Look out of windows to roofs at lower level** – many roof coverings at a lower level (flat and pitched) can often be inspected from an upper window. Ideally, you should be able to open the window and safely lean out. You should also be able to see the majority of the roof covering (say eighty per cent) and all the features that are vulnerable to damp penetration such as junctions with adjacent walls, parapets and penetrating pipework. If not, consider using your ladder or other vantage points as appropriate. **Check for damp penetration, nail sickness in roof void** – same as for D1 (Chimney stacks). This is especially important for flat roofs where access to the roof space is often impossible. **Follow any trails of suspected defects to roof void/underside of flat roofs** – this emphasises the need to link what you see on the outside of a building to what you can see on the inside.
Typical defects	<u>**Pitched roofs**</u> ● roofs too shallow for type of cover; ● spalling/laminating tiles; ● dips/dishing/undulating roof slopes; ● missing, slipped, broken tiles/slates; ● loose hips/ridge tiles, pointing worn; ● leaking valleys; ● moss growth; and ● replaced coverings heavier than original. <u>**Flat roofs**</u> ● lack of fall/ponding; ● asphalt surface crazing; ● blisters, splits and cracks in roof covering; ● moss and debris; ● poor upstands and flashings; and ● roof light, windows and pipe penetrations.

D3 (Rainwater pipes and gutters)

Parts of the building to be included in this element	Gutters, downpipes, hoppers, valley gutters, parapet gutters, gullies.
Normal inspection	**Inspect from ground level using binoculars** – see the section on *Vantage points* for further information. You should not place ladders against gutters. **Consider using a pocket mirror behind cast iron downpipes if severe rusting/cracks are suspected** – this will be useful for all metal downpipes and would usually be done from the ground level only. **View from underneath, as close to wall as possible** – a long view of the gutters is useful to assess their alignment or whether they have any blockages. However, looking from underneath can give you more information about the condition of the joints and the gutters themselves, the gutter supports and the gap between the gutters and the edge of the roof covering. This should be done on all elevations where access to the base of the wall is possible. **Follow the trail from stains, broken downpipes or other suspected leaks to inside** – although it is best to inspect gutters when it is raining, even the British weather does not always oblige. After dry periods, it is still possible to identify which gutters leak by looking for staining/discolouration or algae/plant growth to the wall surface. Once spotted, it is important to inspect the corresponding internal surfaces for signs of dampness that may have penetrated through. Remember to use your damp meter in these locations.
Typical defects	• Rusting and cracked gutters and downpipes; • Leaking joints; • Lack of falls, bends, etc.; • Insufficient brackets and supports; • Leaf clutter and other blockage; • Insufficient downpipes; • Drainage or discharge splashing above damp-proof course; and • Misalignment between roof edge and gutter.

D4 (Main walls)

Parts of the building to be included in this element	External walls (load bearing and non-load bearing), lintels, underlying wall structure (frames), wall foundations, pointing, renders, protective coatings, cavity ties, cavity insulation, externally applied insulation, masonry sills.
Normal inspection	<u>Outside:</u> **All elevations from ground level, using binoculars where necessary, noting constraints such as creepers and close growing vegetation** – the vantage point restriction described previously also applies here. It is also important to note restrictions caused by vegetation as they could limit your assessment. We would also include advertising hoarding and other secondary forms of cladding (such as stick-on-stone, timber and PVCu boarding). **View corners/edges to identify lean, which can be verified with plumb bob or spirit level** – looking along a wall is a very useful way of spotting areas that are bulging or leaning out. Once you have identified a potential problem, a spirit level or plumb line could be used, but this may give you limited information as we mentioned in the *Tools for the inspection* section. **Scratch lightly with a key along occasional mortar joints to identify weakness and/or need for repointing** – this is a useful method for assessing the suitability of the mortar. Where possible, it should be done in a number of positions on each elevation at ground level and to the side of an upper window that you would be opening in any event. The pointing at high level (and therefore inaccessible) is most likely to be in the worst condition and these areas should receive most attention with your binoculars. <u>Inside:</u> **Check wall thickness at window openings and note construction/materials** – this is important for checking structural adequacy as well as providing the information for the RDSAP. **Tap on inside surface to identify construction** – an obvious action that can only help to identify the construction. Remember – a dry-lined brick and block cavity wall can sound the same as a timber and brick cavity wall from the inside. **Modern timber frame construction is usually revealed in roof void and/or at window openings** – you should be looking for plasterboard covered party walls in the roof space, mastic filled movement joints around the window openings and between the different storeys, with cavity weep holes above. System-built properties may also have boarded party walls.
Typical defects	• Leans and bows; • Cracking both inside and outside; • Poor pointing to brickwork; • Cavity wall tie failure; • Rot to timber frames in older buildings; • Single skin construction; • Spalling brickwork; • Thermal expansion/contraction; and • Render failure/surface cracking.

D4 (Main walls) *continued*

Information needed for the RDSAP assessment	A wide range of information needs to be collected about the wall construction, including: • the main type of construction: whether it is stone, solid brick, cavity, timber frame or system-built; and • the type of insulation used in the main walls, the options being: externally insulated cladding, filled cavity (look out for pointed up holes), internal insulation, no added insulation (the wall is as built) and 'unknown'. There is an option to enter the precise U-value, but this should only be done where you know it for certain. **The same questions have to be answered for any extensions to the main building.**

D5 (Windows)

Parts of the building to be included in this element	Frames and sub-frames, windows, glazing, window furniture, sills, glazing mastic and sealant mastic, sash cords and boxes, shutters and shutter furniture, security fixtures and locks.
Normal inspection	<u>Outside:</u> **Use binoculars for upper windows** – the rules discussed previously about vantage points apply. The inspection should focus on the structural opening as well as the window itself, although any faults with the structural opening should be reported in D4 (Main walls). These features should also be inspected from the inside. **Do not pierce timber frames with any instrument to test for rot, use only a finger to check for firmness** – this is a difficult issue. Wet rot in window frames usually develops behind the paint film and can become very serious before the deteriorated wood becomes obvious. Every inspector will have probed a window or doorframe with a pen or set of car keys only to see it disappear into the heart of the wood! Large chunks of timber can fall away, allowing water to get into the building. Our advice is to look for the 'wavy' paint finish to the framing members and avoid any probing. <u>Inside:</u> **Open and close a sample of windows (to test functionality, access to inner and outer frames)** – this clearly indicates that only a few should be opened. We think that you should open one window on every elevation with one or two more on the side most exposed to the prevailing weather. Once opened, you should lean out (safely!) to observe other adjacent elements that you can easily see. **Measure with damp meter around window openings, in particular below sills** – this is especially important where there are signs of water staining and/or mould growth.
Typical defects	• Insufficient structural/tensile strength to support surrounding structure, e.g. in bays; • Defective lintels; • Rot to timber frames and sills – where the windows are in a poor condition, inspect internally for any signs of dampness; • 'Misting' (condensation) between double glazing panels; • Defective seals to double glazing; • Cracked masonry sills, lack of drip groove; • Defective seals around frame; • Broken sash cords; • Defective opening and closing mechanisms – if the windows are sticking or have been adjusted a number of times, look for other signs of building movement in other elements; • No escape from fire; and • Lack of safety glass – where the internal sill is lower than 800mm, look to see if it has been glazed with safety glass.
Information needed for the RDSAP assessment	• The area of glazing compared to a 'typical' property. (Responses include 'normal', 'more than typical' and 'less than typical'). • The proportion of windows that are double glazed. • The date when the double glazing was installed.

D6 (External doors – including patio doors)

Parts of the building to be included in this element	Door frames, sub-frames, door thresholds, doors, glazing and other panelling to doors, door furniture, mastics and sealant, fanlights, draught stripping.
Normal inspection	**Open and close, view frames, and surrounding walls while in operation** – you need to be able to open *all* external doors to properly assess – a sample will not be sufficient. It is important to fully operate larger patio doors including any tilt and turn facility as repair or replacement can be very expensive. Some of the larger doors may be so heavy that the fixings and frames work themselves loose.

Inspect frame and threshold in both open and closed position – look for leakage around the bottom of the door, both closed and open, from the inside and outside.

Note construction/materials and any locked door where seller is not able to provide access – if the door is locked, it should be considered as a limitation and reported accordingly.

Apply damp meter to inside surrounds and base/threshold – this is important because leaks around the doorframe are common, especially on exposed elevations. Try to lift the floor covering just inside the door opening to see if dampness has affected the floors, skirtings, etc. This is especially important with suspended timber floors where dry and wet rot can easily start.

It is also important to assess any glazing in the door. Large panels should be appropriate safety glass, otherwise they could present a danger to users. |
| **Typical defects** | • Rot to timber doors and frames;
• Warping to timber doors;
• Lintels overspanned, but reported under D4 (Main walls);
• Water ingress at threshold;
• Lack of weatherboard; and
• Defective door furniture, e.g. locks, hinges, runners for sliding doors, (but problems with security are not to be reported). |

D7 (All other woodwork)

Parts of the building to be included in this element	Fascias, soffits, bargeboards, eaves ventilation to pitched and flat roofs if through eaves construction, decorative/ornamental timber cladding (e.g. mock Tudor panels and finaels).
Normal inspection	**Inspect from ground floor with binoculars** – see the section on Vantage points for further information.

Inspect through the windows from the inside where practical – this is similar to that described for windows. If you can get a closer look by opening up a window, you should do it. The window can then be one of the samples that you open.

Note construction/materials and refer to C2 if any asbestos containing materials are used – asbestos containing materials are common in this element and need to be reported accordingly.

If there is no ventilation to the roof space through the eaves, then look out for signs of condensation within the roof space and within the adjacent rooms at the junction of the wall and ceiling. |
| **Typical defects** | • Wood rot;
• Warping of timber sections;
• Lack of ventilation provision; and
• Loose fixings. |

D8 (Cladding)

Parts of the building to be included in this element	Any claddings (tile hanging, timber boarding and mock stone) that are fixed or hung to the main structural wall. Any purely decorative timber should be included under D7 (All other woodwork). Render should be included under D4 (Main walls).
Normal inspection	This will be similar to D4 (Main walls). Particular features to consider include any open joints, loose pointing, bulges and unevenness.

It is important to follow the trail of any external defects (such as open joints) through to the inside and check for dampness. |
| **Typical defects** | • Slipped and laminating tiles;
• Rot to timber boarding;
• Warped timber boarding; and
• Loss of 'key' of stone cladding, tiles, etc.

Some claddings may have been applied to cover cracking or other problems with the main wall. Additionally, impervious cladding may stop the transfer of water vapour through the wall, causing interstitial condensation. |
| **Information needed for the RDSAP assessment** | Note the cladding materials and include with reference to the wall construction on the RDSAP form. |

D9 (External decoration)

Parts of the building to be included in this element	Applied protective coatings of all types that need renewal/reapplication at regular intervals, including paints, varnishes and stains.
Normal inspection	**As for the underlying building element/s** – this is taken to mean same as the walls, windows, doors, cladding, and other woodwork it is protecting. You should inspect with binoculars and from appropriate vantage points.
	Enquire from seller when last applied – this can be part of your normal seller enquiries questionnaire (see Appendix F) and can give you an idea of when they need redecorating. Always link the visual information with that given by the seller.
	Note the materials used and where – are the products appropriate for that use/location?
	Follow the trail from peeling and blistered paintwork to wood rot in timber windows, etc.
Typical defects	Peeling and blistered paintwork

D10 (Other)

Parts of the building to be included in this element	This section is to be used for external building elements that do not fall into the preceding elements. In the case study property in Chapter Seven, this section of the Home Condition Report has been used to report on a substandard porch extension, to limit the impact of the structure on other elements of the property.
	Other features that could be included in this element include roof terraces, balconies, large dormer constructions (smaller dormers included under D2 (Roof coverings)), external stairways, metal work, fire escapes and railings that are closely associated with the building rather than the grounds.
Normal inspection	The level of inspection will depend on the type of feature and its location, but the normal rules governing vantage points, use of ladders and checks will apply.
Typical defects	As the features included in this section are quite varied, we have listed some of the essential questions that would help you assess the condition of some of the named elements. (These are in no particular order or priority.)

Roof terraces/balconies

- Is the supporting structure adequate?
- Does the covering have an appropriate wearing course?
- Is there evidence of leakage below the terrace/balcony that is getting into the house?
- Is it properly guarded and is this secure?
- Is the balcony properly supported from the main building?

Large dormers

- Has the main roof structure been properly altered/supported?
- Is the dormer adequately waterproofed, especially the flat roof over it?
- Is the front wall of the dormer properly supported (especially if it is masonry)?
- Is the dormer properly insulated? Are their any signs of mould spotting, suggesting cold bridging/condensation?

External stairs, metal work and fire escapes

- Is the metal work properly protected? Are there any signs of corrosion?
- Are the staircases/landings adequately supported off the main structure?
- Does the design/arrangement meet fire regulation standards?

SECTION E – INTERNAL CONDITION

E1 (Roof structure)

Parts of the building to be included in this element	Structural timber or metal work associated with the roof structure, tie rods and other methods of restraint added to strengthen the structure, connections with the ceiling joists for structural purposes and adequacy of the ventilation to the roof space.
Normal inspection	**'Normal inspection' means physical entry where the access hatch is 3 metres or less above the relevant floor level, unless unsafe or causing damage to other building elements – otherwise head-and-shoulders if possible** – we think that you should make all reasonable efforts to get into the roof space and walk around. Only then can you properly assess features such as chimney breasts and stacks, timber components that may be damp, water tanks, levels of insulation, presence of wood rot and wood boring insects.

Typical restrictions will include:

- if you think the ceiling joists are unstable and will not support you weight;
- particularly thick thermal insulation that obscures the ceiling joist positions;
- possessions in the roof space that prevent you from moving around safely; and
- obstructions posed by the internal 'chords' of prefabricated trussed rafters.

In these circumstances, a 'head and shoulders' is all you will be able to achieve. However, as the roof space inspection is such an important part of the Home Condition Report, this limited approach should be a last resort. In normal circumstances, we think you should be spending about twenty per cent of your inspection time in the loft space. You will be getting dirty and dusty and will probably need to wear your overalls and, in most cases, your facemask.

Such restrictions should be reported, and consideration given to a re-inspection – if the roof space inspection is restricted or prevented, it is important to include this in your site notes, in your Home Condition Report in Section B3 (Further investigations or testing), and at the beginning of Section E (Internal condition). If you think the non-inspected roof space could contain a serious problem, you should consider asking the seller to make the space accessible and carry out a re-inspection later. This will obviously delay the Home Condition Report and possibly affect the fee, so should be done only where necessary. This emphasises the importance of efficient liaison with the seller early on in the process so that access is available when you arrive.

Where there is a 'room in the roof' and the underside of the structure is boarded, leaving only small and inaccessible roof spaces, you will have to form a view based on what defect trails you can see. For example, if the ceilings are heavily stained, there are a number of movement cracks in the plaster or externally, the roof slope shows signs of defection, then your assessment is likely to be more serious. Alternatively, if there are no signs of defects, the need for further investigations will be less and you can come to a clear view. In other words, it is not appropriate to call for opening up work just because you cannot see the full extent of the construction.

Do not force or open access hatches which are screwed down or paint-sealed – hopefully you should have already asked the seller to open any sealed access panels prior to your arrival (see Appendix F). If you arrive and they are still in place and firmly secured, then you should not open them, but make a note of this in your site notes and Home Condition Report.

View also without light/torch to detect holes/daylight shining through – most inspectors would do this as part of their normal inspection routine. However, you should be careful about the judgment you make after doing this. You will be able to see small points of daylight through older roofs that have no sarking felt, but they still do not leak. You should not judge a roof covering just from this one check, but look at other aspects too.

When entering the roof void do not step or put weight on covered joists or any other parts that are not visible and apparently safe – as the insulation of most properties has been upgraded over the last few years, it is likely that you will be unable to clearly see the back of the ceiling joists. You should be able to see the general position of the joists as a series of 'bumps' under the insulation. It is then a matter of feeling your way from joist to joist with one foot while the other is firmly planted on the last joist. This is appropriate as long as you have a rafter or a purlin above to hold on to. How safe this is will depend on the circumstances and you will have to make a decision on a case-by-case basis.

Stored items should not be moved – this is sensible advice because you could damage something. However, it should not be taken too literally. If you can carry out a more extensive inspection of a roof space by moving a small number of, for example, lightweight and well sealed boxes, then we think you should do so.

Do not roll back or otherwise disturb insulation matting – this closely mirrors the HSV Guidance and is linked to sensible health and safety advice, especially where asbestos-based thermal insulation may be present. However, this presents a problem and during a roof space inspection, you will need to:

- discover the thickness of the existing thermal insulation for the RDSAP assessment;
- look at the rear face of a typical ceiling to check the general construction; and
- check the soundness of typical structural connections such as overlapping ceiling joists, junctions of the ceiling joists and the rafter feet, and the support given by a spine wall to purlin struts, etc. |

E1 (Roof structure) *continued*

Normal inspection *continued*	It is arguable whether any of the above checks can be done if the thermal insulation is left in place. Therefore, we suggest the following: • Do not disturb the insulation if you think it is an older type (say pre 1970s) and likely to contain asbestos. • Only lift as much of the insulation as you need to inspect a sample of the features mentioned above (i.e. a corner of a roll). Do not fold back whole rolls of the insulation to give you a complete view. • Always wear your facemask. **Other features to be checked include:** • **chimney breasts** – to be reported under D1 (Chimney stacks); • **evidence of nail 'sickness'/deteriorating tile 'nibs'** – to be reported under D2 (Roof coverings); • **spalling of tiles/slates** – to be reported under D2 (Roof coverings); • **water penetration** – to be reported under D2 (Roof coverings); • **lack of firewall/firebreak to adjoining properties** – to be reported under E3 (Internal walls, partitions and plasterwork) and C2 (Health and Safety risks); • **poor support to water tanks** – to be reported under F3 (Water); • **construction of ceilings (if possible without disturbing too much insulation – see our note above)** – to be reported under E2 (Ceilings); and • **insulation thickness and position** for the RDSAP assessment.
Typical defects	• Overspanned rafters, purlins and other timbers; • Trussed rafters at too greater centres; • Lack of ties/lateral restraint to roof structure; • Split and warped timbers; • Insufficient strength for imposed loading; • Lack of wind bracing to trussed rafters; • Structural stress due to storage; • Unauthorised cutting of timbers; • Wood boring insect infestation; • Inadequate ventilation; • Torn/defective sarking felt/building paper; and • Entry by birds/wasps/bats, etc.
Information needed for the RDSAP assessment	The following information will be required: • The position of the roof insulation, the options being 'rafter level', 'ceiling joist level' or 'no access'. • The amount of insulation, from the following options: None, 12mm, 25mm, 50mm, 75mm, 100mm, 150mm, 200mm, 250mm, greater than 300mm and Unknown'. The same questions are asked about any extensions to the property.

E2 (Ceilings)

Parts of the building to be included in this element	Ceilings including ceiling joists, covings, ornamental plaster moldings, suspended ceilings and any beams that have been installed at ceiling level.
Normal inspection	**Visual Inspection only** – usually from the floor of the room. There is no need to get your ladder out for a closer inspection apart from where there are possible damp patches on the ceiling. Here, you will have to check the area with a moisture meter. In the roof space, lift a small amount of insulation (see discussion under E1 Roof Structure) to identify the ceiling type, because it is important to determine whether it is lath or plaster. **Note if original, suspended or clad** – is there any reason to suspect defects? Older ceilings may have been overclad with an extra layer of plaster, or concealed with a suspended ceiling to hide a serious defect. **Note any beams/concealed beams, etc. indicating altered room layout** – you should check in the rooms above to make sure any beam is in the right position and if not, report under E3 (Internal walls, partitions and plasterwork). **Inspect ceilings beneath bathrooms with extra care** – check apparent damp patches with damp meter if accessible. Make a note of your damp meter readings and cross-reference them with possible plumbing leaks or lack of seals to bathroom installations. This is to be reported under E8 (Bathroom fittings).
Typical defects	• Loss of key to older lath and plaster ceilings, centre roses and cornices. • Cracking to joints in plasterboard ceilings – consider link to possible structural movement. • Water staining and damage. • Asbestos content in decorative finish – the Guidance Notes point out that this is not necessarily a 'defect', but it is important that this type of ceiling should not be drilled or disturbed in anyway. If such a ceiling will have to be repaired or replaced because of other repairs, clear warnings must be included in the report (see further discussion on asbestos in Chapter Three).

E3 (Internal walls, partitions and plasterwork)

Parts of the building to be included in this element	Party walls visible from inside the roof space, stone and masonry work visible within the roof space (but not chimney breasts), partition walls of whatever construction, plasterwork to all walls (including the internal faces of external walls), internal wall claddings, skirtings and dados, internal lintels of internal partitions, internal tile claddings and dry lining.
Normal inspection	**Visual inspection coupled with random tapping to identify construction and detect loose plaster** – light tapping can help identify dry lined walls and in some cases, plaster to solid walls that has lost its backing. Care must be taken not to damage surfaces and decorations.
	Use damp meter around windows, chimney breasts, etc. – we think it is important to test for dampness at the base of internal ground floor walls and the internal face of external walls because these can suffer from rising dampness. Internal walls are often built without damp-proof courses (DPCs).
	Measure to confirm position of beams, etc. where layout has been altered and consider a layout sketch plan if required – although you do not have to carry out a full measured survey, you will need to check 'critical' measurements to make sure upper walls are properly supported (refer to C1 (Legal matters) if permissions would be required). We also think a sketch plan is a vital part of any home inspection and should be included as a matter of course.
	Open and close internal doors to detect movement/settlement after alterations – where structural movement has occurred, the door openings are usually the first to be distorted. Look for doors that have been altered to suit the misaligned shape of their frames. This can occur when the building has been affected by subsidence as well as internal alterations.
	There are a number of gaps in the Guidance Notes, which we attempt to clarify here:
	• Any defects in the party walls should be reported here, including the parts that are within the roof space.
	• Although the main wall section should include faults affecting the structure of the wall, plasterwork issues should be reported here. Taking the case of rising dampness, the problem and cause should be included under D4 (Main walls), but the plasterwork repairs should be included here and properly cross-referenced.
Typical defects	• Damp penetration through the external/main walls.
	• Dampness problems to the internal faces of external walls.
	• Altered layout/removed partitions without adequate support structure.
	• Loss of key to plaster.
	• Partitions that have insufficient key for shelving and other applied loading – we would also add partitions between dwellings, flats and common areas, etc. that are not robust and will allow excessive noise transmission, poor fire resistance, etc.
	• Presence of asbestos containing wall panels, linings and decorative finishes – comments as for E3 (Internal walls, partitions and plasterwork).

E4 (Floors)

Parts of the building to be included in this element	Underfloor structure of timber floors (e.g. sleeper walls, wall plates, joists, etc.), boards or timber sheet and panel flooring, thermoplastic tiles and applied parquet-type surfaces.
	Also, damp-proof membranes, solid floor structures, cement screeds, ceramic or concrete tiles or stone flags, underfloor ventilation, ducted ventilation through solid floors and thermal insulation beneath the lowest floor.
Normal inspection	**Ask the seller if there is a trapdoor giving access to sub-floor void** – hopefully, you would have already asked the seller to open any such trapdoor before your arrival (see Appendix F). If not, ask the seller on arrival so you can inspect it later. If this is not done, record the fact in your site notes and mention it in the Home Condition Report. If the trapdoor is lifted, you should carry out an inverted 'head and shoulders' inspection of the sub-floor void with your torch. An adjustable mirror on a stick can be a great help and it will allow you to see a lot more. You should avoid the temptation of getting under the floor even if the trapdoor is of sufficient size and the sub-floor void is deep enough. You should only get beneath the floor if there are fixed stairs that are safe to use.
	Inspection of the joists is not normally possible, and secondary floor coverings are often applied to the boarding – this is especially true for the upper floors where hardboard may have been fixed over the floor surface.
	Note that fitted carpets should be left in situ, 'wall-to-wall' carpets and rugs, which are not fitted or fixed, should be lifted in corners if practical, without moving furniture/items – you should never attempt to take up fitted carpets whatever the circumstances. Where you can easily lift loose carpets, you should do so. The restrictions imposed by furniture are described previously in this chapter, in the *Moving furniture, panels and floor coverings* section. Nevertheless, we think that it can do no harm to move a few small lightweight items to give yourself a little more space.
	Check 'spring' by jumping lightly or 'drop heel test' (i.e. stand on your toes and 'drop' down hard on your heels) – this is one of the most important tests that can be carried out by an inspector. We have come across a significant number of claims where defects in suspended timber floor could have been identified if the inspector had jumped up and down on it (but not too vigorously)!
	If wearing reasonably flat-soled shoes, you can 'ski' diagonally across carpeted floors to detect localised sinking or crowning – we prefer to do our skiing on a snow covered piste! However, if this helps you identify potential problems, then use this technique. We think the use of a spirit level is far more effective, especially as you should really be wearing safety shoes.

E4 (Floors) *continued*

Normal inspection *continued*	**Check with damp meter if floor boarding is accessible** – this is very important if you are able to lift the edges of the carpet. Sometimes you can push the pins of the moisture meter through a carpet, but the readings can often be inconsistent.

Follow the trail e.g. from lack of ventilation grilles/airbricks to suspended ground floors – a lack of ventilation to a sub-floor void can lead to the deterioration of the supporting structure. This will increase the spring in the floor, which further emphasises the importance of the 'drop heel test'. If you come across a suspended timber floor that does not have sufficient ventilation, deflects excessively when jumped on and has no access for inspection, you should give a clear warning of the possible implications and consider calling for further investigations.

Open and close internal doors to detect movement/settlement after alterations – any movement in the floor could lead to distortion of supported partitions – most noticeable around door openings.

In addition to the above items mentioned in the Guidance Notes, we think that you should link the external inspection to that of the floors. Here are a few examples:

Around the base of the external walls:

- Establish the difference between the internal floor and external ground level, and the relative position of the damp-proof courses (DPC) and the external ground level. If inappropriate, this may need to be reported under this element, D4 (Walls), E3 (Internal walls, partitions and plasterwork, E10 (Dampness) and Section G (Grounds and boundary walls). Cross-referencing between elements is very important and can often be a challenge.
- Estimate the amount and distribution of air bricks and other ventilators to the sub-floor void.
- Look out for external planters, path levels, etc. that could be causing a bridging problem.

At higher levels for other floors:

- Look for areas of poor pointing and rendering or areas of concentrated water run-off that could be allowing water to penetrate solid walls and affect the joist ends.

Typical defects	**In suspended timber floors:**

- Rot, including rot to joist ends to outside walls;
- Lack of sub-floor ventilation – cross reference to E10 (Dampness);
- Wood boring insects;
- Overspanning/lack of sub-floor support;
- Inadequate damp protection;
- Joists damaged/holed by service pipes/cabling;
- Disintegrating particle boarding;
- Deteriorated joist hangers; and
- Loose floor boards.

In solid floors:

- Inadequate compaction of hardcore;
- Breaks/lack of continuity between damp-proof course and damp-proof membrane;
- Lack of adequate damp proofing in older houses;
- Cracks to cement screed; and
- Sulphate attack resulting in 'hogging' of solid floors.

E5 (Fireplaces, chimney breasts & exterior of flues)

Parts of the building to be included in this element	Fireplaces and hearths, chimney breasts in the roof space and rooms (both present and removed), fireplaces closed off and the position and condition of external flues (e.g. balanced flues, flue pipes, terminals to open flues, etc.).
Normal inspection	**Check there is continuity throughout the chimney structure** – you must follow the chimney stack down from the roof, through the roof space and all the floors below, down to the lowest level. Some chimney breasts may 'rake' over and change position, others can change size between floors, but you establish the continuity of support from top to bottom.

If parts of the chimney structure have been removed, the nature of the support is usually concealed and not available for inspection. This may lead to a further investigation under B3 (Further investigations or testing) and an accompanying note made regarding the restriction to the inspection.

'Knock' on chimney breasts, to ascertain structure – some chimney breasts may have been altered, but boxed over in an attempt to hide the work. However, do not confuse this with fireplaces that have been simply boarded over or pipe ducts that have been positioned alongside the chimney breast.

Check ceilings and walls adjacent to possibly unsupported chimney breasts for any signs of stress – this should be part of the support continuity checks described above. Lack of distress does not mean it is adequately supported – you should still ask the seller about the details of the work carried out.

Random checks for dampness – we think that this is an ill-advised statement. Dampness can commonly occur in the following locations and so should be tested for accordingly:

● Around the base of the chimney breast at the junction with the lowest floor. Chimney and associated hearth construction are often not properly damp-proofed. Dampness can sometimes be found in the cheeks of the chimney breast.
● At the junction of the chimney stack and the roof covering – defective flashings can allow rainwater to enter the building and this can affect the chimney breast at lower levels.
● Along the lines of the flues serving lower rooms – if the 'draw' of the flue is not sufficient or the flue is not lined (they don't have to be!), then flue gases from appliances below could be condensing within the flue and soaking through to affect the inside surfaces. Checks for dampness should be made wherever there are stains or discolouration on the chimney breast.

Check there is a draught in open fireplaces which are in use – this is another part of the Guidance Notes that we do not agree with, for two reasons:

● The only effective way to detect a draught is by using a smoke generating appliance or tool. This is not part of the Home Inspector's kit;
● Deciding whether there is enough draught is a skilled judgment. If there is a draught, is it sufficient and what is it sufficient for? There is a significant difference between a little bit of ventilation to keep a flue dry and sufficient draw to stop flue gases of an open fire from spilling back into the room and suffocating the occupants.

This test is best left to the specialists!

Record any suspected and actual asbestos containing materials – the Guidance Notes point out that asbestos containing materials were commonly used around fireplaces, stoves, etc. However, we think that it is impossible to properly determine whether it contains asbestos or not. Therefore, during most home inspections, a material will only ever be a suspected asbestos containing material.

We think a number of other features should be inspected, including the condition and position of external flues, inappropriate installation of replacement fires and 'feature' fireplaces.

The condition and position of external flues – this will include balance flue terminals and the external flues of open flued appliances. The type of issues that need to be checked include:

● the condition of the flues themselves;
● their proximity to other features such as gutters, windows, boundaries, doors and ground levels; and
● their proximity to combustible materials – you should also follow internal flues through the property to make sure they are properly protected where they pass through floors, hot water tank cupboards, roof spaces, etc.

Inappropriate installation of replacement fires – it is important to make sure that any new fire has been properly installed, especially since so many are now available through DIY stores. However, this is a specialist assessment and where gas appliances are involved, you should always ask for evidence that it has been installed by a Council for Registered Gas Installers (CORGI) registered contractor and that it has been serviced regularly.

Older 'feature' fireplaces – the Guidance Notes point out that older fireplaces are often kept as decorative features only. You should not make any comment on whether this can be used as an open fire in the future, since this is a specialist assessment. |
| Typical defects | ● Lack of proper support where chimneys are partly removed;
● Water vapour condensing in flues and penetrating chimney walls;
● Salt staining;
● Poor or non-existent ventilation of redundant flues/chimneys;
● Unguarded/damaged balanced flues;
● Balanced flues too close to combustible materials; and
● Inappropriate installation of replacement fires. |
| Information needed for the RDSAP assessment | You will have to count and record the number of open fireplaces. |

E6 (Built-in fitments)

Parts of the building to be included in this element	Kitchen cupboards and worktops, sinks and their wastes. Appliances such as hobs, ovens, grills, etc. should not be included.
Normal inspection	**Open and close doors/drawers at random, but always inspect the cupboard under sink** – you only open enough of the drawers and doors to get an impression of how well the units fulfil their function. The under sink inspection is important because you can often see: ● the waste pipe to the sink; ● the plumbing connections; ● the rising main and associated stopcocks; and ● supplementary earth bonding between the piped services. **Emptying cupboards is not required unless there is reason to suspect a defect, then ask permission from the seller to empty it or ask him/her to do so** – this is another decision that depends on the circumstances. No one minds moving a few bottles of bleach and one or two packets of washing powder, but when you are faced with a cupboard packed with possessions you should ask the seller to move them. This is another example of giving the owner advance notice of what is required for your inspection. **Note that musty, damp smells may indicate failure in plumbing, walls behind fitted cupboards** – many under sink cupboards smell a little musty, but a strong smell could indicate a particular problem, while many modern sink units will have a hardboard back that will prevent inspection anyway. Like all other limitations, these should be noted and reported.
Typical defects	● Dampness causing deterioration of the base units; ● Damp in the worktops around inset sinks; ● Hinges and handles defective before the base units themselves; and ● Heat damage to worktops.

E7 (Internal woodwork)

Parts of the building to be included in this element	Internal doors and frames, internal parts of windows and frames, architraves, built-in cupboards (e.g. meter cupboards) and wardrobes, skirtings, dado rails, stairs, balusters and handrails.
Normal inspection	**Tread heavily on every step** – this is to check the stability of the treads and should be done on every step. 'Tread heavily' usually means putting all your weight on one foot in the middle of the tread. **Investigate understairs cupboard, which is particularly prone to wood beetle infestation** – the most important location is at the end of the cupboard at the junction of the underside of the stair and the floor. Stored possessions usually obscure this area, so you should ask the seller to move them so you can inspect properly. **Test fixings of banisters/rails by rocking or pushing gently** – for health and safety reasons, a handrail/balustrade should be able to resist a certain amount of lateral force. **Note any unusual gaps between skirtings and floor – cross-reference to E4 (Floors)** – this could suggest problems with the floor or lateral instability of the wall. **Open and close all internal doors – cross-reference to E3 (Internal walls, partitions and plasterwork)** – this could indicate structural movement. **Note any changed layout, particularly in older houses** – you will need to check continuity of support for walls that have been adjusted. We would also include checking for any uneven steps/risers to stairs and exceptionally steep stairs – if these vary too much or are too steep, they could be a health and safety risk and need to be reported under Section C2 (Health and safety risks concerning the property).
Typical defects	● Uneven steps/risers to stairs; ● Exceptionally steep stairs; ● Lack of headroom around stairs; ● Lack of banister/handrail; ● Excessive distance between banister posts/rails, allowing a small child to get their head stuck; ● Wood boring insects; ● Rot; ● Doors binding, warped and otherwise ill-fitting; and ● Skirtings, warped and ill fitting. **Deteriorated skirtings** – where the walls are damp, skirtings can be vulnerable to wood rot, so look for warped/ill fitting/crumbling skirtings.

E8 (Bathroom fittings)

Parts of the building to be included in this element	Baths with taps, shower cubicles and fittings, WCs and cisterns, bidets, splash backs, mastics, sealant and seals.
Normal inspection	**Visual inspection and operation only** – this will include turning all the taps on and off, including the shower and any hose attachments. You should inspect the trap and waste when water is running through it to see if it is leaking. You may need to open the doors to vanity units.
	Do not remove bath and other panels unless seller offers/does so him/herself – these panels are very difficult to remove and replace without damaging decorations or tiling, so they are better left for the seller to remove. If not, you should report it as a restriction.
	We would add a few more inspection routines:
	● check the ceilings beneath baths and showers for water staining, which could indicate leaking appliances;
	● check beneath traps and wastes for leakage;
	● make sure baths are properly supported (especially the larger cast-iron types) and look for signs of deflection in the floor below;
	● check for signs of wood boring insects beneath the toilet and the bath – a common place to find them; and
	● look for cracks in the WC pan and check to see if it is loose/secure.
Typical defects	● Defective seals around baths;
	● Loose WC pans;
	● Leaks/hidden long term leaks; and
	● Cracks.

E9 (Other)

Parts of the building to be included in this element	**This field is to be used for parts of the internal structure – if any – which do not fall into the categories listed above** – cellars are probably the most common element that will be added under this section.
	The following essential issues will have to be addressed:
	● Is the ventilation adequate?
	● Are there any drainage issues? Are there any signs of flooding? Is there a pumped drainage system?
	● Dampness – is the basement adequately tanked or waterproofed?
	● Is the cellar used appropriately? Is it suitable for habitable accommodation?

E10 (Dampness)

Parts of the building to be included in this element	This element covers the general problem of dampness within the property, whatever parts it affects. It covers rising and penetrating dampness, plumbing and appliance leaks and condensation. Dampness mentioned in this section should be cross-referenced with the element that it primarily affects. Only dampness that affects the condition rating should be mentioned here.

Normal inspection	**Internal**
	
	Home Inspectors should be fully conversant with the most vulnerable areas, and Normal Inspection includes:
	
	• base walls, apply damp meter every metre or so depending on furniture; do not omit checking internal partition/party walls, which are or may be built off the ground/oversite concrete;
	• window and external door surrounds; and
	• chimney breasts.
	
	This description of vulnerable areas matches with guidance of other survey types. We would recommend that you do the following:
	
	• When testing the base of the walls, it is advisable to take readings at a few points up the wall preferably to a height of about one metre. This should give you a more complete profile of the dampness and help you diagnose any problems.
	• Take a number of moisture readings in the roof space, including:
	  1. a sample of structural members to test for general levels of dampness (e.g. rafters, purlins, strutts, etc.); and
	  2. timbers that could be exposed to dampness (e.g. rafters around chimney stacks, underside of parapet and valley gutters).
	• Take readings on all wall surfaces that show signs of dampness, such as mould spotting or water stained areas, in whatever position it occurs. This could form part of following the trail of a defect from another element.
	
	External
	
	Note the position and material used for the damp-proof course (if there is one), and distance from ground level – see element D4 (Main walls) for more discussion of this aspect.
	
	Check airbricks or other ventilation apertures – as stated in element E1 (Roof structure), you should not only check the size and distribution of the airbricks, but whether they extend all the way through the wall. This can easily be done by inserting an unwound metal coat hanger through one of the holes.
	
	Follow the trail from excessive condensation to possible problems with the heating system, ventilation, and/or insulation – many inspectors do not see condensation as a defect, but rather something that results from how the occupants live in the property.
	
	It is true that the way people live can affect the level of condensation, but the root cause is usually associated with an imbalance between the heating and ventilation systems, and insulation in the fabric of the building. You should look closely at these issues during your inspection.
	
	Home Inspectors must not restrict their own checks and inspection on the assumption that guarantees or warranties will be enforceable, although the seller should be asked about any specialist treatment undertaken during his/her ownership (cross-reference to C1 – Legal matters) – when evidence of damp-proof course treatment is discovered, some practitioners will stop engaging with defects related to dampness. Instead, they usually recommend that the effectiveness of the guarantee should be checked and any claims made if there is a failure of performance. This is not an adequate approach and where previous treatment is noted, you should still carry out a full inspection and make a full diagnosis. If repairs are required, then the effect of the guarantee should be considered, but it should not be a substitute for clear analysis and recommendations that will resolve the problem.
	
	Where long term dampness is present in a property, you must consider its effect on adjacent elements. Since dampness is an agent of so many forms of deterioration, you must consider:
	
	• chemical changes such as sulphate attack in cement-based products;
	• corrosion and expansion of embedded steel components such as wall ties and steel lintels;
	• wood rot to adjacent timbers, floor joists, skirtings and dado panels;
	• deterioration of plaster and decorative finishes; and
	• increased levels of frost damage to external elements.

Typical defects	• Chemical changes; • Corrosion/expansion of steel reinforcement; • Rot to adjoining timbers – note the ability for dry rot mycelium to bypass relatively long stretches of concrete; • Crumbling plaster; • Discolouration/mould; • Discomfort/detriment to health for occupants; • Odour/musty smell; • Deterioration of decorations; • Blistering wallpaper; • Peeling paintwork; and • Frost damage to low level external brickwork.

SECTION F – SERVICES

F1 (Electricity)

Parts of the building to be included in this element	This element should include wiring circuits, fuseboards, consumer units, electrical fittings, and permanently fixed appliances associated with the electrical system.
Normal inspection	**NOTE: At the time of writing, consultations with the Institution of Electrical Engineers and other organisations were not complete. Therefore, we have included what we think a Home Inspector carrying out this level of inspection should be looking for.**
	Only a visual inspection of the accessible parts of the electrical system should be carried out. Mains switches, test buttons or other controls should not be operated. However, all the light switches should be switched on and off to check for operation.
	The visual inspection will normally include the following parts of the electrical system:
	• the point of entry of the electrical supply, the main fuseboards/consumer unit and any subsidiary switches in other parts of the building, such as the garage or outbuildings; • a sample of the switches, sockets and light pendants in each room; • any fixed electrical fittings or fixtures such as wall heaters or electric fires; • wiring/cabling (where visible) in parts of the property normally inspected such as the loft or basement; and • presence of supplementary bonding in expected locations e.g. beneath the sink, to the water and gas pipes, radiators and water pipes in bath/shower room, etc.
	If any part of the electrical system appears unsafe (e.g. exposed live wires), then none of the switches should be operated, and a clear note made on the site notes and report.
Typical defects	As the electrical system is a specialised installation, it can only be properly assessed by qualified electricians. However, you should be familiar with a small number of visual indicators that can help you to judge (in very broad terms) the suitability of an electrical system.
	This is not intended to substitute a proper test by an electrician, but is meant to simply put you in the right 'ballpark' to confidently give safe, but helpful advice (see the *Further investigation and condition ratings* section in Chapter Three for further discussion of this approach). The visual indicators for electrical systems are described in Appendix E – Condition descriptors.
	If there is no contractor notice fixed to the consumer unit giving details of the last test date or when the electrical installation was installed, the seller should be asked to provide this information. If this is not produced, a note should be made in the report and a precautionary test report called for.
Information needed for the RDSAP assessment	Identify the electrical meter type: single/dual or unknown.

F2 (Gas)

Parts of the building to be included in this element	The gas supplies from the utility company mains into the property, the gas meter, gas distribution pipework throughout the property and all gas fittings and appliances. Where the gas is liquefied petroleum gas (LPG), the element should include the tank or cylinders, any distribution pipework and any ventilation to internal pipe ducts.
Normal inspection	Only a visual inspection of the accessible parts of the gas system should be carried out. Main gas cocks or other controls should not be operated. Where the supply is turned on, the seller should be asked to operate the gas appliances in the property so you can observe them operating normally.
	The visual inspection will normally include the following parts of the gas system:
	• the LPG storage tanks (if applicable);
	• the gas supply's point of entry, the gas cock and the gas meter;
	• visible distribution pipework; and
	• the connections to the various gas appliances including all boilers, water heaters, gas circulators, etc.
Typical defects	Gas systems in a property can only be assessed by CORGI registered contractors. However, you should be familiar with a small number of visual indicators that can help judge (in very broad terms), the suitability of a gas system. This is not intended to substitute a proper test by a CORGI registered contractor, but is meant to simply put you in the right 'ballpark' to confidently give safe, but helpful advice (see the *Further investigation and condition ratings* section in Chapter Three for further discussion of this approach). The visual indicators for gas installations are described in Appendix E – Condition descriptors.
	All gas installations, appliances, and their routine servicing should have been carried out by a registered contractor. There should be a gas completion certificate for each installation and documentary evidence that each gas appliance has been serviced regularly. The seller should be asked to provide these, but if the information is not produced, a note should be made in the report, with a recommendation that the system and appliances be tested. If gas certificates and servicing information are available, then you should inspect the system to check if it has been altered or damaged since the certificates were issued.
	There should be standard paragraphs relating to:
	• any alterations since the completion certificate was issued;
	• any visual defects that are apparent; and
	• appliances not covered by completion certificates referred to above.
Information needed for the RDSAP assessment	Note whether mains gas is available at the property. This is taken to mean either:
	• gas supply at the property or;
	• gas supply in the same street.

F3 (Water)

Parts of the building to be included in this element	The utility company stopvalve, the supply pipe as it enters the dwelling, distribution pipework where visible within the property, external pipework and taps; water softeners, cold and hot water storage tanks (and associated expansion vessels if an integral part of the system), insulation to tanks where required and overflow systems. If the property has a private water supply, the water treatment system should be inspected.
Normal inspection	If the water is on at the time of inspection, all pipework, appliances and fittings should be observed while in normal operation. This includes turning on all the taps and showers and flushing all the WCs. Operation of a 'spa' bath is not considered a practical option.
	We think that the main stopcock to the property should be operated with extreme caution. If it is an older model and looks like it has not been operated for some time, there is a fair chance it could leak, so our advice is to leave it well alone and note the fact in the site notes and report. If the stopcock is more recent (e.g. copper fitting), then you should operate it with care after informing the owner what you are doing.
	If the inspection is unaccompanied or the property is vacant, you should not turn the water on unless a person responsible for the property accompanies you, and this should be mentioned in the report.
	If the lid of the water tank can be easily lifted, inspect the inside to check for sediment and corrosion. Do not do this if you have to dismantle insulation or something similar. You should also check that open vented systems have expansion pipes that discharge over the appropriate tanks.
	Where lead piping is identified, you should refer to current health and safety guidance from the local water authority.
	Other features that should be checked include:
	• overflow pipes to all storage tanks and waste water preventors (cisterns);
	• the amount of insulation to pipework in unheated areas; and
	• the adequacy of the support to the water tanks.
Typical defects	Some of the typical defects include:
	• old galvanised tanks that are rusting and close to failure (220 litres of cold water can cause a lot of damage);
	• mixed materials – if the piped system consists of a mixture of lead, copper and iron pipes, electrolytic corrosion can result in leakage;
	• asbestos water tanks – although asbestos fibres in water tanks pose no known health risks, these tanks can present a danger if they are worked on, damaged or removed, and should therefore be clearly reported; and
	• insulation that could contain asbestos.
Information needed for the RDSAP assessment	Note whether the property has any solar heating installed, along with hot water source details and the type of hot water controls.

F4 (Heating)

Parts of the building to be included in this element	The main heating source (boiler, open fires, gas/electric heaters), heat distribution pipework, circulation pumps and valves, heat emitters (radiators), expansion vessels, ventilation for heating source (if required).
Normal inspection	This should include a visual inspection of all accessible parts of the heating system. If the property is occupied, ask the seller to activate the heating system so that it can be observed 'in use' as all parts of the system begin to get warm. If the property is unoccupied, do not activate the heating system unless the person responsible for the property is present and make a note of this in the report.
	You should open panels and boiler fronts that are hinged and easy to operate. You should only dismantle boiler panels, lagging jackets, etc. if you have the seller's express permission and it does not take too much of your time. Other elements of the inspection include:
	• collecting all the necessary information about the heating source and controls that are required for the RDSAP calculation (see below); • asking the seller if they have details of the installation of the heating system and documents relating to the service history (make a note in the report if the information is not provided); • checking for non-conventional forms of heating, such as heat pumps and solar panels (although these are outside the scope of the Home Condition Report, they should be noted for the RDSAP); and • checking that there is at least some fixed ventilation to the outside air for open flued gas appliances that need it.
	Report where the heating system is unable to properly heat the whole of the property. Examples would include partial central heating systems or where a property only has fixed heating in the living room. A note should be made if there is evidence of secondary heating sources that are required to produce adequate temperatures, such as LPG room heaters, paraffin heaters or on-peak electric fan heaters.
	Other assessments of adequacy are best left to the specialists, but you should ask the seller to provide all details of the heating system, including:
	• boiler manufacturers' instructions; and • boiler service details and/or logbook (Benchmark certificate if installed after April 2001).
	If these are not provided and there is no clear documentary evidence that the system has been serviced in the last twelve months, then you should consider referring for a test – report in B3 (Further investigations or testing).
Information needed for the RDSAP assessment	A wide range of information is required, including:
	• the type of heating source including its proper code; • the type of heating emitter (radiator or underfloor heating); • the type of heating controls; • the immersion water heating types; • the hot water cylinder size; • the hot water cylinder insulation type and amount; • the presence of a hot water cylinder thermostat; and • whether there are any secondary heating types.
	(RDSAPs and energy ratings are discussed further in Chapter Five.)

F5 (Drainage)

Parts of the building to be included in this element	The above and below ground foul and grey water drainage, gullies, inspection chambers, rodding access points, cess pits and septic tanks.
	Soakaways cannot usually be inspected and so are excluded from this section.
Normal inspection	This is a visual inspection without any form of test. You should lift the inspection chamber and other access point covers that are reasonably accessible and can be lifted safely by one person. You should not lift inspection chamber covers that are bolted or firmly wedged into position, partially built or planted over, or too heavy (such as those with thick cast-iron covers or cement/brick paviour inserts).
	Only standard, modern inspection chamber covers, which are reasonably accessible and within the curtilage of the subject property (i.e. not in the public pavement), should be lifted – if you are unable to lift covers, make a note of this in the report.
	The Guidance Notes do not stipulate whether you should lift the cover if the chamber is on land shared with one or more properties. If the drainage is shared, we think you should lift the cover, but for health and safety reasons, take care to not leave it unattended.
	You should also:
	<ul><li>run taps and flush toilets so that you can observe the drains in normal operation in the inspection chamber, but be aware of the health and safety issues of leaving a chamber open when unsupervised. The Guidance Notes do say that you should ' … *call upon the seller's assistance to flush toilets and/or run taps, etc.*';</li><li>consider making appropriate sketches on block plans so you can identify the drainage runs;</li><li>note common or shared drains and private sewers, and cross-reference these to Section C3 (Other risks associated with the property) so the extent of legal liabilities can be assessed; and</li><li>locate and inspect any cess pits/septic tanks (including lifting any access covers), and walk around the full extent of the grounds to locate outfall/drainage field serving any septic tanks.</li></ul>
Typical defects	<ul><li>Extensions, conservatories and vehicular access that pass over the top of the drains, thus causing them damage;</li><li>Large shrubs/trees close to the drains/inspection chambers;</li><li>Substantial growth of lush vegetation (especially nettles!) next to cess pits/septic tanks, areas of waterlogged ground suggesting leaking tanks; and</li><li>Cracking/damage to adjacent buildings that could have been caused by leaking drains.</li></ul>

SECTION G – GROUNDS, BOUNDARY WALLS, OUTBUILDINGS AND COMMON FACILITIES

Grounds

The Guidance Notes state that only a brief description of the gardens and/or grounds is required. The inspection will involve a brief walk around the whole of the grounds. The following information should be noted:

- Obvious and serious defects to paths, patios, steps, drives and hardstandings where they constitute a serious health risk and require building work to rectify. Examples would include serious tripping hazards on a regularly used path or unstable steps to a patio.
- Unusual or unauthorised uses of the garden or grounds. This could include storage of materials used for business purposes or uses that are likely to cause a nuisance, health risk or create disputes with neighbouring owners.
- The location, type and condition of various water features including wells, watercourses, ponds and small lakes. Safety will be a particular concern.
- Additional features that may suggest other types of problems such as landslip or waterlogged areas adjacent to septic tanks.

Boundary Walls

During the inspection of the grounds, you should make a specific note of the property's boundaries, including walls, fences, hedges, ditches, streams, and even earth banks. Retaining boundary walls are especially important as their repair or replacement can be very expensive and result in costly neighbour disputes. Your Home Condition Report should briefly describe the construction, extent and condition of the boundary walls.

While 'walking' the boundaries, if you can see into neighbouring properties you should look out for any features that may potentially be the cause of future problems or disputes, such as:

- large amounts of stored materials or buildings that are too close to the retaining boundary walls (these could over load the structures and result in structural failure);
- ponds, lakes or water courses that could flood the property being inspected;
- livestock or other animals that could pose a threat if they escaped; and
- evidence of contaminated land or commercial/ industrial processes.

This section should be carefully cross-referenced with Section C1 (Legal matters) at the beginning of the report.

Outbuildings

Only permanent outbuildings should be included in this section and typical examples will include:

- outside toilets;
- greenhouses;
- summerhouses and follies;
- tool sheds and workshops;
- old air raid shelters;
- substantial animal cages and runs; and
- timber-framed barns.

Each of these should be visually examined externally and internally, but only if safe and easy to do so. They should be briefly described in terms of type, construction, age and condition. Only serious defects should be identified that require building work to rectify. Safety of the users is the most important consideration as outbuildings can be in a very poor condition. Asbestos-based materials may have been used for older outbuildings and this may be hazardous and expensive to remove. This should be cross-referenced to Section C2 (Health and safety risks concerning the property).

Unauthorised uses must be reported. We have come across many examples of owners using their outbuildings inappropriately, including operating a commercial wood working business in a garage, through to using a tool shed as living accommodation.

A closer assessment should be carried out if the outbuildings are connected to the main property. Faults at the junction of the two can easily lead to structural and dampness problems in the main building.

Garages

These should be visually inspected externally and internally. This will include raising a ladder to inspect the roof covering if appropriate and safe. The type, construction, age and condition should all be reported as well as its size because many modern cars will not fit into older garages. Like other outbuildings, special note should be made of asbestos-based building materials. If the property has an integral garage, then it should be dealt with under the appropriate sections of the main report. Fire separation between the garage and the rest of the property will be the most important issue.

A garage built against a wall of the property will affect the RDSAP rating by reducing heat loss, and will need to be measured accordingly.

Conservatories

The Guidance Notes point out that in terms of defects, repairs and costs, conservatories can be an important and considerable part of the property. Therefore, the inspection should take account of the following:

- The conservatory will need to be measured as part of the RDSAP data collection process. This will also enable you to assess whether the structure would have required building regulations or planning permission when it was first built.
- Heated conservatories will have a considerable impact on the energy efficiency of the property and this should be cross-referenced to the energy section of the report.
- Any inappropriate use including extended kitchens, utility rooms, shower rooms/WCs.
- Assess the impact of the conservatory on the enclosed spaces in the existing house. For example, the level of daylight and ventilation can be drastically reduced. Boiler flues and terminals from extractor fans have often been enclosed by DIY structures.

Leisure facilities

The inclusion of leisure facilities has changed in comparison to other types of surveys. Previously, they were completely excluded, but with the Home Condition Report, although leisure facilities themselves (such as swimming pools) are excluded, the buildings containing them are not. The Guidance Notes stipulate that if they are purpose built, of different construction to the main building, attached (i.e. lean to) or detached, then they should be treated as outbuildings.

If they are of similar construction to the main building and share a number of elements, they should be included within the main body of the report. Use should be made of the 'Other' categories in sections D10 and E9, which are the 'Other' categories for the exterior and interior of the property.

Common facilities

This part of the report should be used to cover communal features associated with the property, including:

- staircases and associated hallways;
- shared garden/drying areas;
- bin stores; and
- communal garages and forecourts, etc.

3 The condition rating process

The content of this chapter will help you to understand and meet the requirements of the following elements of the National Occupational Standards for Home Inspectors:

- **Element 4.3 – Interpret evidence to determine condition ratings**
- **Element 5.1 – Produce complete and comprehensive Home Condition Reports**

(A summary of the different units and elements that make up the NOS in Home Inspection has been included in Appendix B. A complete copy can be downloaded from www.assetskills.org.)

THE PHILOSOPHY OF CONDITION RATING

This chapter explains recent examples of condition ratings, identifying some shortcomings, and sets out several techniques that will help you achieve a consistency in your own condition ratings.

Categorisation and condition surveys – a long history

Condition surveys have always been carried out on buildings. Large organisations use them to collect data about their buildings so they can formulate strategic maintenance policies. Many of these surveys are brief and based on quick external visual examinations. Sometimes called 'broad brush surveys', they can help identify what resources are needed to bring the collection of buildings up to a desired standard.

The use of a ranking system is at the heart of this process, allowing the condition of buildings to be assessed and maintenance priorities established. To do this effectively, information needs to be recorded in a uniform way because subjective descriptions can easily result in misdirected assessments. Terms such as 'good', 'satisfactory' and 'urgent action required' can mean very different things to different people. The NHS Estates were typical of many large property owners and used a letter-based ranking system ranging from A to D, illustrated in Table 3.1.

The drawback with these grading systems is that they only offer a superficial breakdown of condition. A broad range of problems can be included in a single category. For example, consider an asphalt flat roof that has a 'B' categorisation using the NHS style grading system. It could be at the lower end of this category and exhibit only a few minor blemishes and cracks that would cause little concern. Conversely, it could have a number of more significant defects that

would place it higher up the scale. They may not be serious enough to put it within the 'C' category, but the difference between the two conditions could mislead a potential buyer.

Categorising building damage – the BRE approach

The Building Research Establishment (BRE) identified a similar problem in relation to the reporting of damage caused to residential buildings by building movement (BRE 1995). They noticed that a dramatic increase in insurance claims for subsidence damage followed the dry summer of 1976. The BRE investigated a sample of these claims and discovered that the resulting repair works were out of proportion to the severity of the actual damage. The research also revealed that the reporting of the severity of damage was less than satisfactory. According to the BRE, statements like 'extensive cracking to interior walls', can sometimes be the only description of damage given to a property, and the subjective judgments of

Table 3.1: Condition grading system suggested by NHS Estates

Condition Code	Descriptor
A	The element is 'as new' and can be expected to perform adequately to its full and normal life.
B	The element is sound, operationally safe, and exhibits only minor deterioration.
C	The element is operational, but major repair or replacement will be needed soon, that is, within three years for a building and one year for an engineering element.
D	The element runs a serious risk of imminent breakdown.

Reproduced from NHS Estatecode Volume 1, Appendix 2, 1995

individuals can vary considerably. This resulted in properties with a comparable level of damage brought about by similar causes being subjected to vastly different repair schemes.

To make the assessment of damage consistent between surveyors and other professionals involved in subsidence cases, the BRE produced a system dividing building damage into six different categories. The categories ranged from 0 to 5 and used three additional features to help distinguish between the categories:

- a description of the visual damage;
- a description of the repair works that were required to rectify the building damage (ease of repair); and
- the measurement of the width of any cracks.

The BRE emphasised that all three features should be used to classify the damage. The aim of this approach was to give inspectors a common vocabulary, enabling them to make consistent judgments whatever their background and experience.

The English house condition survey – a problem of consistency

The English house condition survey uses condition-ranking systems. Organised by the Office of the Deputy Prime Minister (ODPM), this assessment of the condition of the nation's housing stock is carried out every ten years. One of the most important judgments taken by the surveyors is whether a property is 'unfit'. This is a sophisticated decision that requires a comprehensive knowledge of building condition and what constitutes 'unfitness' in a legal context. As a consequence, there is often significant variability between surveyors. In the 1996 English house condition survey, a number of measures were taken to limit variation in analyses. Close monitoring gave an insight into the variability of surveyors in 'the field', highlighting the following issues:

- The rate of unfitness recorded across the full sample of properties was 8.4%. Despite this, some surveyors found none of their properties to be unfit while others recorded an unfitness level of over 20%. This range exceeded what would have been expected from sampling error alone, demonstrating that the dominant effect was surveyor variability.

- Over one thousand of these surveys were checked by a second, more experienced surveyor. The percentage of this sample judged as 'unfit' after the first survey was of 29.4%. This dropped to 22.4% after the second survey, suggesting that the level of unreliability is around 7%. Although researchers explained the scale of this difference, it does provide more evidence of surveyor variability.

The study concluded that for an overall unfitness rate of 7.5% in the national housing stock, the uncertainty associated with surveyor variability is in the region of 1.8% and exceeds the 0.4% expected as a result of sampling error. Such levels of variability could have significant implications for the Home Condition Report.

Assessing the condition of an electrical system – 371 surveyors and 371 different opinions!

We have been designing and delivering training events for residential surveyors for the last fifteen years. To help participants develop a consistency in their assessment of building condition, we introduced the 'assessment continuum'. This is a graduated scale that uses three condition categories: satisfactory, unsatisfactory, and poor. These descriptive categories have numerical values from one to three and each one is further subdivided into ten increments, allowing more accurate values to be chosen. An example of this continuum is shown in Figure 3.1.

Participants are shown photographic details of a particular defect or deficiency in a residential property and are asked to mark on the assessment continuum where this particular case study should be 'rated'. The results provide an opportunity to discuss the issues raised by the defect and give a valuable insight into the consistency of surveyors' judgments.

In 2003, a series of regional seminars were delivered to 371 surveyors working for a large corporate organisation. The surveyors were asked to 'condition rate' an electrical system of a house, based on written criteria. They were asked not to choose a value on the divide between categories and to keep the value to one decimal place only. We thought that the particular electrical system under scrutiny should be given a value of 1.4 on the continuum. The breakdown of results for the completed assessment continuums are shown in Table 3.2.

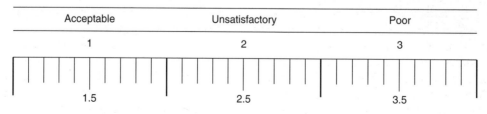

Figure 3.1 – The assessment continuum

Table 3.2: Summary of condition rating statistics

Description	Value
Total number in the sample	371
Average condition rating	1.9
Highest individual rating	2.9
Lowest individual rating	1.1
Most popular value chosen	2.1
Range between the highest and the lowest	1.8

Although training events like this do not properly simulate real decisions, it enables a number of interpretations and conclusions to be drawn. The gap between the highest and the lowest rating is large: twenty-six of the surveyors (7%) considered that the electrical system was at the low end of satisfactory (a rating of 1.5 or below). Nineteen surveyors (5%) rated the system at the higher end of unsatisfactory. Such a wide range of assessments based on the same information is a cause for concern.

The average value of 1.9 (chosen by seventy-seven surveyors) was significantly above our assessment of 1.4 and only sixteen (4%) agreed with us. The most popular figure was 2.1 (22%), which was the lowest possible value in the 'unsatisfactory' category. When asked why, many pointed out that choosing a value in category two would result in a referral to a specialist to check the electrical system – something they preferred to do whatever the visual condition of the system. In our view, this highlights two issues:

- surveyors are not confident about assessing services and prefer to choose the easy option of referring the matter to a specialist; and
- most surveyors would ask for a test of an electrical system for health and safety reasons.

Consequently, this identifies a knowledge and skill gap that many practitioners may have to fill before they can meet the NOS for Home Inspectors.

The Home Condition Report trial and surveyor variability

In December 2002, the ODPM appointed the Building Research Establishment (BRE) to design and implement an independent technical pilot of the revised Home Condition Report. A group of trained inspectors would undertake independent surveys of the same properties to help establish consistent levels of reporting. A sample of twenty properties was selected, providing approximately five hundred building elements to inspect. The sample included examples of flats and houses of different ages, building types, methods of construction and materials. Twenty-five surveyors who had experience of RICS

Homebuyer Survey and Valuation (HSV) reports were selected to carry out the inspections. Each surveyor received a set of guidance notes, attended a two-day intensive training course and received regular updates and further support during the survey period. All the resulting Home Condition Reports were analysed by the BRE, who made the following conclusions:

- The pilot results demonstrated high levels of variability between assessments and condition ratings of the properties by different inspectors. Much of this variation was caused either by inspectors missing or incorrectly assessing defects, rather than putting them in the wrong category.
- More obvious defects yielded clearer reports on how to deal with them, as well as more consistency in inspectors' ratings.
- There were still problems with the rating scale itself, stemming from ambiguities and scope for misinterpretation in the Home Condition Report method. There was no evidence to suggest that narrowing, widening, or reviewing the descriptions of the rating scales would improve the consistency of its application.

The BRE accepted that because of the nature of surveying, there will always be difficulties in translating opinions into a rating scale and there will always be disagreements between inspectors over the ratings they give. Similar to the English house condition survey, there were systematic differences between the individual inspectors, with some very lenient and some very strict. These variations prevented the proposed target of reliability for the Home Condition Report rating being met and aside from differences in the diagnosis of defects, there were also considerable differences in the language used and amount of description offered in the reports.

Conclusions

Home Inspectors must have a sound understanding of building pathology relating to residential properties. They need to be very confident and experienced with the level two type of survey (equivalent to the HSV). This will be particularly important for surveyors who have been exclusively carrying out mortgage valuations for a number of years, as well as other cognate professionals who are less familiar with the residential sector. Home Condition Reports are more technical and focus on 'condition', so additional technical training may be necessary for a significant number of practitioners.

All Home Inspectors should have to undertake intensive and detailed training and assessment so that they fully understand the nature and format of the new Home Condition Report. Guidance notes and training materials should be developed to give examples of how a wide range of building defects can be inspected, rated and reported. It is also important for Home Inspectors to effectively reflect on their performance at regular intervals to measure that performance against national expectations. A level of variability between inspectors will always exist, and further research is needed to clearly establish the limits that are acceptable.

Finally, the prevalent culture of defensive inspection and reporting within the residential sector should be challenged so that future inspectors can strike the right balance between confident assessment, condition reporting and the protection of their own legal liability.

FAMILIARISATION WITH CONDITION CATEGORIES – PITCHING IN THE RIGHT BALLPARK

Before describing the specific nature and format of the condition categories within the Home Condition Report, we think it will be helpful to stay at the conceptual level for a little while longer. Although some readers might find this an unnecessary diversion, it is important that you build up your intuitive skills so you can more 'naturally' allocate appropriate condition ratings in the future.

It's not going to cost you an arm and a leg

In training events, we have found it useful to try to simplify complex concepts to participants. When using the three condition categories, we have considered how readers of the reports will interpret the advice and we think that the public would be able to relate to the following statements:

- **Category One** – It will not cost you anything at all apart from the money you would have to normally spend on maintenance.
- **Category Two** – It is not going to cost you an arm and a leg – just an arm! In other words, you must be prepared to spend quite a bit of money.
- **Category Three** – This **is** going to cost you an arm and a leg – you had better budget for some serious spending!

Although this journey into the vernacular may be too simplistic for some, we think it would be clearly understood by most inspectors and customers alike. It is not based on an accurate estimate of prices or an intuitive knowledge of building costs. Instead, it uses a 'ballpark' approach with regard to the likely impact of defects or deficiencies in a property and their associated costs. Categorising building condition is not this simple, but it does put you close to the right answer. This may be all you need for most condition rating decisions. The next stage is to refine this broad-brush approach so that a more accurate view can be established. The assessment continuum can help with this.

The condition rating continuum – identifying the decision zones

As described previously, we have used the assessment continuum as a training tool. Split into three categories, it exactly matches the ratings in the Home Condition Report. The only additional feature is the tenfold sub-division within each of the categories. These increments have no formal status and should **not** be expressed in Home Condition Report forms, but are used here to help you develop consistent rating skills. Figure 3.2 shows our condition rating continuum, including a brief description of each condition category and along the bottom, three adjectives that summarise and describe each one. These have no official status, but we have included them to help in the assessment and report writing process.

When categorising the condition of any building element, two situations are easy to identify:

- an element that is in very good condition (say continuum values 1.0 – 1.7 or 'it won't cost you anything at all'); and
- an element that is in a very poor condition (say continuum values 3.4 – 4.0 or 'it will cost you an arm and a leg').

Condition rating two is a little more ambiguous because it is in the middle. However, if the defect(s) are properly diagnosed and the condition rating descriptions fully understood, most inspectors should be able to confidently place an element on the continuum between 2.3 and 2.7.

Problems occur within the 'grey' areas that exist between the categories. Making judgments is not a precise science and like the valuation of property, it is a cross between a science and an art! Placing an element on the continuum between 1.8 – 2.2 and 2.8 – 3.2 calls for a deeper understanding of building defects and condition rating criteria, as well as confidence in your own abilities. We call these 'decision zones' and consider them the source of much of the variability that we described previously in this chapter. The remainder of this chapter will offer an approach that will help you achieve a deeper understanding of the condition rating process and give you more confidence in dealing with those 'grey' areas.

HOME CONDITION REPORTS AND THE CATEGORISATION PROCESS – DETAILED GUIDANCE

Before launching into a description of the different condition categories, it is useful to remember how condition ratings in a Home Condition Report might be used. For example, a prospective buyer might have an initial review of properties on the market in an

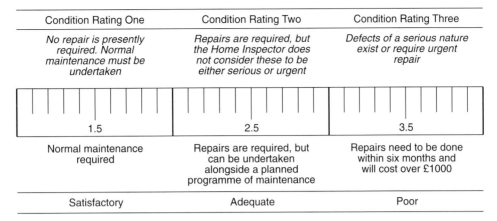

Figure 3.2: The condition rating continuum investigated

estate agent's office and immediately reject any properties that have building elements with a condition rating of three. Alternatively, buyers will use the condition ratings to identify parts of the report and the property that they must pay particular attention to. Similarly, sellers will get an indication of any remedial repairs that they might want to carry out before putting the property on the market, in order to improve their chances of a sale.

The three-point rating standard

The National Occupational Standards for Home Inspectors defines three different rating categories. These have been reproduced below and are further explained in later sections.

HICB Guidance Notes issued in December 2004 added a fourth condition rating of 'Not Inspected', denoted by the letters 'NI'. At the time of writing, the Guidance Notes had not been amended to include an explanation of when this is to be used, though we assume that it should only be used when the

inspection of an element has not been possible at all. Examples could include a pitched roof structure where there is no loft access, a concealed flat roof structure (see the Home Condition Report for the case study property), or a drainage system where there are no inspection chambers or the lids are firmly shut.

Using condition rating categories

Some of these terms will be familiar, but it is important to explain them in more detail.

Defect

An early version of the Guidance Notes defined a 'defect' in a building element as '...*damage, imperfection or fault, which impairs, restricts or limits the functionality, normal maintenance requirements and expected lifespan of similar building elements; e.g. flat roofs are not compared with tiled roofs.*' Therefore, a defect is beyond what would be considered as normal wear and tear. Cosmetic problems and minor

Table 3.3: Condition rating categories and their definitions

Condition rating	Definition	Additional comments
One	No repair is presently required. Normal maintenance must be undertaken.	This rating is appropriate where there are no indications of present or potential defects that require the undertaking of a specific repair. Normal maintenance is not treated as a repair for the purpose of the Home Condition Report.
Two	Repairs are required but the Home Inspector does not consider these either serious or urgent.	This rating is appropriate where repairs are required but the risk of the defect developing into a serious defect is minimal. Repairs may, for example, be undertaken alongside a planned programme of maintenance.
Three	Defects of a serious nature exist or require urgent repair.	A serious defect is one which, for example, is likely to: • cost more than £1000 to repair/rectify; • spoil the intended function of the building element; • compromise the structural integrity of the property; or • affect the health and safety of the occupiers. A defect requiring urgent repair is one which, for example, is likely to: • develop rapidly into a serious defect if not repaired/remedied now; or • cause structural failure or serious defects in other building elements if not repaired/remedied now.

defects that do not affect the expected lifespan of the building element do not affect the condition rating. The Guidance Notes point out that some features may be so unsightly that a layperson may be worried (e.g. very dirty and untidy rooms or decorations that would not be to most peoples' tastes). These will not affect the condition rating, but it would be helpful to include a comment within the report itself.

Normal maintenance

The Guidance Notes define this as meaning '...*work of a recurring nature which is routinely and regularly required to certain building elements, in order to preserve their integrity and functionality.*' This is discussed in more detail later in the chapter.

Deficiency

This is a term that does not appear in the condition rating descriptions, but is discussed in the Guidance Notes and is normally interpreted and used as a comparative description of shortcomings and/or poor quality. Since this can be rather ambiguous and subjective, the Guidance Notes discourage its use in Home Condition Reports.

Planned programme of maintenance

This is used to describe the timescale of the repairs that have been rated as category two. In a formal sense, the term has no direct equivalent. In British Standard 3811, *Maintenance Management Terms in Terotechnology*, 1964, two similar terms are defined:

- **Planned maintenance** – maintenance organised and carried out with forethought, control and use of records to a predetermined plan.
- **Preventative maintenance** – maintenance carried out at predetermined intervals or to other prescribed criteria and intended to reduce the likelihood of an item not meeting an acceptable condition. Preventative maintenance has two components:

  1. Servicing – scheduled work at regular intervals to prolong life and prevent breakdowns (such as annual servicing of boilers).
  2. Repairs and replacements – planned programmes based on observed condition, to repair or replace components immediately before anticipated failure. This approach is more common with larger scale, non-domestic property owners.

Therefore, for the purposes of the Home Condition Report, a 'planned programme of maintenance' should cover both planned and (to some extent) preventative elements that a reasonable property owner could be expected to carry out. Examples would include:

- servicing of gas/oil appliances every twelve months;

- clearing out of gutters, downpipes and gullies every year;
- testing of electrical systems every five years; and
- repainting of external timber/metal surfaces every five years.

Condition rating of multiple elements

Version Eight of the Home Condition Report Guidance Notes introduced the possibility of dividing each element of the building into a number of different sections (currently set at five, although this may be reduced to three). This has been done to help Home Inspectors cope with large or unusual properties. We think that this is a positive development because it is often difficult to concisely describe a number of different elements within one justification box.

Take roof coverings as an example and assume that a property has a main pitched roof covered with clay tiles, an extension roof of concrete tiles and a porch covered with a flat roof. If the clay and concrete tiled roofs are in a satisfactory condition, but the porch flat roof is leaking badly, then the whole of the element would have to be rated as a category three, giving an adverse impression of the property. Once these are separated out, a potential buyer can see that the tiled roofs are both category one and the small flat roof is a category three. Potential buyers can then put the category three in context with the rest of the property, giving a more balanced picture of the property as a whole.

Although the ability to subdivide the elements is helpful, it could become confusing if it is overused. Take windows as an example: it is common to find medium-sized properties with two and sometimes three different types of window. If they are all in a similar condition, they should simply be rated together with a clear description of the different types in the justification box.

To help make this process more digestible, we'll now consider each condition rating category from Table 3.3 in more detail.

Condition rating one

One of the most useful questions to ask is whether a repair is needed. If yes, then the element should be rated two or three. In this respect, the definitions for 'defect' and 'normal maintenance' become important. Some householders may carry out normal maintenance themselves, while others will employ professional contractors. Typical 'normal' maintenance work will include external redecoration, clearing of gutters and gullies, and servicing of gas fires and central heating systems.

There is an overlap between normal maintenance and minor repair. The BRE's view is that the distinction is based on time. For example, consider rainwater guttering to a property. If the gutters were full of debris and needed clearing out, it would be defined as normal maintenance and placed in category one. If one or two gutter brackets were poorly fixed or broken, but not resulting in damaging leaks, then this would be seen as a repair and placed in category two. If a section of the guttering was leaking, soaking the wall below and causing damage internally, the condition could be considered urgent and defined as a category three.

Normal maintenance will also vary between different types of property. Older historic buildings require a different level of maintenance than one more recently constructed. An older cottage that has thick stone built and lime rendered walls with a thatched roof will cost more to maintain than a similarly sized property constructed a few years ago. However, both will only require 'normal' levels of maintenance for its type. This is a common principle of the condition rating process of only comparing *'like with like'*, as suggested by the Guidance Notes. Home Inspectors must account for these differences and interpret 'normal maintenance' as something that is inexpensive and small scale. Each type of property must be judged on its own merits and in comparison to other similar buildings.

Condition rating two

This middle category is the most difficult to define. The distinction that separates categories one and two is the existence of a need for repair. This will normally require the intervention of a professional craft person or contractor (although some householders may still do the repair on a DIY basis). Similar to category one, timing and extent are important issues.

Timing

Take as an example the external joinery to a three bedroom semi-detached house. If the decorations are in a poor condition and a small number of repairs are required (say to a timber sill and an opening casement), and the work can wait until the next external decoration contract is due (say anything over two years), then it should be rated as a category two. By contrast, if the external joinery was rotten and had been letting in water in several places, then the repairs and redecoration need to done as soon as possible (as soon as the weather allows – say within six months), which may put it beyond category two. If the repair work is not carried out, then other parts of the building will begin to deteriorate rapidly.

Extent

The example given above suggested that the replacement of a sill and a casement would constitute a category two level of repair. This would indicate to the reader of the Home Condition Report that some money would have to be spent on window repairs, but not too much. If, on the other hand, the majority of the windows needed repairing and one or two replacing completely, the full extent of the repair work would exceed the category two definition. This would consequently become a serious defect and warrant a category three designation because category two repairs hold a maximum cost of £1000. This is an example of where the home condition rating format could allow the subdivision of an element. In the context of windows, we think this could be used where the windows are made up of different materials or types. So, if there were window frames made of aluminium and some of softwood, you could subdivide the windows element into two different types and give them different ratings and commentary, if appropriate. The same would be true where most of the property has standard casement windows, but has a dormer or skylight window in the roof, with the latter classed as a different sub-element.

In the case study property in Chapter Seven, we put all the windows under one category, whereas we have subdivided the doors to reflect their different types and conditions. Each case must be considered on its own merits, with the allocation of subdivisions only where it will help make things clearer for the reader.

Condition rating three

You will remember that in Table 3.3, we introduced two new terms for condition rating three (serious and urgent), which we will discuss next.

Serious defect
This is an important definition. We have included some commentary under each component part.

Cost more than £1000 to repair/rectify
Using costs to decide condition ratings has its problems. Although many inspectors will be able to estimate the cost of repairs, a significant proportion will not. Unless additional training is undertaken, lack of knowledge in this area could add to inspector variability. This is a controversial criteria that is discussed in greater detail later in this chapter in the section *The cost threshold – estimating the cost of repairs*, where we have constructed a robust costing methodology.

Spoil the intended function of the building element
Every building element will have a number of functions. For example, windows have a primary function to let in daylight, with secondary functions of allowing a view out and providing ventilation. As part of the wall, the window has a number of additional secondary functions:

- strength and stability;
- to keep the weather out;
- to be durable and free from maintenance;
- provide for fire safety;
- resist the passage of sound and heat; and
- provide security.

Not all of those secondary functions are as important as the others. If a defect undermines one or two of these secondary functions, then the condition should not be defined as serious. The *extent* is important and will always be a matter of your judgment. One or two sticking casements would constitute a minor repair cured during a planned programme of maintenance, whereas if all the windows were stuck fast because of swollen and rotten timber, it should be seen as spoiling the function of the building element and therefore classified in category three.

Another difficulty with establishing whether the function of an element has been spoilt can occur with older building elements. These often do not match the performance of their modern equivalents, either through design or construction, or both. For example, take a solid brick wall that is 225mm thick: this is a very common form of wall construction in many parts of the country and is inherently more susceptible to moisture penetration than a modern cavity wall. It has a much higher u-value, making it vulnerable to condensation and leading a number of participants in our training seminars to 'punish' solid walls by placing them in a higher category. This is inappropriate for a number of reasons:

- One of the guiding principles in the rating process is the comparison of 'like with like'. Placing the performance of a solid wall against that of a cavity wall will always skew the final rating decision and so should be avoided.
- You should always look at the condition at the time of the inspection. If a solid wall is not letting water through or allowing condensation to form, then it can only be judged as 'satisfactory' and rated accordingly.
- Speculating that solid walls will always be more vulnerable to defects than cavity walls in the future will result in subjective value judgments and lead to inspector variability.

However, solid and cavity walls *are* different, especially when they begin to deteriorate. For example, poor pointing on a solid wall is more likely to lead to problems and require a more urgent response than a cavity wall in the same condition. In this way, a solid wall will often change to a higher category more easily than an equivalent cavity wall and is illustrated by the case study property in Chapter Seven. This property has cavity walls where the mortar joints were in a relatively poor condition. However, there was no evidence of dampness internally and we rated the walls

as category two because we felt that there was little risk of rapid deterioration. If this had been a solid wall, the risk of dampness penetration would have been higher and consequently, we may have rated it as a category three.

As another example of an older building element, let's consider a prefabricated timber truss roof structure without proper lateral bracing. Early forms of truss rafter roofs often have less lateral bracing than current building regulations require. In theory, this could leave the roof structure vulnerable to distortion and damage, especially during stormy weather. So, should this be given a higher condition rating because of a design deficiency? There are two issues:

- If it is an older roof (say more than twenty-five years) and the slopes are true and even with no signs of distortion, then a lower category would be appropriate because the roof has withstood the test of time (and many storms) without any damage. A recommendation to provide lateral bracing at some time in the future could be made in the report, resulting in a category two rating.
- If the roof is more recent (say less than five years old), then the emphasis will change. Although there might not be any visible damage, it would not have been tested under a full range of conditions (e.g. full snow load and high winds), so must be evaluated more critically. Additionally, because lateral bracing has been part of the building regulations for many years, the construction may not have full approval. In such cases, a category three rating might be applicable with a higher level of urgency expressed in the report itself.

Compromise the structural integrity of the property

The phrase 'structural integrity' conjures up an image of unstable walls or distorted roofs that are on the verge of collapse, yet it is a very broad term that should be applied equally to all building elements. The dictionary meaning of 'integrity' is *'the condition of having no part or element taken away or lacking; completeness' (Shorter Oxford Dictionary*, 2002). Therefore, for a defect to 'compromise integrity', it would need to have a pronounced effect on an element, potentially leaving it unstable. Examples include:

- a ceiling that is close to collapse;
- part of a wall that has distorted so much it is unable to properly support weight from above;
- several roof components that have distorted and resulted in the roof slope becoming uneven;
- a floor that vibrates excessively during a 'drop heel' test;
- a window that is in such a poor condition it is letting water get into the property, and parts of it are close to falling out; or
- dampness at the base of a wall that is ruining plaster finishes and causing wood rot in the skirtings and adjacent floor joists.

It is impossible to give an exhaustive list, as you will have to make judgments on a case-by-case basis.

Affect the health and safety of the occupiers

The rating of a building element is influenced not only by condition, but also by the impact a defect may have on the health and safety of the occupiers. There are a number of dangers in the home and it is important that 'run of the mill' risks are not allowed to influence the rating. Examples of building defects that do pose a threat to the health and safety of the occupiers include where:

- there are insecure parts of the building that could fall onto building users;
- there is the threat of a gas explosion or electrocution;
- there is serious risk of contamination from overflowing sewers, high-risk asbestos materials, etc.;
- there are unguarded balconies or insecure handrails; or
- there are loose or uneven treads to a staircase.

It is all a matter of fact and degree, but there should be a clear link between the condition of the element and the threat to the occupiers.

Urgent repair work

The Guidance Notes give two examples of defects requiring urgent repair work, which are outlined and described below.

Develop rapidly into a serious defect if not repaired/ remedied now

In the explanatory notes for an early trial of the Home Condition Report, the BRE provided a definition of urgent repair work as that which needs to be repaired within a few weeks or months and certainly within six months. We think this is a workable interpretation that should be adopted. If a relatively insignificant defect has the clear potential to develop into a serious defect within six months, then it should be classed as urgent. You should not be speculative in this judgment – not all minor gutter leaks will result in rampant dry rot after only one winter season! Most buildings are generally durable, resilient structures and in reality, few defects develop so swiftly.

An important aspect of 'urgent work' is that it does not rely on costs and a defect can still be urgent without being expensive. A typical example would be a leaking joint on a gutter that is allowing a lot of water to flow down the face of a solid brick wall. This may affect the internal surface of the plaster, decorations and adjacent timber components within a couple of months. The cost of repairing the leaking joint will be relatively low, but should be done within weeks rather than months in order to prevent further deterioration. Other examples of urgent work include:

- Large amounts of water entering the building through a roof leak. This will affect the ceiling below, causing it to come away from its fixings and bulge downwards. Further leakage could result in partial or complete collapse.
- Extensive and/or intense dampness at low level that is affecting the plaster finish and a number of joist ends and skirtings.
- A foul drain that is blocked and resulting in sewerage overflowing into the garden.

It is interesting to note that subsidence related defects, although often serious, rarely become urgent. This is because few properties change rapidly and become close to collapse due to foundation related problems.

Cause structural failure or serious defects in other parts of the building if not repaired/remedied now

The definition of structural failure is similar to 'structural integrity' in that it includes defects that affect multiple parts of the building, including:

- a leaking gutter that gives rise to unstable plaster and wet and dry rot;
- a leaking roof that is affecting the roof timbers and the ceiling below;
- a plumbing leak that is beginning to affect the floor finish, floorboards and floor structure;
- building movement that has prevented a number of doors and windows from opening and closing, leaving a small portion of the wall as unstable; and
- dry rot that has caused a number of floor joists to collapse.

To come within this definition, the consequences of the defect have to be serious and the deterioration has to occur relatively quickly. If we take the leaking gutter example, the leak must be considerable and soaking through the wall to affect internal surfaces. If the same amount of water were flowing down the face of a cavity wall, the level of urgency would be different because the damage would be much less. So, do not be over zealous when applying 'serious' or 'urgent' definitions to defects, but reserve them for defects that have a clear impact on the building.

Condition rating decisions and inspector judgments

The previous explanations articulated the different condition categories described within the Guidance Notes and National Occupational Standards, and we hope that you will become more confident about applying the criteria as you work through this book. Nevertheless, one of the main difficulties that you will always face is a range of properties in all types of condition. No set of rules can cater for every situation and you will have to use your own technical judgment in many cases.

When exercising this professional judgment, the Guidance Notes suggest that an inspector should take into account a number of factors. These have been described below and appear in **bold**, with our additional commentary below. Condition ratings should:

- **Refer to condition only, not reflect purely cosmetic issues that have no effect on longevity or performance** – It doesn't matter what you think about the way people have 'improved' their property; if it doesn't affect the condition then it does not affect the rating. This is different from an assessment with a valuation component. For example, where a property had been visually altered in a way that might affect value (say stick-on stone cladding), it would be taken into account when valuing the property, but in the Home Condition Report, if the cladding is not affecting durability, then it has no impact on the rating.
- **Take into consideration the cost of repair** – See **Condition rating three** for more discussion on this aspect.
- **Reflect any detrimental effect on surrounding building elements** – See **Condition rating three** for more discussion on this aspect.
- Reflect performance – **How well will the building element keep performing its function?**
- **Compare 'like with like', e.g. not the life expectancy of a flat felted roof with a pitched, tiled one** – Inspected properties should not be compared with an ideal property in a perfect condition, but one that is equivalent.
- **Assume that normal maintenance will be undertaken in future** – You must always assume the person in charge of the property is a 'reasonable' owner, even if you suspect they may not be!
- **Be consistent** – Try and adopt the same approach, property-to-property, area-to-area.
- **Follow general accepted building practices** – Do not bring your own subjective opinions to the assessment. We have found that many practitioners have their own highly individual constructional preferences that often fly in the face of current practice. Make sure you are familiar with current research and construction practice and apply those standards, not your own.
- **Be reasonable – perfection is not the norm** – This is self-explanatory and you should not set unrealistically high standards.
- Not reflect quality unless it impairs on performance, life expectancy or normal maintenance – **This is especially true with DIY elements within a property. Although you might find some property improvements extremely distasteful, do not let them affect your assessment unless they really do affect the longevity of the element.**
- **Disregard individual taste or fashion** – Bright orange walls may give you a headache, but it will not affect the condition rating.

- **Take health and safety aspects into account** – See **Condition rating three** for more discussion on this aspect.

The relationship between a serious and urgent defect

Before we leave the definitions of 'serious' and 'urgent', it is worth emphasising the relationship between the two. For example, a defect can be:

- serious but not urgent – where the repair can be categorised as serious, but does not need doing within the next six months;
- urgent but not serious – where the scale of the repair is small, but needs doing within the next six months; or
- urgent **and** serious – where the repair is serious and it needs doing quickly.

The important point here is that all the above examples will be defined as category three defects, although their nature and extent vary considerably.

The cost threshold – estimating the cost of repairs

The Guidance Notes have introduced the cost of repair as one of the criteria for rating decisions. This is the first time this has been used so widely in the residential property sector. Although the use of a cost threshold has its problems, it has the potential of giving a common vocabulary to inspectors across the country. However, there are some dangers to be aware of. For example, the cost of repairs varies across the country. In one training seminar, a participant pointed out that most repairs within the M25 motorway would automatically be category three because prices are inflated by the 'London' effect. It is easy to have sympathy with this view, but official figures do not confirm this difference. Regional variations in the cost of building work are provided by the Building Cost Information Service and expressed by multiplying the estimated cost of the work by a regional 'location' factor. At the time of publication, this was set at 0.91 for Scotland and 1.2 for Greater London. Using the BCIS figures, the cost of replacing the guttering to a terraced house would be £550. In Scotland this would be adjusted to £500.50, while in London it would be £660. Although the difference is significant, it is not sufficient to change the category rating.

It is worth remembering that the cost of repair is independent of the property's value. Although homeowners' attitudes towards costs will vary (usually because of income), £1000 buys the same amount of repairs on the posh side of town as anywhere else. For practitioners more familiar with the valuation process, this concept may be difficult to grasp. A £1000 roof repair on a £750000 detached property would have very little impact on the value of the property or the buyer's decision to purchase. The situation for a £60000 two up, two down terraced property in a low value area would be very different because a four figure repair would affect its value and probably discourage many potential buyers. These considerations have no place in the condition rating process and the £1000 repair limit should be considered in isolation.

We think £1000 is a reasonable 'psychological' threshold. Although it may appear arbitrary, we think that the change from three figures to four would signify 'seriousness' in the eyes of many potential homeowners. In addition, if you consider what constitutes £1000 worth of repairs, most inspectors would consider the defects that caused them as being serious.

As previously discussed, many experienced practitioners in the sector may not have a comprehensive knowledge of the cost of repairs to residential properties. This could result in further condition rating inconsistencies as Home Inspectors resort to subjective and inaccurate estimates. The other problem that costs introduce is that it gives sellers and buyers a measure by which they will judge the accuracy of your rating decisions. Imagine the situation where a new owner of a property organises the repairs to a particular element that you had identified in a recent Home Condition Report and rated as a category two, but the builder's final bill comes in at well over the cost threshold. Since the level of this cost threshold will be in the public domain, once the building costs exceed £1000, the owner may feel aggrieved and submit a complaint. Whether this complaint is justified depends on the facts of the case. For example, the builder may have done far more work than was required or used materials of a higher quality than were really needed. There may be many different explanations why the £1000 cost threshold was exceeded, but property owners will still have a measure that they will use to judge rating decisions. This potential area of conflict cannot be avoided as long as the cost threshold remains. To maintain a sustainable defence, Home Inspectors will need to:

- properly identify and assess the condition of the elements;
- objectively estimate the cost of any repairs and make a note accordingly in your site notes; and
- after considering all of the rating criteria (in addition to the cost information), properly rate the element.

Although this will not stop conflicts, it will give you a properly documented and transparent decision making process which is the basis of a good defence.

However, the *BCIS Housing Repair Cost Guide* has been compiled to help surveyors provide guidance on costs of repair works and improvements identified in a residential survey. Although the Home Condition Report has a different structure and purpose to a residential survey, we think that this guide will help provide Home Inspectors with the costing consistency that will be needed when putting reports together. Chapter Six provides further discussion on how BCIS guides can provide a useful resource to assist in the rating process.

The final point we would like to make about this cost element in the rating process is that it should not be applied too literally. Costs are just **one** of the criteria that will help you decide whether a defect is serious or not and should not be viewed as the sole determinant of a rating. Additionally, costs are not quoted in the Home Condition Report, so no reader will even see your estimates let alone be relying on them. Used in this way, we think the cost of repairs will be helpful to Home Inspectors and encourage a measure of consistency between properties.

Further investigations and condition rating

The emphasis of the Home Condition Report is that the Home Inspector should come to a clear view. The Guidance Notes reinforce this and clearly state that '…*Home Inspectors must not call for specialist testing only to cover themselves*'. This is a reaction to previous surveys that referred customers to numerous 'specialists' for further investigations. After paying several hundred pounds for a survey report, many people were disappointed to find that they still had to organise further specialist inspections before they could be fully informed about the condition of the property. There will be many cases where you cannot fully assess every defect or deficiency and the Guidance Notes acknowledge this, giving two typical examples:

- where there is a suspicion that a visible defect may have affected other, concealed building elements; and
- where it is not possible to ascertain the extent of a visible defect within the confines of the Home Condition Report inspection.

In such cases, the Guidance Notes state that Home Inspectors must '…*recommend that a further investigation is undertaken*', emphasising another example of where Home Inspectors will have to exercise their technical judgment.

Whatever the circumstances, the important feature of the Home Condition Report is that a building element will always have to be given a condition rating even where a call for further investigations is fully justified. There is no provision for not giving a rating until these further investigations have been carried out. This is a critical judgment and we'll now consider three specific examples (building movement, services and concealed areas) to help illustrate the principle.

Building movement – condition rating and further investigations

Imagine a property that has been affected by building movement and consider two different situations:

- At the time of inspection, if all the visual evidence of defects is relatively minor and it is apparent that the damage occurred a long time ago (i.e. the classic case of the 'long-standing, historic movement'), then a condition one rating would be given without any call for further investigations.
- If the damage was relatively minor, had happened recently and there were local indicators that suggest it might get worse (e.g. a nearby mature tree, an older leaking drain), further investigations would be justified. To allow for this situation, the Home Condition Report has been designed to allow the allocation of a condition rating. The situation would be described in the 'justification' box, while a referral for further investigation is separated and put at the front of the report in section B3. By doing this, the reader can clearly see that the defect needs further investigation, but they can get an indication of how serious it might be.

This matches another approach that is recommended by the BRE when assessing damage to property. The BRE have developed the concept of the 'present condition survey', where a surveyor records the condition at a particular point in time, ignores how it might develop in the future and the information is then used in a more complete diagnostic process at a later stage. The situation is very similar with a Home Condition Report – there is no purpose in speculating how serious building defects will become in the future, as this will simply introduce more variability into the rating process. It is much more helpful to give an objective assessment of what can be seen at the time of inspection and refer the matter to someone who can give a more detailed and accurate assessment.

When determining the condition rating, the level will change depending on the amount of visible damage. Using Table 1 from BRE's Digest 251 (*Assessment of damage in low-rise buildings*), we have matched possible condition rating categories to different levels of building damage, illustrated in Table 3.4. When using our suggested approach, you should remember that:

- if the damage is recent and likely to get worse, you should always recommend a specialist referral in section B3 of the Home Condition Report; and
- the decision is based on what you can see at the time of the inspection and the future development of the defect should not drive your decision at this stage.

This approach goes back to the concept of 'pitching in the right ballpark', discussed at the beginning of this chapter. Sellers still might be left with the task of organising further investigations, but at least they will have a good indication for the likely scale of any problems.

Services – condition rating and further investigations

In the past, many residential practitioners offered little or no comment on the condition of the service systems in their reports. Instead, they often referred their clients to specialists almost as a matter of course. Not only was this expensive, it could also delay the sale of a property, especially when additional reports were recommended for damp, timber, etc.

At the time of writing, consultations with important stakeholders in the residential sector about the content of the Home Condition Report and Home Information Pack are incomplete. In relation to services, some commentators would prefer to see gas and electricity tests as a mandatory part of the Home Information Pack, allowing Home Inspectors to comment on the reports carried out by the qualified specialists. Other commentators would like to see gas and electricity removed from section F of the Home Condition Report altogether. Until these decisions are taken, the inspector's role is to inspect and comment on the condition of services in the property, and the following section aims to provide a safe strategy for doing this.

How far can inspectors go?

The inspection methodology for services has already been described in Chapter Two, along with precise inspection routines for service systems. The problem faced by Home Inspectors is that services are a specialist field. For example, electrical regulations have changed dramatically over the last decade and keeping pace with the Institution of Electrical Engineers' (IEE's) Regulations and subsequent amendments is a challenge for qualified electricians. There are similar changes within gas and water regulations, making it practically impossible for Home Inspectors to keep up to date with these highly technical requirements. Two other factors impose further restrictions on Home Inspectors:

- The majority of service systems are hidden from view and have to be assessed on the small proportion that an inspector can see.
- Faulty services can quickly result in serious health and safety risks for building users. The fear of electrocutions, fires, suffocation and gas explosions often results in many practitioners staying on the side of caution when assessing services in a property.

Consequently, a more balanced approach is required and the first step is to assess your own level of knowledge so you can establish your own skill limits.

Table 3.4: A comparison of BRE's damage categories with Home Condition Report rating categories

BRE Categories					
0	**1**	**2**	**3**	**4**	**5**
Negligible hairline cracks	Fine cracks that can be easily filled during normal decoration. Cracks rarely visible in external brickwork.	Cracks easily filled. Re-decoration probably required. Some external re-pointing may be required to ensure weather-tightness. Doors and windows may stick slightly.	The cracks require some opening up by a mason. Re-pointing of external brickwork and possibly a small amount of brickwork to be replaced. Doors and windows sticking.	Extensive repair work involving breaking-out and replacing sections of walls, especially over doors and windows. Window and doorframes distorted, floors sloping noticeably.	A major repair job required involving partial or complete re-building. Beams lose bearing; walls lean badly and require shoring. Windows are broken with distortion. Danger of instability.

Home Condition Report Categories		
Category One	**Category Two**	**Category Three**
The level of damage in this rating category would probably not need repairing. If it did, then the repair would be considered as 'normal maintenance'. If the damage indicates foundation movement (e.g. tapering diagonal cracks), then a category two or three rating should be considered. Category one should be reserved for minor thermal/moisture movements that have no structural significance.	This level of damage would certainly require a repair, but in most cases it would be small scale, not urgent and could wait until the next planned programme of maintenance.	Damage of this magnitude would always need repairing and in most cases, this would need to be done soon. It is likely that this type of damage is caused by foundation movement and therefore could be serious.

BRE categories described in full in *BRE Digest 251: Assessment of Damage in Low Rise Buildings with Particular Reference to Progressive Foundation Movement, 1981.*

Establishing a balanced approach

If you are not operating at an appropriate level, you may be making serious errors of judgment. However, the lack of knowledge is not the only danger – some knowledge can literally be life threatening! In our training seminars, we have encountered a significant number of practitioners who have some in-depth, but patchy technical knowledge about service systems. Although some of this may be accurate, their other views are often based on misconceptions or misunderstandings. This creates a false confidence that can entice practitioners to go beyond their role and make specialised technical judgments that are misleading at best, dangerous at worst.

We do not want to sound too dramatic, but it is important to work within safe but helpful skill boundaries. To help you assess your own skill levels, we have outlined what we think an inspector should know about services. In respect of water, electricity, gas, heating and drainage systems, an inspector should be able to:

- describe (in general terms) the main types of service systems used in residential property and know how they function;
- identify the main components of the most common service systems;
- understand what can go wrong with service systems;
- identify the most important visual indicators that give an insight into the condition of the service system as a whole;
- outline the latest regulations and statutory controls (including the most significant recent amendments) governing the installation, maintenance and testing of service systems; and
- explain the role and duties of the various qualified specialists who install, test, and maintain service systems.

The problem of changing standards

A service system classed as satisfactory ten years ago will now get an adverse report from a specialist even if it is in a satisfactory physical condition. This was recently illustrated when we inspected an electrical system in a property that had been rewired fifteen years ago and had not been inspected or tested since. Visually, the system seemed to be in an adequate condition and although there were a few minor defects, in our view these did not warrant extensive repair. Since there were no serious or urgent defects, we would have applied a category two condition rating.

To check these conclusions, a qualified electrician carried out a thorough visual safety check (not a full test). The electrician gave a positive assessment of the system and stated that '...*although some parts of the system were dated there are no serious problems that require urgent attention*'. The electrician's report went on to mention that a few elements needed upgrading and listed twelve repair items together with an estimate for just over £1100! The majority of this work related to changes in electrical standards and not to the condition of the system.

Looking at the cost of the repairs, it could be argued that this system should have been rated as category three. Faced with a bill of this magnitude, we could imagine a potential buyer questioning the validity of a category two rating. However, when we consider the case more closely, there were only a few visual defects that a Home Inspector should have spotted. It is not that anything was missed, just that a skilled person with specialist knowledge spotted more. Also, none of the deficiencies were urgent because they made the system dangerous to use, but existed due to changes in electrical standards. Finally, not all of the twelve repair items were necessary. After further questioning, the electrician admitted that two of the items reflected personal preference and these might not have been identified by other electricians. Omitting these from the quote would have reduced the cost to just below £1000.

We still think the condition rating of two was correct, but our assessment missed the need for a precautionary test. If the system was rewired fifteen years ago, it is well overdue for its periodic inspection. Therefore, in addition to the category two rating and reporting on the general state of the system, we should have advised in section B3 of the Home Condition Report that a precautionary test should be carried out. This would satisfy the Home Inspector's role by:

- applying a condition rating and commenting on the system based on the visual indicators at the time of inspection;
- not unduly 'punishing' the system because some of it was concealed or not having the necessary specialist knowledge to assess it fully, and
- recommending a precautionary test because one was due and changing standards would have outdated the system.

If we had found more obvious and serious defects providing a trail of evidence to more serious problems (e.g. dangerous DIY alterations or exposed live parts of the system), then a condition rating of three would have been appropriate, together with a recommendation that the system be fully tested.

Applying the rating

Using this and other experiences, we have drawn up some guiding principles that may help you assess service systems. They only provide general guidelines because each case must be judged on its own circumstances. Since service systems are potentially dangerous, a relatively minor fault alone may push a system into category three if it poses a significant danger. This is an example of where a defect can be urgent, but not serious.

Category one ratings will be appropriate where:

- there are no visual indicators of a defect or deficiency;

- the system appears to meet current standards (as far as a Home Inspector can judge);
- there is clear documentary evidence that the system has been properly installed, maintained and recently tested; or
- there is no evidence of DIY alterations or damage since the last test was carried out.

Under these circumstances, there would be no need to advise that a precautionary test is required.

Category two ratings are appropriate where:

- there are only a few visual indicators of minor defects, which do not pose a serious health and safety risk;
- the system appears to meet recent standards, although it might not conform to the very latest amendments/regulations;
- there is clear documentary evidence that the system has been properly installed, maintained and recently tested, but it may now have exceeded its latest test/service date by a short period; or
- there is no evidence of DIY alterations or damage since the last test was carried out.

Under these circumstances, there would be a need to advise that a precautionary test is required.

Category three ratings are appropriate where:

- there are several visual indicators of major defects or deficiencies that **do** pose a serious health and safety risk to the building users;
- the system **does not** appear to be up to current standards;
- there is **no** documentary evidence that the system has been properly installed, maintained or recently tested and now exceeds its last test/service date by a considerable period; or
- there **is** evidence of DIY alterations and/or damage since the last test was carried out.

Under these circumstances, there would be a need to strongly advise that the whole system is tested as soon as possible.

These guiding principles have been expressed generically so that they can be applied to all service types. To see how these principles are applied to individual services, see the *Specific elements* section of Chapter Two and *Condition rating descriptors* in Appendix E.

Concealed areas and further investigations

The Guidance Notes give an example of wood boring insects. Within the limits of a normal inspection, an inspector should be able to recognise and actively look for signs of woodworm. If nothing is spotted, then a specialist test should not be called for just because conditions for its development exist.

The use of further investigations will always be a balancing act that is difficult to get right. There are clear indications that the philosophy of the Home Condition Report represents a step change from previous types of survey. Inspectors are expected to be confident technical assessors on the condition of residential property who do not hide behind precautionary referrals to qualified specialists. During one of our training seminars, we created the following sound bite that tries to express this new approach:

'Don't three it just because you can't see it!'
Although many of you might consider this crass and too simplistic, it exposes a negative approach adopted by many practitioners. You must always look at the available evidence and then come to a rating judgment. Two hypothetical examples are outlined below:

A roof space that could not be inspected:

- A category one rating would be appropriate where the roof covering is in a good condition, the roof slopes are level, and there are no stains/roof leaks on the ceilings directly beneath. However, you should clearly indicate in Section E of the Home Condition Report that the area has not been inspected, and warn that the condition rating is based only on those parts that could be inspected.
- A category two or three rating would be appropriate where the roof covering is in poor condition, the roof slopes are undulating or 'dishing', and there are a number of water stains on the ceilings below. Additionally, a clear recommendation should be included that access to the roof space should be provided and a full inspection and report produced.

An inspection chamber lid that could not be lifted:

- A category one rating would be appropriate where there are no adverse indicators over the line of the drain run (e.g. large trees/shrubs, vehicular access, new extension to the building), no evidence of leaks or overflow and there is probably access to most drainage runs for clearing purposes.
- A category two or three rating would be appropriate if some of the above indicators were present. A clear recommendation should be included that the inspection chamber should be lifted and a full inspection and report on the drains carried out.

These are just two typical examples of the many areas of a residential property that can remain concealed during an inspection. This approach should be applied to other concealed elements that you encounter.

APPLYING CONDITION RATINGS

This section will now show how to apply condition ratings in real situations. We will first consider a few techniques (condition rating flowchart, questionnaire and continuum) that have been designed to simplify the rating process, before examining a number of photographic case studies that will help you to develop your new skills and knowledge.

The condition rating flowchart

We have produced a flowchart that breaks down condition rating into a systematic process, and is the first step to help make your rating decisions more objective. These steps have been drawn from the Guidance Notes and the Advisory Notes produced by BRE during the early Home Condition Report trials.

The process is simple: Inspect and assess the building element and answer the identified questions, to gain an indication of which rating is appropriate. For example, if the element is in a satisfactory condition and does not need any type of repair then a category one rating is appropriate, with no further consideration necessary. Conversely, an element that needs some sort of repair intervention may receive a 'yes' response and require further consideration. Depending on the circumstances, a yes response to further questions may indicate that a category three rating is appropriate. Nevertheless, this is not a precise science and not all positive responses will automatically result in a category three rating: it is all a matter of context and judgment. Therefore, we find this 'either/or' approach too crude as it does not match the real decisions that inspectors have to make. The next section describes the condition rating questionnaire that has been designed to help you make more sophisticated decisions.

The condition rating questionnaire

The questions from the condition rating flowchart have been reproduced in this 'questionnaire'. You should assess the building elements in the same way as before and tick the appropriate response. The responses are graded from **unlikely** to **very likely**. If something was unlikely to happen, it would be appropriate to place a tick in column one. If you think something was very likely to happen, it would be appropriate to place a tick in column three. Column two is for borderline cases.

After you have responded to all the questions, add up the responses in each column to get a total. If most of your responses are in column one, then the appropriate condition rating is likely to be category one and no further consideration is necessary. If most

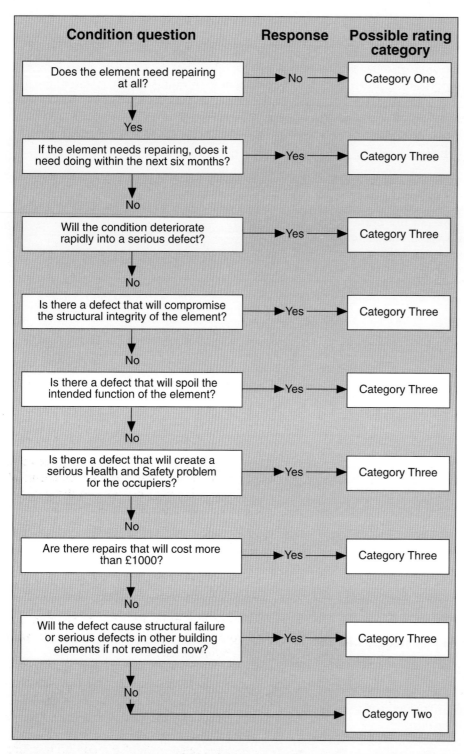

Condition question	Response	Possible rating category
Does the element need repairing at all?	No	Category One
If the element needs repairing, does it need doing within the next six months?	Yes	Category Three
Will the condition deteriorate rapidly into a serious defect?	Yes	Category Three
Is there a defect that will compromise the structural integrity of the element?	Yes	Category Three
Is there a defect that will spoil the intended function of the element?	Yes	Category Three
Is there a defect that wlil create a serious Health and Safety problem for the occupiers?	Yes	Category Three
Are there repairs that will cost more than £1000?	Yes	Category Three
Will the defect cause structural failure or serious defects in other building elements if not remedied now?	Yes	Category Three
		Category Two

Figure 3.3: Condition rating flowchart

of your ticks are in columns two and three, then your condition rating will be moving towards category three. If, on the other hand you have mostly ones with a few twos, a category one condition rating would be appropriate. Condition rating two will be somewhere in the middle.

The questionnaire is merely a tool to help put you in the right ballpark and aid your decision making processes. It is in no way intended as a replacement for your own professional judgment, which should be based on a complete analysis of the building element's condition.

The condition rating continuum

Placing a building element in the appropriate category is one of the main objectives of the Home Condition Report. However, because a range of different conditions are covered within each category it would be useful to know exactly where within a category you have placed the building element. This will give you a better understanding of your own condition rating skills and to facilitate this, we have included our condition rating continuum that allows you to express your assessments on a graduated scale. As you can see

	Questions	Response		
		Unlikely		Very likely
		1	2	3
1.	Does the element need repairing at all?			
2.	If the element needs repairing, does it need doing within the next six months?			
3.	Will the condition deteriorate rapidly into a serious defect?			
4.	Is there a defect that will compromise the structural integrity of the element?			
5.	Is there a defect that will spoil the intended function of the element?			
6.	Is there a defect that will create a serious Health and Safety problem for the occupiers?			
7.	Are there repairs that will cost more than £1000?			
8.	Will the defect cause structural failure or serious defects in other building elements if not remedied now?			
	Total number of responses in each category			

Figure 3.4: The condition rating questionnaire

in Figure 3.5, each condition rating category has been subdivided into ten further increments with the following values:

- Category one: 1.0 – 1.9
- Category two: 2.0 – 2.9
- Category three: 3.0 – 3.9

CONDITION RATING OF ROOF COVERINGS – A PRACTICAL EXAMPLE

To illustrate how these different techniques can be used, we have put together some examples of roof coverings from three different properties. These are typical examples of their type and will help to identify the main differences between the condition rating categories.

Briefing for the condition rating exercise

The photographs in Figures 3.6 to 3.14 show the tiled and slated coverings of three different roofs. For the purposes of this practical example, only the roof coverings will be considered. The chimneys, gutters, and roof structures will be ignored as they are covered in other parts of the Home Condition Report form. We have included just a small number of photographs to illustrate the roof examples and they should be taken as being typical of the roof as a whole.

Before you turn to read our analysis of the roof examples, you should work through the following

exercises yourself. You will benefit far more from this practical example if you first form an independent view before comparing your opinions to those of our own and reflecting on any differences.

Instructions

Study the photographs of the three properties and do the following for each one:

- List the most important features of the condition of the roof coverings that will influence your condition rating decision.
- For each different roof covering, work through the condition rating flowchart and then answer all the questions in the condition rating questionnaire. Add up your responses and propose an overall condition rating for each roof covering.
- Using the graduated scale of the condition rating continuum, choose a more precise value for the condition rating. For the purposes of this exercise, you should:
- Express your answer to one decimal place only.
- Not choose whole numbers on the border between adjacent categories, (i.e. you are not allowed to choose the values 1.0, 2.0, 3.0, or 4.0). This may seem petty, but it forces you into a positive decision rather than sitting on the fence!

Make a note of this information and only then go on to the feedback sections to discover how we rated the examples.

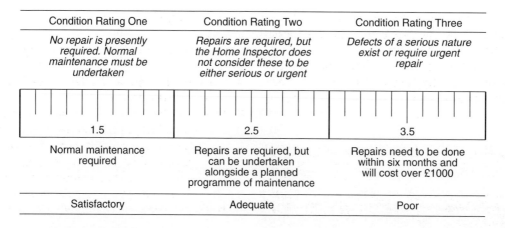

Condition Rating One	Condition Rating Two	Condition Rating Three
No repair is presently required. Normal maintenance must be undertaken	*Repairs are required, but the Home Inspector does not consider these to be either serious or urgent*	*Defects of a serious nature exist or require urgent repair*
1.5	2.5	3.5
Normal maintenance required	Repairs are required, but can be undertaken alongside a planned programme of maintenance	Repairs need to be done within six months and will cost over £1000
Satisfactory	Adequate	Poor

Figure 3.5: The condition rating continuum (re)investigated

The next section will include a brief description for all three roof covering examples, with each example accompanied by three photographs.

Roof covering A – property details

This is a clay-tiled roof of a house built during the inter-war period. The most important features include:

- A covering supported by a traditional timber 'cut' roof structure that is adequate for its purpose.
- No missing or cracked tiles. The roof slope is even and well laid, and the ridge and hip tiles have recently been rebedded/repointed – although not too neatly!
- (Assume an internal inspection has revealed that there is no sarking felt). The tiles are back pointed (torching) and there are no roof leaks. The nibs on the back of the tiles are in good condition and only a few tiles have been replaced in the past.

Roof covering B – property details

The roof of this refurbished cottage was recovered with slate approximately twenty years ago. The most important features include:

- A generally even roof slope. The internal inspection reveals that there are no roof leaks and the covering has sarking felt beneath.

Figure 3.7: Roof covering A

Figure 3.8: Roof covering A

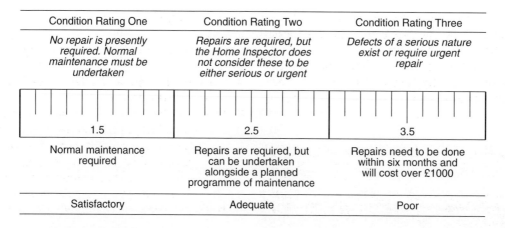

Figure 3.6: Roof covering A

- Externally, a small number of slates have slipped and three are missing. These are generally located around the eaves and the verges.
- A few slates (less than ten) have their corners snapped off. The ridge tiles are adequately bedded, and there is no evidence of previously replaced slates.

Figure 3.9: Roof covering B

Figure 3.10: Roof covering B

Figure 3.11: Roof covering B

Roof covering C – property details

This slate roof covers an older property that was built in 1850. The most important features include:
- An uneven slope and a large number of slipped and cracked slates.
- Evidence that several slates have been replaced in the past and ridge tiles that need repointing.
- The internal inspection of the roof space reveals that the slates are laid over sarking felt, but this is an old and brittle type that has a number of tears and splits.
- Water has been penetrating the sarking felt and has badly damaged one of the ceilings below.

Figure 3.12: Roof covering C

Figure 3.13: Roof covering C

Figure 3.14: Roof covering C

Roof covering A – feedback

Condition rating questionnaire

All the questions are relatively easy to answer and there is little doubt over the responses. No repairs are required and there is no suggestion that the roof would deteriorate in the near future. The condition rating questionnaire shows eight 'Unlikely' responses and this is clearly a category one condition rating.

Condition rating continuum

This is not a marginal decision and so the continuum value will be towards the lower end of category one. We think 1.2 or 1.3 is about right. What rating did you give?

As with many roofs, you could forecast that the level of repairs will increase in the future, but this is too speculative to influence the rating decision. Any minor problems that may occur will be repaired from time to time as part of normal maintenance work.

Roof covering B – feedback

Condition rating questionnaire

Although the condition of this roof could be described as 'adequate', it does need some repairs that are beyond 'normal maintenance' and so places this roof covering in a category two condition rating. The repairs are not urgent because water is not penetrating the fabric of the building. The repairs can be delayed for some time (say two or three years) without any adverse effect. The cost is likely to be less than £1000 as it will be a straightforward job for a roofing contractor, and so a condition rating of two would be safe.

Condition rating continuum

Like roof covering A, roof covering B is not a marginal decision. With six 'unlikely' responses, one in the middle and only one 'very likely', this rating will be towards the lower end of category two – we think around 2.3.

	Questions	Response		
		Unlikely		Very likely
		1	**2**	**3**
1.	Does the element need repairing at all?	◉		
2.	If the element needs repairing, does it need doing within the next six months?	◉		
3.	Will the condition deteriorate rapidly into a serious defect?	◉		
4.	Is there a defect that will compromise the structural integrity of the element?	◉		
5.	Is there a defect that will spoil the intended function of the element?	◉		
6.	Is there a defect that will create a serious Health and Safety problem for the occupiers?	◉		
7.	Are there repairs that will cost more than £1000?	◉		
8.	Will the defect cause structural failure or serious defects in other building elements if not remedied now?	◉		
	Total number of responses in each category	8	0	0

Figure 3.15: Condition rating questionnaire for roof covering A

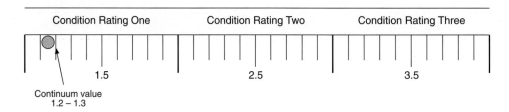

Figure 3.16: Condition rating continuum for roof covering A

Questions	Response		
	Unlikely **1**	**2**	Very likely **3**
1. Does the element need repairing at all?			⊙
2. If the element needs repairing, does it need doing within the next six months?		⊙	
3. Will the condition deteriorate rapidly into a serious defect?			
4. Is there a defect that will compromise the structural integrity of the element?	⊙		
5. Is there a defect that will spoil the intended function of the element?	⊙		
6. Is there a defect that will create a serious Health and Safety problem for the occupiers?	⊙		
7. Are there repairs that will cost more than £1000?	⊙		
8. Will the defect cause structural failure or serious defects in other building elements if not remedied now?	⊙		
Total number of responses in each category	6	1	1

Figure 3.17: Condition rating questionnaire for roof covering B

Roof covering C – feedback

This roof needs repairing urgently. Water is penetrating the building and if this is not stopped, other parts could begin to deteriorate. The poor state of the slates will leave them vulnerable to storm damage that could result in even more damage. It is likely that small areas of slates will have to be replaced because so many have slipped or cracked.

Condition rating questionnaire

This roof covering is much worse than roof coverings A and B. It needs urgent repairs that cannot wait until the next maintenance cycle. A general overhaul within the next few weeks or months is required, although complete renewal will be more cost effective in the medium term. In theory, a more serious defect could develop that threatens the structural integrity of the building, but this is not a positive certainty. The function of the covering is clearly in danger of being spoilt (i.e. it does not keep the rain out!) and likelihood of slates

falling off could endanger occupants and passers by. The cost of repairs could easily be above £1000 and replacement of the entire roof covering could be anticipated within the next five years if not repaired in the short term.

However, the problem does not need further investigation. A Home Inspector should be able to fully appraise the condition of this roof and come to a firm view within the scope of the Home Condition Report. There will be no need to call in a roofing contractor for the purposes of assessment, and it will be the report reader's decision whether to get an accurate estimate for the cost of repairs.

Condition rating continuum

The combination of three middle responses, with five 'very likely' responses in the condition rating questionnaire clearly puts roof covering C into a category three condition rating. Since the answers to questions four to six are more strongly positive, we think it should be in the lower half of category three. A rating of around 3.3 seems about right.

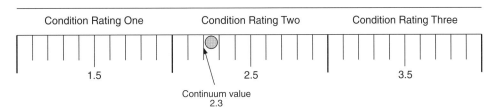

Figure 3.18: Condition rating continuum for roof covering B

	Questions	Response		
		Unlikely		Very likely
		1	**2**	**3**
1.	Does the element need repairing at all?			⦿
2.	If the element needs repairing, does it need doing within the next six months?			⦿
3.	Will the condition deteriorate rapidly into a serious defect?			⦿
4.	Is there a defect that will compromise the structural integrity of the element?		⦿	
5.	Is there a defect that will spoil the intended function of the element?		⦿	
6.	Is there a defect that will create a serious Health and Safety problem for the occupiers?		⦿	
7.	Are there repairs that will cost more than £1000?			⦿
8.	Will the defect cause structural failure or serious defects in other building elements if not remedied now?			⦿
	Total number of responses in each category	0	3	5

Figure 3.19: Condition rating questionnaire for roof covering C

Figure 3.20: Condition rating continuum for roof covering C

Reflection on your performance

Each of these roof coverings is a typical example of their type. Using the condition rating descriptions, they sit comfortably within each one and most Home Inspectors would choose the correct category. If your continuum rating responses are within the following values, we think you have made appropriate assessments.

- Roof covering A – anything below 1.5
- Roof covering B – between 2.2 and 2.5
- Roof covering C – between 3.2 and 3.5

Compare our assessments to your own – hopefully they are close. If not, go back to the questionnaire and compare where your responses diverged from our own. We will never claim that our assessments are the absolute correct answers, but they are reasonably close. The important part of any exercise like this is to reflect on your own performance and understand why you have come to a different decision. You may be convinced that your responses are the correct ones and if you have arrived at that point by following clear, objective, rational and consistent reasoning, then that is your judgment and you should stick to it.

DEALING WITH BORDERLINE DECISIONS

The vast majority of building elements will be easy to rate. However, what if roof covering A had a few more defects? What if the ridge tiles were loose, or three or four clay tiles were cracked or missing? The roof could still be described as 'satisfactory', but a few repairs would be needed (although not urgently). This might change the position of the rating on the continuum, but would it stay within category one or would the repair requirements nudge it into category two?

Decision zones

The difference between a rating of 1.8 to 1.9 and 2.1 to 2.2 could be considered within a normal margin of error. No amount of objective analysis can help in some borderline cases. The decision will often rely on the inspector's intuition and which category 'feels' right. This may sound like a mystical process, but it isn't. Dealing with marginal issues is a skill that requires a deeper understanding of the rating criteria and experience in their application. Figure 3.21 shows an annotated version of the condition rating continuum. On this diagram, we have identified two different types of theoretical 'decision zones'. These include:

- **Clear judgment zones** – based on the definitions of the different categories; these are the zones that most inspectors should have no difficulty in judging. There should be little difficulty in placing an element of a building within one of these zones.
- **Marginal judgment zones** – these occupy the 'grey' area between and most inspectors will find it challenging to make an assessment in these regions.

Looking at the continuum as a whole, each category has the following number of 'marginal' increments:

- Category one – two marginal increments
- Category two – four marginal increments
- Category three – two marginal increments

This helps explain why assessments in category two are often difficult. The overlap with the other two divisions reduces the size of the central clear judgment zone and reduces certainty.

One method of building your confidence with marginal cases is to identify the critical point at which it will change from one category to another.

Transition between condition rating categories one and two

The critical question that separates categories one and two is 'Does the element need a repair that is beyond what you would expect under 'normal' maintenance?' Let's assume roof covering A has a small number of tiles that are cracked or missing, but water is still not getting into the roof space. If the roof had roofing felt beneath the tiles, then it would probably stay on the category one side of the divide. The repairs could wait until the owner next employs a roofing contractor as part of normal maintenance.

If the roof did not have any secondary protection against water penetration (i.e. no roofing felt) and the water was kept out by older mortar torching or just

good fortune, then an appropriate rating would be in category two. The owner would have to repair the covering, but as it is not yet leaking, it would not be described as urgent and so would be tackled as part of a planned programme of maintenance.

Transition between condition rating categories two and three

The critical questions are:

- Will the element present a serious health and safety risk to the occupiers of the property?
- Does the element have to be repaired sooner rather than later (i.e. within the next six months)?
- Will the cost of repair comfortably exceed £1000?

We think health and safety, urgency and costs are the defining issues with category three. We have used the term 'comfortably' because it would be unreasonable to rate something in category three just because the repair is likely to cost £1,050. Few inspectors can be so confident about their estimating skills.

Conclusion

To conclude on this point, making clear rating decisions in these marginal cases will always be difficult and subtle differences in assumptions will result in variations in rating decisions between different inspectors. Since condition rating is not a precise science, a certain amount of variability will always occur. In the face of this uncertainty, the best you can do is adopt an objective and transparent decision making process that is properly documented in your site/file notes and reflected in your report. Then, if third parties ask you to explain your decision you will be able to show a coherent link between what you saw and the decision you made.

OTHER ISSUES RELATED TO CONDITION RATING

There are a number of situations where applying a condition rating to building elements can be difficult. The remainder of this chapter will look at those situations and consider prescribed methodologies that can provide a solution while also maintaining consistency.

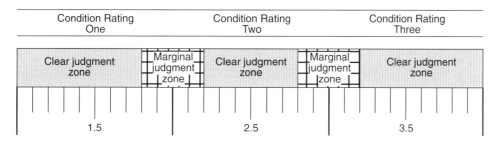

Figure 3.21: Condition rating continuum and decision zones

Widespread defects that affect multiple parts of the building

It is rare for a defect to affect just one part of a building. For example, consider a leak around the bottom of a chimney stack caused by a faulty flashing. As well as being a problem with the flashings, the problem may also affect:

- the trimming rafters around the damp brickwork where wet rot and timber infestation could develop;
- the brickwork of the chimney in the roof space;
- the ceiling joists and associated trimmers around the chimney breast;
- the plaster ceiling to the bedroom below; and
- the wall plaster in the bedroom.

Each one of these problems has a separate entry in the Home Condition Report. If the defect is not treated carefully there could be unnecessary repetition between the different sections. During early Home Condition Report trials, the BRE also discovered that inspectors often over emphasised the seriousness of this type of defect by rating all the affected elements too highly. To reduce such problems, the BRE prescribed the following simple steps:

- **Step One** – Determine a 'primary' element that contains the source of the problem. In our leaking chimney stack example, this will be Section D1 (Chimney stacks).
- **Step Two** – The main description of the problem should be included under the primary building element in the normal way. This description should also briefly include any consequential damage that has (or is likely to occur) to other parts of the building.
- **Step Three** – The consequential damage to the other parts of the building should be mentioned under the relevant element. Each description should be linked to the main description under the primary element with a simple cross-reference. For the leaking chimney stack example, the problem should be mentioned under:
  - Section E1 (Roof structure) – trimmers and chimney stack brickwork;
  - Section E2 (Ceilings) – trimmers and plaster;
  - Section E3 (Internal walls, partitions and plasterwork); and
- **Step Four** – Apply a condition rating to the primary element. In the chimney example, if a lot of water is entering the roof space and could cause serious damage to the ceilings below, then the repair will need to be done quickly and a category three condition rating would be appropriate. From a financial point of view, the cost of repairing the leak may not be so high. For example, the *BCIS Housing Repair Cost Guide* estimates that

replacing a flashing around an average chimney would be in the order of £550. However, the combined costs of all the repairs to the different elements may exceed the £1000 limit. You should not allow this to affect the rating of the primary element.

- **Step Five** – Apply condition ratings to the other affected elements. The BRE rightly point out that consequential damage should not normally be given a condition rating of three because some inspectors have often repeated the three rating against the other elements to make sure the original defect was accounted for. This would give a very negative impression of the property and is likely to be disproportionate to the real impact of the defect. Therefore, if a primary element has been given a category three rating, the consequential damage would usually be given a rating of one or two. A simple example would be the damage to the plaster ceiling. If this could be simply sealed and decorated over, then a condition rating of one would be appropriate. If a small area of plaster had come away from its backing and was stable, but had to be replastered, then a condition rating of two would be appropriate. On the other hand, if the ceiling was in imminent danger of collapse, then a category three rating should be applied to the ceiling element in its own right.
- **Step Six** – Include a description of the problem in Section B2 (Accommodation) as described below.

Other examples include:
- an infestation of wood boring insects that affect the roof timbers, some dado panelling, floorboards and floor joists;
- sulphate attack of concrete that has caused a number of floors to swell, distorted a number of internal partitions as a consequence and pushed out the foundation brickwork at low level below the DPC; and
- condensation dampness caused by poor insulation that affects walls, ceilings and windows in a number of different rooms.

To make sure that these types of problems are brought to the attention of the report reader, this standard section has been included at the front of the report (Section B2). Defects should still be described under the usual sections in the normal way, but emphasised here. The Guidance Notes suggest that this section should include a cross-referenced list rather than a descriptive narrative.

Other problem defects and deficiencies

The various pilot schemes that have been carried out over the last few years have helped to highlight a number of typical situations that inspectors have had difficulty in rating.

Asbestos

The Guidance Notes are clear that Home Inspectors will not be Licensed Asbestos Surveyors and will only have to report on *'readily identifiable asbestos containing materials.'* The Guidance Notes go on to say that if a Home Inspector identifies asbestos containing material, they should comment both under Section C2 and the relevant building element. The one drawback with this approach is that without testing a material, it is impossible to confidently identify materials as containing asbestos. In our view, you should adopt this approach where a particular component is highly likely to contain asbestos. Although it is not appropriate to go into technical detail, typical indicators will include:

* age of the material;
* appearance; and
* use of the component.

Even if you are certain a component does contain asbestos, it does not automatically result in a condition rating of three. For example, if an asbestos containing material is in a stable condition and in a position where it is unlikely to be disturbed, then a lower condition rating will be appropriate. Whatever the circumstances, where you suspect a material may contain asbestos you **must** mention this in the report. This is because you cannot be certain that it will not be disturbed in the future and you need to warn owners and potential buyers that it exists.

The case study property in Chapter Seven has a number components that may contain asbestos fibres and you should see the Home Condition Report to see how these are handled.

In the case of flats, the position is somewhat different. Under the *Control of Asbestos at Work Regulations* 2002, there should be a 'dutyholder' for the block as a whole. This person should have organised a survey of the common areas, identified any asbestos containing materials and established a plan outlining how this can be safely managed. There should be a conspicuous notice displayed in the common areas clearly detailing these arrangements. If there is not, the issue should be highlighted in Section C1 (Legal matters) of the Home Condition Report, as the implications could be expensive.

Internal decorations

Early versions of the Home Condition Report included internal decorations as an element that should be condition rated, but this has since been omitted completely. The only exception is external decoration because they protect the underlying material from deterioration, and so are considered as an element in their own right. One slightly grey area to consider is textured decorative coating that may contain asbestos fibres. As asbestos containing materials have to be treated with care, this issue is described in more detail in the section above.

Poor DIY alterations

Most experienced inspectors will be familiar with how a well intentioned DIY project can become a disaster waiting to happen (in fact, many inspectors might be responsible for carrying them out on their own properties)! Far from enhancing the amenity of the property, the effects of poorly executed building work can range from aesthetic catastrophes through to deficient repairs that are life threatening.

In general, if these substandard DIY jobs do not pose a threat to the building or the occupants then they should be considered as cosmetic and so would **not** contribute to any condition rating. They might be included in the report, but they should not contribute towards the rating decision. Examples could include:

* poorly applied, unfinished or 'distinctive' decorations that the vast majority of the population would find unacceptable;
* half finished hard landscaping projects in the garden; or
* a variety of fitted, non-matching cupboard fronts to the kitchen units;

Conversely, where homeowners have altered a building element and left it in a dangerous, half finished condition, it should be reported under the appropriate element and given a suitable condition rating. Examples of this type could include:

* an extended electrical system that clearly does not conform to current standards;
* a loft conversion where important structural roof timbers have been cut through to fit a roof window; or
* a raised flower bed in the garden that extends above the damp-proof course level.

Deficiencies in service provision

In early drafts of the Guidance Notes, the BRE stated that house condition ratings were not intended to promote a particular standard of provision. In other words, if a thirty year old property still has its original bathroom, kitchen fittings and decorations that are in a satisfactory condition, then these should not contribute to the rating.

Contemporary regulations and tastes may have overtaken some of those elements, but this does not put them into a category three condition rating. Examples illustrated in the case study property in Chapter Seven include:

* a kitchen that has older fitted cupboards, appliances, etc. that are in a satisfactory condition, but well below the current level of provision expected in a new house; and
* a bathroom that has basic, dated fittings that are still adequately performing their function.

Here, the kitchen units would be considered slightly old-fashioned by most potential buyers, but they still work. A pink bathroom suite may positively put people off the property, but since the appliances are in an adequate condition and only require small scale repairs, they receive a category two condition rating.

Removed amenities

Where an amenity or a service once existed, but has been removed by a previous owner **should** be considered as being in a poor condition, according to the BRE. The most common examples include removed bathroom and kitchen fittings, missing internal doors, and even removed boilers and electrical fittings! Some of the removed items may themselves result in a danger to the property and the occupants and should therefore be reported appropriately under Sections B and C2 of the Home Condition Report. Elsewhere, they should be rated as if they are damaged items.

Security of property

When the Housing Bill was passing through parliament, a major concern was raised over the security of inspected properties. If a Home Condition Report identified substandard door and window locks or other security devices, some commentators were worried that criminals might be able to use the Home Condition Report to identify vulnerable properties. To avoid this happening, the Guidance Notes state that such features should not be mentioned in the Home Condition Report and Home Inspectors will '... *advise sellers separately if significant or unusual security risks are identified during the inspection, in order to avoid such information entering the public domain.*'

The Guidance Notes are not specific about when or how this should be done, but we think that the following risks should be communicated directly back to the seller or their agent:

- vulnerable parts of the property such as lourve windows, loose or rotten window casements and thin panelled doors;

- lack of security devices that are usually recommended by police authorities and/or insurance companies; and
- parts of the property that are particularly vulnerable to break-ins such as windows and doors that open directly onto public access ways, etc.

The precise method of communication is not specified, but we recommend that it should be by letter, fax or email. Whatever form of correspondence is used, you should always keep a copy with the site notes for the property.

CONDITION RATINGS AND THE HOME CONDITION REPORT – APPLYING CONDITION RATINGS TO DIFFERENT ELEMENTS

Characteristics of different condition rating categories for each element heading of the Home Condition Report are included in Appendix E. Before proceeding, it is worth outlining the limitations of the information contained in Appendix E:

- Only typical examples have been included. No attempt has been made to include unique or regional variations.
- The descriptions relate to elements that would fall in the mid-point of the category described. You will have to use your own judgment if the reality is slightly better or worse than that described in this section.
- The descriptions are our opinion and carry no formal or official status. These have been put together with care and are designed to assist you in the initial rating decisions that you will be facing. They are not a substitute for your own thoughts and decision making processes. In other words, do not use them blindly, but do use them to help give an objective basis to your own rating decisions.

4 Writing the Home Condition Report

The content of this chapter will help you to understand and meet the requirements of the following elements of the National Occupational Standards for Home Inspectors:

● **Element 5.1 – Produce complete and comprehensive Home Condition Reports**

(A summary of the different units and elements that make up the NOS in Home Inspection has been included in Appendix B. A complete copy can be downloaded from www.assetskills.org.)

In this section, we have used different examples to illustrate good and bad report writing styles and techniques. The case study property featured in Chapter Seven includes a full Home Condition Report together with full explanations and justifications for the ratings. We are conscious that there is increasing use of tablet PCs and palmtop devices to produce site notes and there will inevitably be software that will convert site notes into a report format. However, as with a calculator, unless you understand the multiplication tables then you have no idea whether the calculator is producing accurate results. Therefore, we have attempted to produce a framework for best practice that can be used as a benchmark whatever your approach to making site notes and final reports.

GOOD PRACTICE IN REPORT WRITING

The Guidance Notes state *'The Home Condition Report is based on a visual inspection and provides a statement of condition, on the date of inspection'*. The report is the product of your inspection and in very simple terms, this is what the customer buys. They do not buy your site notes or what might have been in your head at the time. You are as good as the report and it is no good if the customer does not understand it; you have one opportunity to crystallise all your notes and thoughts to convey the right message. There is an additional complication over previous practice because you are now working for at least two opposing parties – the actual buyer and seller, so it will be important to use a writing style that can be understood by all.

Think of the reader

The structure of the Home Condition Report guides both the reader and the writer. The writer needs to respond in a methodical way and thought should be given to how best convey the necessary messages within the various sections. Summaries within sections B1 and B2 of the Home Condition Report have to capture the whole flavour of the property inspected, rather in a similar way to how headlines and opening paragraphs of newspaper articles attempt to encapsulate the entire context of the article in a few words. For a property in a satisfactory condition, you might write:

'The property is in a satisfactory condition overall, but with a few defects that are typical for its type and age.'

Alternatively, for a property where you need to highlight a serious feature, you might write:

'The property is generally in a satisfactory condition for its type and age. However, there is some evidence of movement on the rear extension that appears to be continuing and will need to be investigated further by a specialist.'

The important factor here is that some people may only read the summary sections of a report, so if you do not indicate that something is wrong, this may lead to awkward situations later. At this level, you do not need to qualify the term 'specialist' as that will come later on in the report.

The structure of the Home Condition Report allows you to provide signposts for the reader not only in the summaries, but also in the condition ratings. The significance here is that the Home Inspector must clarify what the rating means. For example, Home Inspectors are able to split any building element into a maximum of five sub-elements so that the condition of each different part can be isolated and not affect the rating of the other parts of the element. For each sub-element, the comment in the justification box needs to:

- establish the precise nature of the defect; and
- establish the extent to which the defect affects the sub-element.

The satisfactory condition of the rest of the element can be emphasised in the other sub-elements. If the commentary does not meet these needs, you might mislead the customer into thinking that the property is worse (or better!) than it actually is.

Accuracy, brevity and clarity (ABC)

The ABC of report writing refers to accuracy, brevity and clarity. Part Two of the Guidance Notes state that in the comments section of the Home Condition Report, ' … *Home Inspectors should be as precise as reasonably practical* … '. Later, in the *Poor examples of report writing* section of this chapter, we provide examples that do not achieve these objectives, causing confusion and in some cases undermining the credibility of the inspector.

Transparency and objectivity

There is a need to be transparent in what you have seen and what you could not see, especially if the customer expects that you should have seen it. Regrettably, this means that reports will not always be as brief as would be liked. In order to demonstrate what not to do, we have provided the following excerpt from the drainage section of an actual report:

'Drainage appears adequate with falls and crossfalls apparent at the front and back of the property. There was some evidence of a blocked drain in front of the property and we recommend you get this checked out.' (Total words: 37)

In an attempt to be transparent, the surveyor has turned an assumption into a statement of fact, but how could the surveyor possibly know the type of falls without a plan or CCTV drainage survey? Aside from this, the comment is also contradictory. A better alternative would be:

'The foul drainage from the property appears to run through an inspection chamber in the drive into the public sewer located under the road outside the property, and this is partially blocked. The drains should be cleared by a drainage contractor and then a CCTV survey commissioned to establish the cause of the blockage and if any remedial works are needed.' (Total words: 61)

THE HOME CONDITION REPORT – A SPECIFIC APPROACH TO REPORT WRITING

The Home Condition Report is a standardised format that is operated under licence and cannot be changed in any way. It is formatted using boxes, which give a clear split between the various sections. The first part of the report is a summary of the property, its accommodation and the overall findings of the inspection, together with any additional investigations that are required. This is then followed by the details of each element within the property along with their individual ratings. The report framework is broken down in Table 4.1 and offers a benchmark to the structure of all Home Condition Reports. It gives logic to how the report can be prepared and more importantly, understood by the customer. Unfortunately, not all defects fit nicely into the defined categories, so there has to be some cross-referencing.

Table 4.1: Breakdown of a Home Condition Report

Section of the report	What does the section include/refer to?
A	Terms of Engagement, setting down the basis upon which the report has been prepared
B	Summary of general information about the property – address, accommodation, construction, overall condition, summary of ratings, further investigations and details of any foundation movement
C	Matters that need referring to the conveyancer, that are a health and safety risk or pose some other risk, such as flooding
D	Refers to the external elements of the property, such as the roof and main walls
E	Refers to the internal elements of the property, such as floors and ceilings
F	Refers to information regarding utility services
G	Refers to additional elements of the property, such as outbuildings and grounds
H	Includes the energy rating for the property

A full report has been included in Chapter Seven

The Guidance Notes are specific about how the report should be written. It must be:

- in plain language with properly formed sentences, paragraphs and punctuation;
- free of technical jargon (if any expression is not in common use, an explanation is essential); and
- easily understood by the lay reader.

Sections D through to F give an elemental approach that is understood by most customers. Within these elemental sections, there is a split that shows the element's rating along with the justification for the rating. It is important that the Home Inspector breaks down the information in the justification box into sentences or paragraphs that provide the following information:

- Identification and description of elements in general terms:
  'The main pitched roof is covered with concrete tiles over a secondary waterproof barrier of sarking felt'.
- Assessment, explanation and analysis of what problems exist:
  'Although the main roof is not leaking, there are a number of defects:
  ○ The ridge and hip tiles are in a poor condition and need replacing.
  ○ The roof slopes are covered with moss that may lead to the deterioration of the roof tiles. This needs removing and will result in reoccurring maintenance in the future'.
- Prescription of courses of action – what needs to be done, by when and by who?
  'A roofing contractor should do this work'.

In the last section, there is no need to be specific about the timing of the repair as the condition rating will provide the reader with that information. If you make sure that every justification box is structured around these headings, the whole report should meet the appropriate standards.

Reporting on a typical defect

Consider a semi-detached property with low level dampness in the solid main external walls and at ceiling level on a chimney breast in the front bedroom. Assume that the property has solid floors, timber skirtings and a few timber ceiling joists that are in contact with damp masonry. To properly report on a defect of this type, you will have to mention the dampness in a number of different elements. These have been summarised below:

D1 Chimney stacks (Rating 3)
The chimney stack to the front roof slope is made of brick and is in a poor condition. The cement around the base of the chimney pots (flaunching) and the mortar between the bricks (pointing) needs renewing. The waterproofing between the chimney stack and the roof covering (flashing) is leaking and causing dampness problems in the front bedroom (see E2).

These defects should be repaired by a roofing contractor to prevent any further deterioration.

D4 Main Walls of the property (Rating 3)
The main walls are constructed with solid brickwork and are plastered internally. The base of the walls are damp and this may be caused by a breakdown in the damp-proof course (see E3).

This dampness needs to be investigated further by a specialist (see B3). This needs to be repaired as soon as possible to prevent further deterioration in the building (see B3).

E2 Front bedroom ceiling (Rating 2)
The plaster ceiling in the front bedroom has been affected by a leak around the base of the chimney stack (see D1). The surface layer of part of the ceiling has fallen off and will need to be replaced when the leak has been repaired. A general builder should do this work.

E3 Internal walls, partitions and plasterwork – Interior of gable wall (Rating 2)
The base of the inside of the main wall is damp and that has spoilt the plaster and decorations in a number of areas. This is probably caused by dampness due to a faulty damp-proof course. Timbers in contact with damp surfaces can also become affected by wood rot. At the time of our inspection, there was no visible evidence of this, but it may be concealed (see D4).

E5 Fireplaces, chimney breasts and exterior of flues – Chimney breast to Front bedroom (Rating 1)
The chimney breast is part of the main wall structure and is affected by dampness (see D1 and E3). The stained area should be sealed before decorations are applied.

E7 Internal woodwork (Rating 1)
Dampness is affecting the lower part of the main external walls and below the chimney stack (see D1 and D4). In these areas, timber components are likely to be in contact with damp brickwork and could become rotten. Although this was not apparent at the time of our inspection, it could be concealed and so should be investigated in accordance with previous recommendations (see B2).

E10 Dampness (No rating on this element)
The property is affected by dampness in the following locations:

- The base of the walls at low level on the ground floor (see E3). This is likely to be caused by a faulty damp-proof course.
- The chimney breast in the rear bedroom on the first floor. This is probably caused by a leak around the base of the chimney (see D1).

Both these problems are serious and need repairing to prevent further deterioration. It should be noted that any timbers in contact with damp areas may become affected by wood rotting fungus. This cannot always be detected by visual inspection as the rot may start on the concealed side of the wood (see also B3).

B3 Further investigation

The dampness affecting the ground floor should be investigated further by a specialist registered with the British Wood Preserving and Dampcourse Association. This should establish the precise cause, extent of the damage and remedial action necessary.

(Note: the dampness to the chimney stack is not included in the further investigation because you should be able to completely identify the cause and extent of the damage.)

Dampness is always seen as a serious problem; it is unsightly, shows that there are defects in the structure and, if not repaired, it will only get worse. It is not the intention of this section to discuss condition ratings, but we have included a brief rationale in relation to our example:

- The primary elements of the main walls and chimney stack have been rated as a category three because they are directly affected by the defects, meet the serious criteria and could be expensive.
- The plasterwork is essentially cosmetic and is unlikely to cost £1000 to repair by element. Although unsightly, it is not as urgent as the main defect and has therefore been given a category two condition rating.
- The chimney breast is not actually defective. It may be wet, but this is unlikely to impair its function and the sealing of any water stains can be completed within 'normal maintenance' programmes.
- The woodwork is showing no actual defects and although rot may be revealed by further investigation, the current condition appears to be satisfactory. However, a warning has been given because of the potential seriousness of wood rot.

(Note: There could be other issues related to the property which may affect the ratings, although we have only focused on the dampness. Clearly, other aspects cannot improve the rating.)

Our theoretical example shows how two relatively common defects must be carefully and systematically reported. The same defect has to be mentioned in several different elements, each time emphasising the different aspects, but without being overly repetitive or missing anything out. Several other examples are included in the case study property in Chapter Seven.

REFERRING TO 'SPECIALISTS'

At some point, you will have to request further investigations because something is beyond the scope of the report or your expertise. If you know the cause and extent of the defect, then the action is merely to get the work done and you can specify the type of contractor who would be best suited do the work, such as a general builder or a roofing contractor. As well as having the ability and qualifications to carry out the work in hand, it also indicates that the work might be of a higher standard.

Where you require an investigation because it goes beyond your expertise, then you are really calling for a 'specialist' or someone devoted to a single branch of their profession or subject area. As a consequence, it is inappropriate to refer to a general builder as a specialist, but it would be within this definition to refer to a company who specialise in the treatment of damp. However, we would recommend that the term be reserved for those organisations that add value to the investigation, rather than merely quote a cost for some works without doing a thorough investigation to establish the cause and extent of the defect.

Wherever possible, you should quote relevant specialisms or qualifications such as 'building surveyor' or 'structural engineer' because they carry a specific meaning. Someone to check the gas heating system would need to be CORGI-registered or from an equivalent body. If you do not state the qualification, you are exposing yourself to criticism if the buyer or seller chooses 'Fred' from around the corner who is some kind of handyman and does not produce the right sort of investigation. There are a number of specialist organisations included in the glossary in Appendix A.

USE OF STANDARD PARAGRAPHS VERSUS FREE TEXT

The Guidance Notes mention the use of standard paragraphs. It is likely that most of the entries in Sections B, C and H of the Home Condition Report will be generated by reporting software and the phrases will be mandatory. Although 'preferred text' will be produced for Sections D, E and F, there will be considerable opportunity for free text entry.

It is important to note that standard paragraphs or 'preferred text' provide a useful benchmark, but in all cases, **standard paragraphs should be amended to fit the circumstances and requirements of the client/s**. Standardisation is not always appropriate, but does provide a basis upon which amendments can be made.

Use of standard paragraphs is going to be helpful initially, especially to those who have been so used to advising the buyer of negative points about the property, and who are now faced with making fundamental changes in the way they report. This is no small undertaking – the new Home Condition Report paragraphs attempt to provide positive advice without leaving situations unresolved, while at the same time, trying to minimise the potential liability to the Home Inspector.

Any Home Inspector doing a number of Home Condition Reports is likely to use a form of standardisation, although they may try to reject the concept. Descriptions on various standard types of property do not change and it would be folly to try to devise a different phrase for each situation. Insurers like standardisation because they can then be sure that if you identify a defect, the standard action paragraph will protect you and them because it clarifies to the customer what has to be done.

Customers who review a number of reports will no doubt see similarities, and the suggestion has been made that they will think the service has been 'dumbed down'. This has to be resolved by good public relations and it should also be noted that until lenders achieved standardisation, underwriters had to put their own (sometimes difficult to understand) interpretation into reports. The issue here was that they were not always interpreting the reports correctly, and the context of the surveyor's comments or advice could subsequently change or become unclear. Therefore when using free text, ensure it has structure and can be understood, and when using standard paragraphs, ensure they correctly fit the circumstances.

CHECKING THE REPORT

A final, but important piece of guidance is to cross check the report thoroughly. Regrettably, it is common practice to sign reports at the end of what can be a very busy day and to rush certain processes just to meet the post. We have seen so many reports that include mistakes ranging from basic grammatical and spelling errors, through to whole parts of the report being completely missed out. So, take time out to check!

PARTICULAR ISSUES IN REPORT WRITING

In this section, we have reviewed a number of issues that keep cropping up in reports that we have read. These are in no order of priority.

Technical terms

Technical terms have a place, but do not expect a layperson to understand them. If they are used, they must be explained. The simplest solution is to keep technical terminology to a minimum. For example, consider the use of the phrase, '*The torching in the roof space is falling away*'. This would communicate better as '*The cement mortar (torching) used to the underside*

of the tiles within the roof space is falling away'. Another classic is '*The benching in the inspection chamber is in a poor condition.*' A layperson might be puzzled why a bench would be down the drains! A better alternative would be '*The cement surface at the base of the inspection chamber (benching) is in a poor condition.*'

From these examples, you can see that we have included the technical term in brackets after the jargon-free description. We have done this for two reasons:

1. By linking the technical term with the jargon-free alternative, you will be able to use just the technical term in any further elements; and
2. Many buyers and sellers might well use the Home Condition Report to organise the necessary repairs. Contractors often recognise the technical terms more easily when compared to the jargon-free phrase.

Some inspectors may want to attach a glossary of technical terms to their report, but this is not a feasible option because the reporting software will not allow uploading such a resource to the national database. Table 4.2 includes some other technical and legal terms found in reports, together with their more people-friendly alternatives. It might seem like we are being pedantic over some of these, but it is easy to get so familiar with words and phrases used in your working environment that you could forget that ordinary people simply do not use them anymore. Other examples are taken from the Plain English Campaign website that we recommend all Home Inspectors should regularly visit (www.plainenglish.co.uk).

Use of English

We don't consider ourselves to be experts on the English language and so have to be very careful when we attempt to give you advice on how to improve yours. However, the Plain English Campaign provides some worthwhile advice and the following tips are based on some of the ideas on their website (www.plainenglish.co.uk).

Listing information

The listing of information is a good way of splitting complex information and sits well within the Home Condition Report format. If you want to make a series of related points, you can make a list that provides a more direct way of communicating with the reader:

Dampness affects the house in the following areas:

- the rear lounge;
- the front chimney breast;
- the bathroom ceiling; and
- the rear bedroom wall.

Table 4.2: Terminology to avoid when compiling Home Condition Reports

Words and terms to avoid	Alternatives
efflorescence	white salts
purlins	main parts of the roof structure
F&E tank	small tank that is part of the heating system
pointing	mortar between the bricks
flaunching	cement at the base of chimney pots
sarking/roofing felt	secondary water proof barrier/layer
additional	extra
commence	start
comply with	keep to
we <u>would</u> advise …	we advise
consequently	so
the <u>subject</u> property	the/this property
ensure	make sure
dwelling/dwellinghouse/residence	property, house, flat
in accordance with	under, keep to
curtilage	grounds, land, land around the house
in respect of	for
elevation	wall, front/rear/side of house
in the event of	if
vendor/purchaser	seller/buyer
on receipt	when you get
circa	about/around/approximately
particulars	details
albeit/notwithstanding	although
regarding	about
amongst/lest/whilst	among/in case/although
prior to/ongoing	before/continuing
enjoys the benefit of	has
before legal commitment to purchase	before exchange of contracts

However, this has to be balanced with the requirements stated in the Guidance Notes, that the report must be written with '…*properly formed sentences, paragraphs and punctuation.*' Some reports can degenerate into a series of notes and thoughts bearing a striking similarity with site notes rather than a full and comprehensive report. Needless to say, this should be avoided.

Sentence length

Most commentators agree that the ideal sentence length is between fifteen and twenty words. We would prefer something towards the lower end of the scale. Longer sentences are very difficult to follow and many inspectors are likely to use them when they are trying to explain complicated issues. However, no matter how difficult the topic, long sentences can always be broken down. Although the longest sentence we have ever come across had 168 words in it, the one below weighs in at an impressive 59:

'*There are a series of regular header bricks provided to the offshoot walls and as such, taking into account the width of the walls these are referred to as 'snapped headers' whereby these provide the bond between the inner and outer leaf brickwork to the cavity walls whereas more modern construction methods are to provide cavity metal wall ties.*'

This was taken from a building survey report and putting aside any technical inconsistencies, it is extremely difficult to follow and does not really tell the reader much anyway. Most computer text editing applications include spelling and grammar checking facilities that can be set to measure your average sentence length (see the *Using spelling and grammar checkers* section).

Past or present tense

The reader of the report will be aware that you have only seen the property when you carried out the inspection, so avoid using the phrase '*at the time of the inspection*'. If you are describing something about the property that existed only a few days or even weeks ago, then use the present tense:

'*The property is semi-detached. … the roof is covered with slates/tiles. … the house has cavity walls. … etc.*'

This sounds much better than:

'*The property was semi-detached. … the roof was covered with slates. … etc.*'

If you are describing something that you actually did during the inspection, then use the past tense:

' *… the roof space was inspected . … damp meter readings were taken … inspection chamber covers were lifted … etc.*'

Use of first person

In the context of the Home Condition Report where you are writing for yourself, you should write in the first person, e.g. '*I advise*' or '*I noticed that the gutters are full of debris*'. However, many practitioners prefer a style that is written in the first person plural, e.g. '*we advise*' or '*we noticed …* '

'Appears' to be so negative

One particular phrase that readers of inspection reports find frustrating is the use of ' *… appears to be …* ':

- the roof appears to be slate;
- the rear wall appears to be damp;
- the house appears to be semi-detached; or
- the wiring appears to be in PVC cabling.

For many inspectors, this term slips in so easily, almost without being noticed. It is often used where an inspector is unclear or not completely confident about a certain issue. This is not unreasonable, but try to be more positive. Consider the following alternatives:

- the roof is covered in a type of slate covering;
- the rear wall is damp;
- the house is semi-detached;
- where visible, the wiring is in modern PVC cabling.

If you really are doubtful about a particular issue, then use the word '*probably*' because it sounds less evasive than '*appears*'.

Using spelling and grammar checkers

Most computer text editing applications have a facility that checks text for spelling mistakes and grammatical errors. For example, Microsoft Word can automatically assess the readability of a report and express a rating that is based on the average number of syllables per word and words per sentence. Two scales are used:

- **The Flesch Reading Ease Score** – this rates the text on a hundred point scale. The higher the score, the easier it is to understand. For most purposes, you should aim for a score of between sixty and seventy.
- **The Flesch-Kincaid Grade Level Score** – this rates text on a US grade school level. It's not completely suitable for the UK market, but does give an indication of how easily your writing can be understood. For example, a score of eight means that an eighth grader (a fourteen year old) should be able to understand your writing. The ideal score is between seven and eight.

Microsoft Word also gives the average number of words per sentence and the total amount of words in the text sample. We have used the example of poor report writing that was used previously in this chapter:

'*There are a series of regular header bricks provided to the offshoot walls and as such, taking into account the width of the walls these are referred to as 'snapped headers' whereby these provide the bond between the inner and outer leaf brickwork to the cavity walls whereas more modern construction methods are to provide cavity metal wall ties.*'

The report extract returned the following scores:

> Number of words: 59
> Words per sentence: 59 (because there is only one!)
> Flesch Reading Ease score: 19.3 (should be 60–70)
> Flesch-Kincaid Grade Level score: 12 (should be 7–8)

Such poor scores are not surprising. Expressed differently, the scores improved:

'*The walls of the rear part of the house are made of solid brick and contain rows of 'snapped' headers. These bricks are designed to give the wall strength. Modern cavity walls use small metal ties for the same purpose.*'

The revised report extract resulted in the following scores:

> Number of words: 40
> Words per sentence: 13.3
> Flesch Reading Ease score: 87.5 (should be 60–70, but the higher the better)
> Flesch-Kincaid Grade Level score: 4.3 (should be 7–8, but the lower the better)

We have used less words and shorter, clearer sentences. Although we're not completely happy with the passage, it is now much more readable and understandable. Using these readability features can help you reflect on your writing style. They can make your reports more accessible, but they are not a precise science. It is a mistake to write text to suit the spelling and grammar checker 'scores' of text editing applications. By following the logical direction of a computer program, you can easily end up with sentences that have lost all of your meaning. Instead, you should use them as a tool to improve your natural style so that you automatically produce clear, concise, well-expressed reports all of the time.

To activate the **Readability Statistics** feature in Microsoft Word, click on the **Tools** menu and then **Options**. Next, click the **Spelling & Grammar** tab of the dialog box and make sure the **Show readability statistics** box is ticked at the bottom, before clicking **OK**. When you next finish a spelling and grammar check, you will be presented with your document's readability statistics in a popup dialog box.

POOR EXAMPLES OF REPORT WRITING

In this section, we have selected some typical examples of poor report writing style. They have been selected from reports that have come to our attention either because they were challenged by clients or were identified during quality control procedures.

Example One

This first example was in a Homebuyer Survey and Valuation (HSV) report. The site notes comprised handwritten sheets of paper with no format or structure; no section headings or action points were identified. We struggled to work out how this particular surveyor approached the dictation of the report because it was not clear which parts needed to be highlighted for action and whether they had all been included. Ideally, the surveyor should tick off the action points as they are dictated. Additionally, we could not be sure when all the parts relevant to any one element of the property had been included, as the site notes were so haphazard. Showing just one section on internal joinery gives an impression of the remainder of the report:

> *'The dining kitchen has wooden unit doors with modern worktops, the joints being dealt with by masons mitres although these are separating slightly. There is an inset polycarbonate sink and drainer which is in satisfactory condition.*
> *The staircase is sound to tread and the handrail is secure. It should however be braced to the top balustrade to resist flexing.*
> *The extractor works in the cloakroom. There is an Edwardian style cloakroom suite which is of good quality and has a high flush WC.*
> *The bathroom has a gold effect glass shower cubicle, the tiling being slightly dated and loose around the bath and shower. Ideally, all should be tiled over with a more modern tile which will protect the existing.*
> *With the exception of Georgian glazed doors to the lounge and kitchen, internal doors are the modern colonial style. There is an aluminium patio door to the rear lounge.'*

In the Home Condition Report, the elements covered in this sample report would include D6 (External doors, including Patio doors), E3 (Internal walls, Partitions and Plasterwork), E6 (Built-in fitments), E7 (Internal woodwork) and E8 (Bathroom fittings). However, the HSV is no less structured and the surveyor should not have wandered away from the kitchen units (which would legitimately be in this section) and onto bathroom fittings, tiling and then patio doors (which should come within the *External joinery* section). The only explanation for this is the lack of structure to the site notes.

Looking at the content of the individual sections, it would be sufficient to state:

E6 (Built-in fitments)
'The dining kitchen has wooden unit doors with modern worktops and inset sink. These units are serviceable.' (Rating 1 or 2)

E7 (Internal woodwork)
'The staircase is sound to tread and the handrail is secure. It should however be braced to the top balustrade to resist flexing. With the exception of Georgian glazed doors to the lounge and kitchen, internal doors are the modern colonial style and are in satisfactory condition.' (Rating 2 for the repair to the balustrade, but this may also need mentioning in C3 Health and Safety Risks)

E8 (Bathroom Fittings)
'The extractor works in the cloakroom. There is an Edwardian style cloakroom suite which is of good quality and has a high flush WC. The bathroom has a gold effect glass shower cubicle.' (Rating 1)

We would question the inclusion of the extractor, but this may be relevant as to the form of ventilation. Under E3 (Internal walls, Partitions and Plasterwork), it would be relevant to refer to the loose tiling and risk of potential damp/leakage. However, the suggestion of 'tiling over the existing' is not worthy of further consideration, (but appealed to our sense of humour)!

Example Two

This second example highlights the following issues:

- too much detail and the need to avoid minor matters;
- the risk of changing the context of the report by going outside the scope of its Terms of Engagement; and
- the changes necessary for those who are more used to relating condition to value.

This again focuses on the internal walls and partitions of a property and has a direct correlation to Section E3 (Internal walls, Partitions and Plasterwork) of the Home Condition Report:

'Internal walls are a combination of blockwork/brickwork, which are plastered, painted/wallpapered. Some of the internal walls are 110mm thick and we could not confirm the material of which they are constructed without opening up the wall. The bathroom wall is partly tiled. The tiles would benefit with some grouting. Replace ceiling between bathtub and wall in the bathroom. Box off exposed pipework in the bathroom. Torn wallpaper in bedroom one needs replacing. Wallpaper in stairwell poorly done. Resecure wallpaper in stairwell. Box off exposed copper piping in stairwell. Two walls in kitchen are partly tiled. Part of kitchen walls are wallpapered and in poor condition and needing attention.
Generally, the floor carpet in various spaces within the property needs replacing. Doors and architraves are in a basic condition. Most of the internal doors open silently when tested.'

It is not the intention of the Home Condition Report to report on minor matters and decorative issues; they should only be mentioned if they have serious impact upon the condition of the property. Essentially, most buyers can identify whether the decorations are a problem. They could have an effect on value, but remember we're working with a condition report and not a valuation. Decorations may be mentioned, but only if they are damaged as a result of another defect.

Having stated what the wall construction is, the surveyor goes on to state that this could not be confirmed! This takes transparency too far and causes confusion.

Including a reference to the floor carpet seriously changes the context of the report and takes it beyond the scope of the Terms of Engagement. If you are going to note such cosmetic matters, there will be an expectation that you will cover all cosmetic matters.

The woodwork should be included within E7 (Internal woodwork). When producing a more effective report, apart from posting the various different elements into the relevant sections, it is essential to focus on the important aspects:

E3 (Internal walls, Partitions and Plasterwork)
'The internal walls are probably of brick or blockwork. Cosmetic attention is required to some of the wall finishes.' (Rating 1)

E7 (Internal woodwork)
'Doors and architraves are in a basic condition. Copper pipework is exposed in places where it would normally be boxed in.' (Rating 2)

The 'boxing in' does not fit logically in Section F (Services), but it could equally go in Section E9 (Other). The rest of the original report is irrelevant, although some comments may be put into the site notes. The grouting would only be an issue if it was the cause of damp penetration and this is clearly for the Home Inspector to make a judgment, although in the context of the report quoted, it is unlikely that this was the case.

Example Three

Sometimes there is a tendency to be too objective and not helpful enough. In this example, the extract was included in the Windows section of a report:

Where the original windows have been replaced, we cannot specifically confirm that satisfactory support has been given to the masonry above.

This is clearly factual, but is it an issue? A possible additional comment in this case may have helped:

'…which is a common failing with this type of design. There was no evidence to suggest that the support was inadequate.'

This report was undertaken before the need for building regulation approval on replacement windows, so that would be of no help. This sort of situation always poses a dilemma because it is likely that the windows have not been in there long enough to prove themselves. However, the apparent condition is clearly stated and it shows that the Home Inspector has given thought to the situation. There is no reason to ask for further investigation and the notorious 'trail' of suspicion has not been triggered. If there was evidence, such as details of a contractor who had previously done this, or some (even minor) cracking, then a recommendation for further investigation would be appropriate.

Example Four

These following examples highlight some of the problems with using standard paragraphs in general terms. The issues are self-evident and should be avoided. In this example, the surveyor had a standard paragraph for chimneys and was so keen to use it although it was not needed. In the context of the Home Condition Report, this warning of future maintenance potential is considered unnecessary:

'Chimney stacks are particularly exposed to the weather and so regular maintenance must be carried out to ensure their stability and weather tightness. A chimney was not apparent on the subject property.'

In this next example, the surveyor forgets that the property being inspected is a first floor flat, but still feels the need to advise there was no rising damp:

> *'Where access could be obtained, moisture readings were taken internally at regular intervals and we found no sign of significant rising or penetrating damp in this property.'*

In this final example, the surveyor has thoughtlessly tried to string a number of standardised paragraphs together and produced some classic gobbledegook. The property has a projecting party wall above the roofline that also acts as a firebreak:

> *'The party firewall, where visible, appears reasonably sound. However, it is weathered. The party firewall is unlikely to contain any damp-proof course and this could lead to water penetration and possible timber and masonry decay. If regular maintenance is carried out then bearing in mind the age of the property, it is not cost effective and not warranted at this time. It is likely, nevertheless, that damp will penetrate from time to time and on-going repairs will be required both externally and internally.'*

Is it sound or not? It is weathered so there is reason to believe the lack of damp-proof course is having an effect? There is a requirement for ongoing maintenance, so there will probably be a scaffolding cost. You are left with a damp issue that will not improve. Therefore, a better way of reporting could be:

> *'There is solid brick party wall projecting above the roofline that is weathered and will require ongoing planned maintenance. It may be prudent to budget for the installation of a damp-proof course to prevent further deterioration. Failure to carry out frequent maintenance without additional preventative measures will result in damp penetration. A general builder or roofing contractor should carry out remedial works.'*

Even after trying to make this clearer, its advisory nature takes it beyond the remit of the Home Condition Report.

Summary of report writing section

In this section, we have considered what can happen if there is a lack of structure right from the start of the inspection and how this can be transposed to the final report. We have reviewed how the context of the report can be unnecessarily extended and how to avoid this, as well as problems associated with raising issues, but not prescribing advice or solutions. Finally, we have looked at the dangers of being too regimented and using standard paragraphs without much thought of what was intended or carrying out a final quality check.

COMPLETING SECTIONS B AND C OF THE HOME CONDITION REPORT

In terms of skills and knowledge, Sections D and E are the most important parts of the Home Condition Report and most of a Home Inspector's time will be spent on getting them right. However, both sellers and buyers will often only read the summary in Section B and come to a judgment despite how many warnings they receive to read the whole report. Therefore, Sections B and C contain vital information that will help the reader and their advisers to gain a broader view (in some cases their only view) of the property. Consequently, we have described how the most important parts of Sections B and C should be completed. As the Home Inspector initiative evolves, software will be developed that produces mandatory standard text for many of these sections, and choices will have to be made between the options presented.

Completing Section B – summary of general information about the property

Most of this information is self-evident and you can view an example of completed information in the case study property's Home Condition Report in Chapter Seven. Rather than describe each section in detail, the most important aspects are emphasised below:

Postcode
It is vital that the correct postcode is entered, as this is required before the property can be uploaded to the national database.

Date of construction
Although the precise date of construction may not be known, you should be able to place it in the correct era and estimate its age to within a fifteen to twenty year margin. This is important for a number of reasons:

- you will need to know the date of construction to calculate the costs of reinstatement for insurance purposes;
- it will help you to establish the property's construction type and the sort of defects you can expect; and
- it is a requirement of the RDSAP protocols.

Flats, maisonettes and other commonhold/leasehold properties
The Guidance Notes define a flat, studio, bedsit, apartment, or maisonette as an individual home that is contained in a larger building and shares some building elements with other units. The storeys or

floors are defined below and for the purpose of stating the number of floors in each block, each one counts as one floor:

- ground floor – at or immediately above the outside ground level to the front;
- the floor above the ground floor is the first, then the second and so on; and
- the floor below the ground floor is the basement or if it is not completely below ground level it may be referred to as lower ground floor.

Commercial use

This part of the report refers to uses such as retail premises, offices and workshops. You should give a brief description of the type of use, the approximate percentage of the block that it occupies and where in the block (in relation to the property you are inspecting) it is situated.

Accommodation

The different rooms are summarised in the table at the top of page five of the Home Condition Report. All the rooms that are used for residential purposes should be included. Conservatories are considered as an outbuilding in Section G of the Home Condition Report, but here they should be included as a room.

A room that is not suitable for habitation should be listed as 'Other'. Examples could include a low ceiling converted loft space or a semi-basement room with no windows. The RDSAP requires a count of the number of rooms in the property, though this will not exactly match the formal definition of habitability presented in the Guidance Notes.

If these substandard spaces are being used and marketed by the current occupiers as habitable space, a clear note should be made in Section B1 (Overall condition of the property).

Construction

The description of the construction under this heading should be very brief. The Guidance Notes suggest that this should be no more than two lines for each element and free from technical jargon. The following example is given:

'Main roof is pitched and covered with concrete tiles; extension roof flat with felt covering.'

We would add others:

'The walls are brick faced and assumed cavity construction.'

'Windows are a mixture of the original timber single glazed and newer PVC double glazed units.'

'The floors are of a solid construction throughout the property and are probably made of concrete.'

In the description of the walls in the above example, we have used the phrase 'brick faced' and 'assumed

cavity construction'. This is because although the brick bond and the thickness may suggest a cavity wall, it might not be. It is difficult to be precise on a non-destructive inspection. Therefore, terminology that is more cautious has been introduced. The Guidance Notes rightly point out that terms like 'traditional', 'conventional' and 'typical' should be avoided as they carry little meaning for the average reader. In due course, once the Home Condition Report software becomes available, you will be able to choose from standard phrases.

System-built construction

Unless specifically excluded by the legislation, all types of system-built properties are to be covered. In terms of the Home Condition Report, system-built properties are defined as:

'...any type of construction where the main framework and/or larger building elements, are pre-fabricated off-site and then assembled or erected on-site.'

This can apply to the older types of system-built dwellings commonly built after World War Two as well as the newer varieties that have been developed over the last few years. It should also include varieties like Wimpey No-Fines and Laing Easiform that are poured concrete rather than pre-fabricated. Therefore, the term 'system-built' should not be automatically associated with poor or below standard.

The inspection of this type of property is discussed in more detail in Chapter Two, but it must be emphasised here that if you do not feel confident in this area you should decline the instruction to provide a Home Condition Report.

Tenancy occupation

Where lodgers or other occupants seem to be sharing the same 'household', it should be mentioned in this section. This is common where students or other people are living as a single household. Evidence could include locks on bedroom doors, separate food storage in the kitchen or cooking appliances in the bedrooms.

Summary of main services

For all four boxes in this section, 'yes' or 'no' answers are appropriate and refer to whether the property is connected to the gas, water and drainage services supplied by the usual utility companies and local authorities.

If these are not connected, you should ask the seller what type of provision exists. This information should be confirmed (if possible) by your own on-site checks during the inspection, and cross-referenced to the appropriate parts of Section C1 and Section F. This information is important because it helps the legal adviser to check that services have all the appropriate consents and approvals. This is also especially important in rural areas.

Garages and outbuildings

A garage is defined as '...*a building, for which the principal use is to house a car or cars*'. This may seem obvious, but they are sometimes too small to hold a modern car and should be noted accordingly.

Conservatories

These are defined as '...*enclosed, purpose-built extensions with a translucent roof...*'. It is only in this part of the form that this type of space is treated as being part of the main property. The condition of a conservatory is otherwise reported under Section G.

Outbuildings

In the context of the Home Condition Report, 'outbuildings' refers to permanent outbuildings and are defined as '...*permanent structures that are used in conjunction with the main property...*'. Legally, they are considered as part of the 'land' and will not be removed when the property is sold.

One of the boxes in this section of the report asks you to include the use of the outbuildings and you should report any non-residential use. The example given is a small workshop used in connection with the seller's business. This is important because uses of this type may require planning or other permissions and approvals.

Roads and footpaths

The roads and main paths serving the property must be identified and their condition assessed. If they are not 'made-up' (properly surfaced with a robust and durable finish), then they could be a considerable maintenance liability, especially if the owner is solely or partly responsible for their upkeep. In these cases, it is important to cross-reference to Section C1 for the legal adviser to check.

Conservation area/listed building

Most inspectors should be familiar with the conservation areas in their area of operation, but probably not all the listed buildings. Where a property is older or has unique architectural features (which might be relatively modern), it is important to cross-reference to Section C1 for the legal adviser to check.

The overall condition of the property (Section B1)

The Guidance Notes state that this section should briefly summarise the overall condition of the property and should be no more than four or five lines. This section should be completed after completion of the other sections, when an overview of the property as a whole can be given. Although short, this summary takes great skill to construct and it should be consistent with the developing view given in the rest of the report. The following advice may help:

- Focus on the overall condition of the property that is suggested by the relative numbers of the different

categories. In Figure 3.2 in Chapter Three, we use three adjectives for each of the different condition ratings. These could be used to describe the property as a whole.

- The philosophy of the Home Condition Report is to identify defects of an urgent or serious nature. Therefore, in this summary you should briefly describe those elements that you have rated as category three.
- Try to imagine the condition of a property of this type and age. Consider how this compares with the property that you have just inspected. Is it above or below this average?
- Keep to condition-related issues, do not drop in the property's marketing attributes as this is now a completely separate process.

Following these rules, we have constructed the following examples:

'*The property is in a satisfactory condition for its age and type. However, some elements are in need of routine repairs, including the gutters and the redecoration of window frames.*'

'*The property is in an adequate condition for its age and type, but there are a number of elements that need repairing, including:*

- *walls that need repointing;*
- *internal walls affected by dampness that need to be investigated and repaired; and*
- *the electrical and heating systems need testing and may require updating.*'

'*The property is in a poor condition for its age and type as there are a number of serious and urgent defects. These include the recovering of the roof, the replacement of the bathroom fittings, repair of the windows and the possible replacement of the heating system.*'

Whatever approach is adopted, the most important rule is consistency.

Summary of ratings (Section B2)

This is a summary of the different ratings in the report. Eventually, the software packages used for writing the reports will automatically generate this section. The information is likely to include:

- the total number of parts of the property that have been given condition ratings;
- the split of elements between ratings one, two and three; and
- a listing of those elements that have a condition rating of three.

Widespread defects that affect other parts of the property (Section B2)

This aspect has been fully described and discussed in Chapter Three. This section should include only a cross-referenced list rather than a descriptive narrative. Examples could include:

Infestations of wood boring insects were found in the roof timbers (Section E1), the internal wall panelling (Section E3) and the floor timbers (Section E4).
Condensation dampness and mould growth affects several of the ceilings (Section E2), walls (Section E3), and window frames (Section D5).
The spreading of the roof structure has distorted roof timbers (Section E1) and caused cracking in the ceilings (Section E2) and walls (Section E3).

Further investigations or testing recommended (Section B3)

The general approach to this section of the report is fully discussed in Chapter Three. The most important aspect is to distinguish between 'further investigation of an observed defect' and 'precautionary testing'.

Further investigation of an observed defect

This recommendation will be made either when a visible defect may have affected other concealed elements, or when it is not possible to determine the extent of a visible defect within the confines of the inspection. Typical examples might include:

- where a serious, long term roof leak around the base of the chimney may have caused wood rot in roofing timbers that are concealed by the ceiling of a room within the roof space;
- where dry rot affects timber skirtings of a ground floor room and the adjacent timber floor is covered with a fitted carpet; and
- where there is recent and extensive cracking to external walls, that is likely to be caused by foundation movement, or where there is no degree of certainty as to the cause and likelihood of further movements.

In cases like this, further investigations should be recommended and the information you include should be as helpful as possible. In earlier versions of the Guidance Notes, the BRE suggested that you should include the type of investigation required and the qualifications or expertise of the practitioner who should be employed for the task.

Where your advice recommends that further explorative work on a likely defect is required, you should try to give an overview of the nature of the investigation, based on whether it will focus on monitoring over time, testing of components, a more invasive examination, and if specialist skills or a specification for work are needed. You should also include what should be determined or discovered from the additional investigation.

You should also give some indication of the urgency of the proposed investigation. Examples could include:

The roof timbers around the base of the leaking chimney should be exposed and inspected by a recognised timber treatment specialist (member of the British Wood Preserving and Damp Proofing Association). This should be done as soon as possible. The floor timbers in the ground floor rear room should be exposed and inspected by a recognised timber treatment and damp-proofing specialist (member of the BWPDA). This should be done as soon as possible.
A qualified structural engineer or chartered building surveyor should inspect and report on the cracking to the rear wall.

Precautionary testing

Precautionary testing is limited to those situations where a specialist installation is beyond your ability to assess, or there are clear indications that although there might not be serious or urgent problems, an element might be below current known standards. This recommendation will almost exclusively be limited to service systems and typical examples include:

- an electrical system with no visible part presenting a risk, but has no evidence of recent testing and is clearly below current standards;
- any gas installation that has not been serviced by an approved organisation within the last twelve months; and
- an older septic tank that appears to be performing adequately, but the seller has no evidence of the original installation details or maintenance arrangements.

If any of these were exhibiting a dangerous, urgent or serious defect or deficiency they should be included in Section B3 (Further investigations), where more information and a greater emphasis can be given. There should be examples included in the report that:

- a contractor registered with the National Inspection Council for Electrical Installation Contracting (NICEIC) has tested the electrical system;
- gas appliances such as the boiler and room heater have been tested by a contractor registered with CORGI; and
- the septic tank has been inspected and tested by a qualified water engineer or other specialist contractor with experience of this type of work.

The various specialist organisations and their contact details are included in Appendices A and H respectively.

Foundation-related movement (Section B4)

As foundation-related defects are so important, aside from this section (B4), they are mentioned and emphasised in a number of different sections of the

Home Condition Report, including any elements that are damaged by the foundation-related movement (Sections D to F) and Section C3 (Other risks associated with the property).

In this section you should summarise any movement that may have been caused by subsidence, settlement or heave in the foundations. As the Guidance Notes point out, if the structure has been damaged by other causes, such as failed lintels or lack of lateral restraint to gable walls, then these should be included under the relevant building element. The Guidance Notes also point out that sellers and buyers will be concerned by all types of cracking regardless of whether it is active or not. Therefore, if you see building damage that is of no concern (i.e. longstanding and non-progressive), then you should mention it in this section, giving appropriate reassurance. Typical examples would include:

'Foundation movement has probably caused the internal and external cracking to the rear. This has occurred recently, is likely to get worse, and needs investigating.'

'The cracking and distortion to the walls to the rear is long standing and is of no structural significance.'

Completing Section C – Other matters

Legal matters (Section C1)

The Guidance Notes make it clear that Home Inspectors will not be required to carry out any searches for planning permission, building regulation approvals or any other statutory information held by public authorities. This section is for the physical evidence that has been found during the inspection that might have a legal implication. The appointed legal advisers can then check this section further.

When a house is sold, a number of standard searches will seek to find out the usual range of information. The role of the Home Inspector is to be the eyes and ears of the legal adviser and highlight particular features that need to be investigated further. The standard searches can then be adapted in an attempt to resolve any specific questions.

There is also an important link between the information provided by the seller and what can be seen during the inspection. If there is a contradiction, the Guidance Notes suggest that the physical signs should be listed, with a supporting comment such as, *'It is understood from the seller that the necessary permissions have been obtained.'* A relatively new extension to a property might be a typical example. If the seller states verbally that they *'…have all the proper permissions, but I've lost the paperwork'* and the standard of construction does not meet the building regulation standard, it is important to point this out. The legal advisers will need to ask the local authority whether the rear extension has got the required permissions and approvals. The wording could include:

'The seller was unable to provide any documentation to show that the rear extension has all the necessary approvals. As the standard of construction does not meet the current building regulation standard, legal advisers should check whether this specific feature has been properly approved.'

Other matters that should be raised under this section if appropriate, include:

- whether unmade roads serving the property have been adopted by the highways authority;
- the maintenance liabilities of shared drives, fences that are obviously in poor condition and common drains;
- whether 'permission to discharge' has been granted by the Environment Agency for any septic tanks;
- inappropriate alterations to a listed building or one in a conservation area;
- work to the party wall/party boundary wall that may require prior approval of the neighbour; and
- gates in boundary fences that suggest a possible right of way.

Health and safety risks concerning the property (Section C2)

The health and safety risks to the occupants of a property are one of the factors that a Home Inspector will have to consider when rating a building element, and this section is intended as a summary of any risks. The Guidance Notes define health and safety risks as those that:

- require repair or building works in order to eliminate them;
- are 'serious' risks; or
- are unusual when compared to other properties of a similar age and type.

The judgment will always be a challenging one as minor, 'everyday' risks should not be included. The main description of the problem should be included under the building element that the risks are most closely associated with. This section is to highlight and cross-reference these problems and the Guidance Notes give the following examples:

- risks inherent from the design of buildings/ building elements, e.g. unfenced roof terraces;
- risks from building materials, contaminated land and substances, e.g. asbestos, radon or high aluminium concrete;
- risks caused by deterioration of building elements, e.g. seriously rotten casement windows on the first floor or external render falling from high levels;
- risks caused by inappropriate use of buildings and services, e.g. using a damp cellar as sleeping accommodation;
- risks from services, e.g. defective electrical installations, gas or heating appliances; and
- poor provisions of escape from fire, e.g. insufficient size of opening windows in bedrooms.

The problem of asbestos is emphasised by the Guidance Notes and you should be aware of the current advice from the Health and Safety Executive (HSE) and other authoritative bodies. This is discussed in more detail in Chapter Two. If asbestos is present, it should be mentioned in this section and described in more detail under the building element it is most closely associated with.

Other risks associated with the property (Section C3)

The Guidance Notes state that this section will be of particular importance to sellers and buyers, lenders and future insurers. Therefore, this section should focus on those risks that are usually included in building insurance policies, including past or current subsidence, flooding and major structural repairs that have been carried out.

Evidence of these risks will usually be assembled from the information provided by the seller, details of your own inspection, local knowledge and property-related information from publicly accessible databases and websites. You should carefully monitor this developing area because more information is coming into the public domain. Although some of this may not be very precise or useful, it is likely that many sellers and buyers will access it, meaning Home

Inspectors need to be aware of the same information. The following information is currently available online and free of charge:

The National Radiological Protection Board (www.nrpb.org) – this gives important information about the level of radon in all areas across the country. It also includes information on electromagnetic fields and radiation.

The Environment Agency (www.environment-agency.gov.uk) – this gives important information about flooding risk, searchable by postcode. It also includes information on water and land quality.

Landmark Information Group (www.landmarkinfo.co.uk) – this is a commercial website offering digital mapping, planning and environmental risk information.

These information sources have been used to generate a profile for the case study property in Chapter Seven. If you operate in a well-defined geographical area, you will have no doubt already built up a small, but accurate database of your own. In our view, unless you know the characteristics of the area you are working, you should check these information resources for every home inspection you carry out.

5 Energy ratings and the Home Condition Report

INTRODUCTION

The collection of data and the provision of an energy performance certificate are an integral part of the Home Condition Report. The certificate contains:

- an energy rating for the property;
- benchmarks to set the energy rating into context; and
- suggestions for improving the property's energy rating.

The government's approved method of assessing a property's energy performance is known as the Standard Assessment Procedure, or SAP. The SAP is just based on energy costs for space and water heating. A SAP rating is required for all new build properties and those that are undergoing significant material alteration (such as the addition of an extension to the property).

The SAP has a scale from 1 to 120. From an energy perspective, the lower values represent poor efficiency, while a score of 120 is excellent. The English House Condition Survey (2001) has shown that a typical SAP for an average house in England is about 51. A new house built to current building regulations would score around 95.

SAP AND THE EUROPEAN DIRECTIVE

In 2002, the European Union produced a directive (2002/91/EC) aimed at promoting improvements in the energy performance of buildings across member countries. The main elements of the directive include:

- the establishment of a framework for a common methodology for calculating the energy performance of all buildings;
- the application of minimum standards of energy performance for new buildings, and renovated buildings with a total surface area over 1000m²;
- certification schemes for new and existing buildings and provision of these certificates to occupants; and
- inspection and assessment of boilers and heating/cooling installations.

The directive also requires that a valid energy performance certificate be produced for all properties at the time of sale. This is the reason why the SAP rating has been made part of the Home Condition Report, with many commentators suggesting that the need to conform to this directive is one of the driving forces behind the *Housing Act*. Without the Home Information Pack and the Home Condition Report, the government would have to bring in specific measures to collect energy performance information.

THE REDUCED DATA SAP (RDSAP)

To ensure there is a consistent approach to the collection and processing of SAP data, the Federation of Authorised Energy Rating Organisations (FAERO) was established in 1998. This brought together all of the government-authorised energy rating scheme providers and currently includes Elmhurst Energy Systems, MVM Consultants and National Energy Services. The aims of FAERO are to:

- promote the use of authorised and quality-assured SAP energy ratings in all areas of the domestic housing market;
- ensure high standards of technical competence and customer satisfaction; and
- develop standards and procedures to ensure consistency and accuracy.

One of FAERO's main tasks is to develop the reduced data SAP (RDSAP) methodology that will calculate the energy performance of a property based on the data collected during the home inspection. At the time of writing, the data requirements have been finalised, but guidance has not yet been issued on exactly how the data is to be collected. Consequently, this section is based on our interpretation of what information is available and we expect this to develop and change with the confirmation of formal guidelines.

HOW THE ENERGY PERFORMANCE CERTIFICATE WILL BE PRODUCED

Although it will be some time before Home Information Packs are assembled and Home Condition Reports with

RDSAP reports produced, the process is likely to be as follows:

- A 'pack assembler' will commission a Home Condition Report from a licensed Home Inspector.
- The necessary data for both the Home Condition Report and the energy rating will be collected at the same time. The energy data will be integrated with the Home Condition Report data so that processing one set of data produces both the Home Condition Report and energy rating report. This data would then be processed most probably online by the Home Inspector.
- Once processed, an energy performance report is generated and it is at this stage that the inspector will check the recommendations and remove those that are inappropriate for the property.
- When the Home Inspector is satisfied with both the Home Condition Report and the energy performance report, both can be signed off and sent to the pack assembler.

This process will provide the seller and potential buyers with a clear view of how the property's energy performance can be improved.

DATA COLLECTION AND INPUT

If you are familiar with other methods of SAP data collection, the RDSAP will be similar, but not exactly the same. You should review the measurement and collection methodologies of the new system once the guidance has been published. The data required for the RDSAP is likely to be broken down into a number of different sections, each with subsequent considerations.

This section outlines the nature of data requirements in its broadest sense. Further information in relation to heating and water can be found in the *Specific elements* section at the end of Chapter Two.

A complete set of data along with a home energy report has been compiled for the case study property and included in Chapter Seven . This has been created using the software provided by one of the three approved energy-rating providers, Elmhurst Energy Services Limited.

SECTION H OF THE HOME CONDITION REPORT: THE HOME ENERGY REPORT

The software used for the SAP calculations and report produces the energy performance certificate, which will become part of the Home Information Pack. The report includes a summary of the data collected by the Home Inspector which was used to calculate the SAP rating. A summary of the property's energy performance related features is also included. Table 5.1 illustrates the scope of the SAP report in more detail.

Table 5.1: Information requirements for the RDSAP

RDSAP section	Considerations for the Home Energy Report
Built form	- Whether the property is a house, bungalow, flat or maisonette - Whether the property is (semi) detached, mid/end-terrace, etc. - Whether the property has any extensions, a conservatory, or loft conversion - The number of rooms in the property
Property dimensions	- Floor areas, heights and heat loss perimeter - Shelter factors including garages and conservatories (especially if they are heated) - Heated/unheated corridors in flats
Constructions	- Main construction and insulation - Extension construction type and insulation - Main roof construction and insulation - Extension roof construction and insulation
Windows	- Area of glazing compared to the average for its type - Proportion of glazing that is double glazed - Date of double glazing
Heating systems	- Main heating type and controls - Secondary heating type and controls - Water heating type - Hot water cylinder type and insulation - Hot water cylinder thermostat - Electricity meter type
Other details	- Number of open fireplaces - Presence of solar panels

Energy rating and typical running costs of the property

This section of the SAP report presents the following information:
- the cost of electricity per year;
- the cost of gas per year;
- the cost of other fuels (if appropriate) per year;
- the level of carbon dioxide emissions (CO_2) per year; and
- energy consumption in kWh/m^2 per year.

The energy performance certificate

Figure 5.1 shows the relative efficiency of different types of homes. It is similar to that used for electrical white goods (such as washing machines) and should be understood by the public. The average SAP rating for newly built homes is shown in comparison to the SAP rating for the property in question.

Measures to reduce the running costs and improve comfort

This section makes recommendations for improvements to the property. For each measure, it provides the following information:

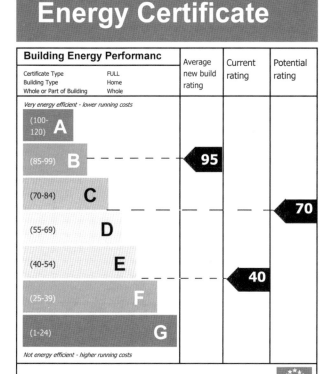

Building Energy Performanc		Average new build rating	Current rating	Potential rating
Certificate Type	FULL			
Building Type	Home			
Whole or Part of Building	Whole			

Very energy efficient - lower running costs

(100-120) **A**

(85-99) **B** — — — ◄ **95**

(70-84) **C**

(55-69) **D** — — — — — ◄ **70**

(40-54) **E**

(25-39) **F** — — — ◄ **40**

(1-24) **G**

Not energy efficient - higher running costs

GB 2004

Directive 2002/91/EC

Figure 5.1: Home energy certificate

- a description of the measure;
- the amount of money saved per year; and
- the improvement in the energy rating.

This section is broken down into 'lower cost' and 'higher cost' measures. It will also include another section that will make specific recommendations related to helping the environment.

The coloured bar chart of the energy performance certificate displays the actual energy rating of the property in comparison to its potential rating if all the improvement measures were implemented.

The second part of this section goes on to explain the measures in more detail. Each improvement is accompanied by a short explanatory paragraph that is generated by the SAP software. The Home Inspector will not be able to adjust this in any way.

The final section includes general information about the energy rating itself, the energy survey that has been carried out and how to contact the Home Inspector if the reader needs further technical information.

An energy performance report for the case study property has been included in the sample Home Condition Report in Chapter Seven.

WILL YOU NEED FURTHER SAP TRAINING?

All of the government-authorised energy rating scheme providers offer accredited training courses for those who are interested in energy assessment of residential property. Many of these will be of interest to Home Inspectors who want to get a deeper understanding of Standard Assessment Procedures and energy issues in general. At the time of writing, a SAP qualification is not a mandatory part of the Home Inspector qualification and does not have to be taken. Candidates simply need to prove to the assessment centres that they can collect the correct data, send it to the energy assessor and make appropriate recommendations based on the output from the energy report.

As the RDSAP requires only straightforward data, it is our view that many experienced practitioners will be able to prove they are competent in this area with minimal instruction, so this area could be included in more general Home Inspector training courses. The following statements may help you assess what level of training you will need.

You will require only minimal training if you:

- are familiar with the SAP methodology and some of the theory behind the energy calculations;
- have taken a previous SAP training course (any level); and
- have given advice to clients based on information provided in an energy assessment.

An accredited SAP training course will be useful if you:

- do not know much about the SAP methodology and very little about how the computer software calculates the SAP value;
- have never taken a training course or attended a CPD seminar on the SAP process; and
- have never given SAP-based energy advice to clients.

An approved training course will enhance your profile and provide evidence that you are competent in this area, but it is worthwhile balancing its worth against the cost and time taken to attend.

THE CASE STUDY PROPERTY – DATA COLLECTION

At the time of writing, fully agreed procedures and protocols for the RDSAP, associated software programs and energy reports had yet to be agreed by FAERO. In an attempt to give you an insight into the energy rating process, this section presents and explains the information that needs to be collected for a SAP rating to be produced. The data collection methodology and software used are from one of the licensed energy rating companies recognised by the government, Elmhurst Energy Systems. For convenience, we have used the details of the case study property in Chapter Seven. We must emphasise that the final version of the RDSAP will be different to what you see in this section, but in our view, the differences will be minor.

Description of the data on the SAP survey form

The following information illustrates the data required to complete the RDSAP energy rating survey form, published by Elmhurst Energy Systems. The rating survey form is split into a number of sections to reflect certain elements of a property. These sections require the user to input a corresponding value, enabling the software to calculate an overall rating based upon all inputted data. The different sections and their respective values are listed below in **bold**, along with relevant screenshots from the online energy rating service.

- The **property type** would be entered as a **bungalow** that is **detached**.
- **Number of storeys** – one.
- **Date Built** – 1946.

Page 1: Property Type

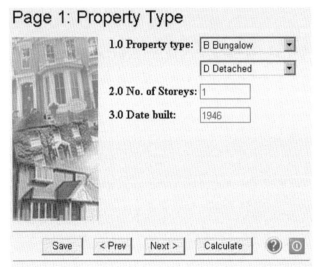

Figure 5.2: Property type

- **External perimeter** – using the measurements for the reinstatement/insurance calculations (see the *Calculation of reinstatement costs for insurance purposes* section in the Chapter Seven case study), Figure 5.6 shows the perimeter measurements. The calculation is:

3.2 + 3.1 + 3.9 + 3.1 + 5.2 + 7.0 + 9.1 + 2.8 + 3.2 + 4.2 = **44.8 linear metres**.

- **External floor areas** – using the reinstatement/insurance calculations (see the *Calculation of reinstatement costs for insurance purposes* section in the Chapter Seven case study), the floor area is 96.02 m². However, the external floor area for the SAP calculation does not include the area of the rear entrance extension or the front porch because both are unheated. The calculation is therefore:

96.02 – (4.4 + 2.39) = **89.23 m²**.

- The **Average Storey Height** of the bungalow is **2.41 metres**.

Page 2: External Perimeter

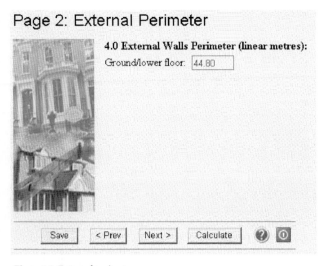

Figure 5.3: External perimeter

Page 3: External Floor Areas

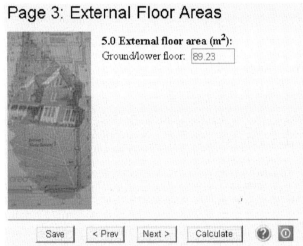

Figure 5.4: External floor areas

Page 4: Average Storey Height

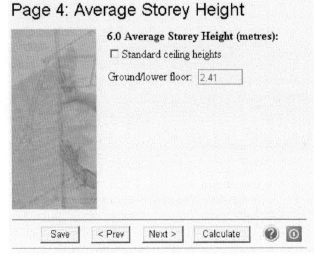

Figure 5.5: Average storey height

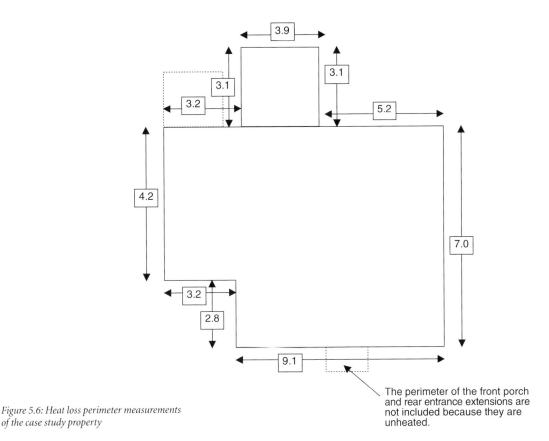

Figure 5.6: Heat loss perimeter measurements of the case study property

The perimeter of the front porch and rear entrance extensions are not included because they are unheated.

- **External Wall Type** – there are two external wall types: the wall to the original house and the wall to the lounge extension. The software takes account of the extension by calculating the area of the 'secondary' wall type. The program will automatically deduct this from the total wall area of the property. The area of the secondary wall type must be expressed as a 'net' area (i.e. with any window openings deducted). The calculations are:

Area of lounge extension wall (secondary wall)

Wall including patio door

Wall area	$3.9 \times 2.41 = 9.39\text{m}^2$
Patio door	$2.3 \times 2.1 = 4.83\text{m}^2$
Adjusted Wall area	$9.39 - 4.66 = 4.56\text{m}^2$

Other two walls (same dimensions)

Wall area	$3.1 \times 2.41 = 7.47\text{m}^2$
Window	$1.8 \times 1.2 = 2.16\text{m}^2$
Adjusted wall area	$7.47 - 2.16 = 5.31\text{m}^2$

Total area of secondary wall
$$4.56 + 2(5.31) = \mathbf{15.18\text{m}^2}$$

- **Roofs** – there are two types of roof to this property:

  i. the main pitched roof over the majority of the property, which has a layer of thermal insulation **75mm** thick; and

  ii. the flat roof over the lounge extension, which has an unknown level of insulation that is assumed to be approximately fifteen years old. The software guidance notes relate thickness

Page 5: External Wall Type

Figure 5.7: External wall type

of thermal insulation to date built and for 1989, this is given as **75mm**. The area of the lounge extension (3.9×3.1) has to be entered so the program can automatically deduct from the other.

- **Main Ground Floor Type** – the program calculates the area of the floor from the perimeter measurements, so the only information required is the floor type. In this case it is a **solid**, **uninsulated** floor.

- **Number of External Doors** – the number of external doors should be included here even if they open into unheated but covered spaces. The case study property falls into this category as the front and rear doors open into the front porch and rear entrance extension respectively. The patio doors

Page 6: Roof Type and Ground Floor Type

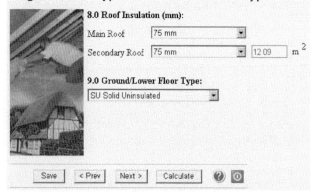

Figure 5.8: Roof type and ground floor type

are classed as windows because of the large proportion of glazing, so the value for external doors will be **two**.

- Percentage of windows with **Double Glazing** – all windows to the property are double glazed so the value here will be **100%**.
- **Draught Proofing** – this assessment covers all windows, doors, rooflights and loft access hatches. In the case study property, all windows have effective seals, but the two doors and loft hatch do not. Due to the high number of windows, we have entered a value of **90%** in this section.
- **Number of Open Fires** – there are **no** open fireplaces in the property.

Page 7: Doors, Windows and Open Fires

Figure 5.9: Doors, windows and open fires

- **Space and Water Heating** – this section includes the main heating system, its controls, any secondary heating system and the water heating system.
- **Main Heating System** – there are two possible ways of entering data for the heating system:

 i. record the details of the boiler and the information that can be obtained from the Seasonal Efficiency of Domestic Boilers in the UK (SEDBUK – www.sedbuk.com) database; or

ii. use the 'code' tables in the software guidance manual and choose the default efficiency associated with that type of system.

We have adopted the latter approach. The system consists of a floor mounted open flue gas boiler, but the age of the boiler is impossible to determine with any level of accuracy. In the coding choices, the important threshold is 1979 because before that time, the level of efficiency drops to 55% while after 1979, efficiency is 65%. In our view, this boiler could be over twenty-five years old and if not, it is certainly on the threshold. When faced with this doubt, the software guidance recommends that the worst case should be assumed. Therefore, the pre-1979 value has been selected, for which the coding is **BGM**.

- **Main Heating Controls** – the most important issue here is whether the system has a boiler interlock. This feature will ensure that the boiler shuts down when there is no demand for heat from either the hot water or heating circuit. Boilers without an interlock that continue firing even if there is no demand are wasteful and achieve a lower efficiency value. The heating system belonging to the case study property has a room thermostat, thermostatic radiator valves (TRVs) on all radiators, a cylinder thermostat on the hot water tank and a programmer. Although we still cannot be sure that the system is wired up to provide the boiler interlock, it has all the components so we have assumed it is. Therefore, the heating control code is **CBD** (programmer, room thermostat & TRVs).
- **Secondary Heating System** – if the main heating system is uncapable of bringing the property up to acceptable temperatures (i.e., 21°C in the living room and 18°C in other areas), then the details of a secondary heating system should be entered. As there are radiators in every room of the case study property, but no other forms of fixed heaters or open fires, no secondary heating system has been entered.
- **Water Heating** – the main heating boiler supplies the hot water and so the code is **HWP** (from the main/primary heating system).
- **Underfloor Heating** – there is **no** underfloor heating.
- **Hot Water Cylinder** – the property has a hot water cylinder that has a thermostat. It has a **foam** insulation that is approximately **25mm** thick. There is only one immersion heater.
- **Electricity Tariff** – the property has a **standard** tariff.

The final page of the online energy rating service informs you that the data has been successfully saved and allows you to preview the final report online and export the report as a PDF.

Page 8: Space and Water Heating

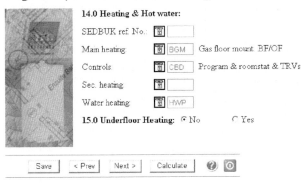

Figure 5.10: Space and water heating

Page 9: Hot Water Cylinder and Electricity Tariff

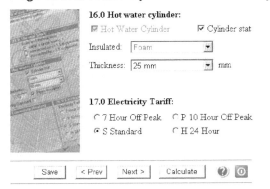

Figure 5.11: Hot water cylinder and electricity tariff

Click Calculate to save entered data and to calculate

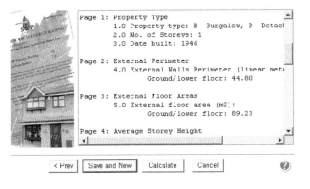

Figure 5.12: Calculation page

Calculation results

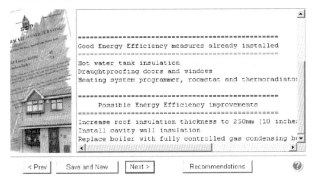

Figure 5.13: Calculation results

THE CASE STUDY PROPERTY – SAP RATING AND ENERGY REPORT

The data shown on the RDSAP energy rating survey form was processed through Elmhurst Energy Systems' online facility and it produced the information displayed in Table 5.2.

Table 5.2: Energy rating and typical running costs of the case study property

SAP rating	40
Estimated annual heating cost (including VAT)	£466
Carbon dioxide emissions (tones per annum)	6.2

The report also expresses the actual and potential SAP rating on a relative scale (see back to Figure 5.1) and gives details of possible energy efficiency improvements, which are summarised in Table 5.3.

Table 5.3: Possible energy efficiency improvements

Improvement options	Annual savings	Estimated cost	Payback years
Increase roof insulation thickness to 250mm (10 inches)	£39	£337	8.6
Install cavity wall insulation	£82	£274	3.3
Replace boiler with fully controlled gas condensing boiler for heating and hot water	£101	£1440	14.3

SAP rating of the case study property

By any definition, the energy efficiency of the property is 'poor'. This is despite all the windows being double glazed – a feature that many members of the public would see as being very energy efficient. The case study property's low SAP rating can be explained due to the following reasons:

- The proportion of heat loss floor and roof space area is high in relation to the living space. In other words, a detached bungalow loses more heat than an equivalent detailed two-storey property.
- The walls are not insulated and because the property is detached there is a high proportion of heat loss wall area.
- The old boiler is inefficient.

Recommendations for improvement

The software program automatically recommends the most effective improvement options, including increasing roof insulation, installing cavity wall insulation and replacing the boiler with a condensing boiler.

- **Increasing roof insulation** – The low level of roof insulation (75mm thick) provides a good opportunity for improving the energy efficiency of the property. Increasing the thickness to 250mm will save a respectable £39 per year, but due to the relatively large roof area, the installation cost is relatively high. The pay back period of over eight years is longer than a two-storey property, though it would still be worthwhile carrying out the work.
- **Installing cavity wall insulation** – The lack of any insulation within the wall makes this a favourable option as it is a relatively straightforward and low cost method. The high savings and quick payback make this the best investment of the three leading options.
- **Replacing the boiler with a condensing boiler** – On an annual basis, this improvement saves the most money. The difference in thermal efficiency between the existing boiler and a new condensing boiler is very significant, but the installation cost is also high. This improvement would give the longest payback period. It is not worth carrying out this improvement on its own, but because the Home Condition Report showed that the existing boiler is approaching the end of its useful life, it is an option worth considering when the existing boiler finally breaks down.

Although there will be no opportunity to include your own commentary on these energy issues in the Home Condition Report, you may get enquiries directly from potential buyers. Therefore, you should be able to give a broader explanation of the possible options, rather than simply relying solely on the automatically generated paragraphs.

6 Insurance and repair cost assessments

The content of this chapter will help you to understand and meet the requirements of the following elements of the National Occupational Standards for Home Inspectors:

- **Element 5.1 – Produce complete and comprehensive Home Condition Reports**

The performance criteria is based on ability to calculate and state estimated minimum reinstatement costs for insurance purposes.

(A summary of the different units and elements that make up the NOS in Home Inspection has been included in Appendix B. A complete copy can be downloaded from www.assetskills.org.)

INTRODUCTION TO THE BUILDING COST INFORMATION SERVICE (BCIS)

The Home Condition Report requires the Home Inspector to produce a figure that can be used by purchasers to advise their chosen household insurer of the full rebuilding cost of the property. Home Inspector guidance recommends the use of BCIS's House Rebuilding Cost Index for the Association of British Insurers (ABI) to provide guidance figures for the rebuilding cost of a property.

You can find more information regarding the House Rebuilding Cost Index at **www.bcis.co.uk**. The information given in the guidance figures provides a general indication of rebuilding costs for many common properties within the UK, though it is not appropriate for all property.

The guidance figures are based upon a full rebuild of a property, so they assume and take into account the following:

- total demolition;
- clearance of the site, with rebuilding of the property from the foundations upward; and
- rebuilding of the property to its existing design, with similar standards to the existing building, using modern materials and techniques.

The property also needs to meet current building regulations and other statutory requirements, so if the building does not conform, necessary adjustments have to be made. Also, the guidance figures provided in the standard tables are based on specific examples of houses of average quality, which were built using standard construction methods. The guidance figures are not applicable to:

- properties built of stone or materials other than brick;
- properties with basements, cellars, or more than two storeys;
- properties with special design features, historic or listed buildings, or properties larger than the examples; and
- properties other than of average quality.

However, the guidance figures do give supplements for certain features, such as thatch, basements and cellars, stonework, very small properties such as 'starter' homes and those with increased roof pitch. Some properties benefited from cheaper build costs principally due to economies of scale when they were actually built, such as modern timber framed houses. In respect of reinstatement, these costs cannot be accommodated because it will be a one-off construction.

UNUSUAL PROPERTIES

Where a property has unusual features or is dissimilar to properties typical of its construction period, the BCIS guides are inappropriate and you should refer the property to a specialist such as an architect, quantity or building surveyor.

The kind of features and rebuilding work not covered in the guidance figures includes:

- highly ornate plaster covings and ceilings in a period property which may have to be reconstructed in similar materials, especially if the property is listed; and

- significant retaining walls which are not standard construction and probably require engineering calculations and designs for reconstruction to ensure they fulfil their purpose.

The guidance figures offer examples and considerations of features such as variations in ceiling height from the accepted figure for the age of the property, and how this affects various building elements and services. For example, an increase in ceiling height of 0.5 metres for a semi-detached house will add twenty-seven per cent to the cost of the stairs, nine per cent to waste pipes and thirteen per cent to built-in cupboards. Therefore, you should know what ceiling height is expected. If there is a significant variation, either compare the building to another age category or seek specialist advice. A small semi-detached house built between 1946 and 1979 would be expected to have a ceiling height of 2.4 metres, whereas a large detached house of the same period would be 2.67 metres.

ESSENTIAL INFORMATION

You should have copies of the following publications:

BCIS Guide to House Rebuilding Costs

While it is not a substitute for professional judgment, a copy of the current guide is an essential reference for undertaking insurance reinstatement cost assessments.

Rebuilding costs are presented for 648 examples in eight main tables, expanding the tables associated with this section for three quality specifications and four measurement options. Additional advice is given for attics, additional storeys, cellars, garages, stonework and thatch, conservatories, flats, timber framed houses, 'starter' homes, additional bathrooms and kitchens, external works and drainage. The text is illustrated throughout with tables showing how costs change in different circumstances.

BCIS Regional Supplement

This supplement to the guide gives separate tables of costs for each of the English Government Office Regions (with Merseyside included in the North West), Scotland and Wales.

Guide to the Rebuilding Cost of Flats

This guide contains rebuilding costs for low and medium rise modern blocks of flats, and houses converted to flats.

An alternative to these printed publications; *BCIS Rebuild Online* can calculate rebuilding costs for individual properties and produce tables adjusted to date and location. It also includes further details of the adjustments available. You can find out more at **www.bcis.co.uk**.

UNDERTAKING THE ASSESSMENT

Since the BCIS give guidance to customers on how to calculate a basic reinstatement cost on their website, it is not difficult for the informed customer to challenge the professional assessment.

All measurements should be gathered using a metric tape. Calculate the gross external floor area of the house in metres squared (m^2). That is the area measured to the external face of the external walls and should include all floors (in most cases you can measure the ground floor area and double it). Where there are extensions, then look at the property as a series of blocks as fortunately, most property is rectangular or square. Where there is an irregular shape such as a bay window, then consider geometric shapes, using common sense. All measurements should be taken in accordance with the RICS *Code of Measuring Practice*.

The Code of Measuring Practice requires for all integral buildings such as garages, conservatories and all areas within the external envelope to be measured. The BCIS publications give additional guidance on how the following areas should be treated:

- integral garages should be measured as part of the main building and included within the full calculation;
- conservatories are treated individually and given a rate in the guide for standard design; and
- additional storeys such as attics should be incorporated on a value of seventy per cent of that used for the main floor area, assuming the storey sits over the whole of the floor area below (with shallow areas of roof space included within the measurements).

A block plan of the property should be drawn on your site notes and measurements noted. A separate calculation should be made alongside the drawing to show what rates have been applied to different parts of the property, such as attic rooms. A block plan sketch for the case study property is included at the end of this chapter in Figure 6.1.

The rebuilding cost (in $£/m^2$) is obtained from the tables in the guides, which reflect age and quality of property. There may be times when a property is not characteristic of its age band, so rates may therefore need to be adjusted accordingly. This may happen where a house was originally constructed pre-1920, but has been substantially reconstructed to more modern standards using more modern materials.

There is a table for each age band of house: pre 1920, 1920 to 1945, 1946 to 1979 and 1980 to date.

SELECTING THE APPROPRIATE REGION

Regions refer to Government Office Regions (GORs) with the addition of Scotland and Wales. With effect from April 1997, the GORs replaced the Standard Statistical Regions as the primary classification for the presentation of English regional statistics.

The cost of building work in Northern Ireland is considered by the guides to be considerably lower than in the rest of the UK. Tables are provided that cover this differentiation.

SIMPLE STEPS TO ACHIEVE THE REINSTATEMENT COST

1. Obtain the rebuilding cost in £/m^2 from the tables in the guides and select the size by referring to the typical areas shown. Having found the appropriate rate, make any necessary adjustments for quality.
2. Multiply the gross external floor area in m^2 by the rate to give the estimated rebuilding cost of the house.
3. Add the cost of rebuilding any garages, outbuildings, walls, fences, etc.
4. The figures in the table are priced at January levels of the appropriate year. For an approximate adjustment to current prices you can use the **ABI/BCIS House Rebuilding Cost Index** at www.bcis.co.uk/costind.html.

To illustrate how this approach can be applied to a real building, we have used the case study property in Chapter Seven. The calculation of the floor area and all other assumptions are shown in part four of the case study.

ESTIMATING THE COST OF REPAIR WORKS

As discussed in Chapter Three, a building element's repair cost is just one of the criteria that will help you determine the element's overall condition rating. We have included an example of how you can use the *BCIS Guide to House Rebuilding Costs* to provide a little objectivity to your estimates. We are not suggesting that you go through this process for every element on every property. Instead, you might want to do this when:

- the cost of repair is likely to be on the £1000 borderline;
- costs are likely to be a determining factor in the rating decision; or
- you want to develop your estimating skills.

Our example is based on repairs to the rear chimney of the case study property in Chapter Seven. Here is the text from section D1 (Chimney stacks) of our sample Home Condition Report:

'The rear brick built chimney stack serves the open flue boiler in the kitchen. Although it is structurally sound, there are a number of defects:

- *the mortar between the brick joints are deteriorating and need replacing (repointing);*
- *the lead waterproofing at the junction of the chimney and the roof covering (flashing) is leaking and needs replacing; and*
- *the cement around the top of the chimney (flaunching) and the chimney pot has deteriorated and needs replacing.*

A general builder or a roofing contractor should do this work as soon as possible because water is leaking into the kitchen below.'

The repair works will include repointing, reflaunching, one new chimney pot, and new lead flashings and soakers, including the back gutter. The relevant section of the *BCIS Guide to House Rebuilding Costs* (C5 – the exterior: chimneys) presents descriptions and prices for a number of different repairs, listed in Table 6.1.

Table 6.1: Chimney repair and cost estimates

Type of repair	Estimated repair cost
Repointing of a two metre high chimney with decayed mortar (one pot stack)	£520
Replace lead flashing all around chimney including back gutter, stepped flashing and apron	£420
Replace chimney pot	£485
Reflaunch the chimney	£420
	Total: £1845

On face value, the cost of repairs alone would put the chimney element into a category three condition rating. However, detailed scrutiny of the pricing document reveals that all of the separate estimates include access costs such as scaffold, which inflates the total cost by a considerable sum. The builder will only have to provide one scaffold from which all the repairs can be carried out. Therefore, the estimated repair cost total of £1845 includes quadruple counting!

To get a more realistic price, these access costs will have to be removed and this is where the process becomes more subjective. The estimates in the BCIS Guide to House Rebuilding Costs do not identify the access costs, meaning that you will have to establish these yourself. We have maintained the access costs for repointing, but all the others have been reduced by what we consider is an appropriate amount. The total recalculated costs are now £1040:

- repointing costs   (£520.00);
- replacing flashings (£220.00);
- new chimney pot   (£100.00); and
- reflaunching   (£200.00).

This presents a potential problem for rating the condition of the element. If the flashings had not been leaking and some of the other key questions had not suggested a high level of seriousness, would the £1040 cost total be sufficient to require a category three condition rating? This will be confused by the varying nature of the building industry. Some contractors will submit estimates that exceed £1000 by a considerable amount, whereas others (who may not use the appropriate safety equipment) will charge much less. Sellers and buyers will also exert different pressures: the former trying to show that the costs will be less than £1000, while the latter will be only too keen to point out costs that exceed this magic figure!

This example provides just one illustration of the difficulty in handling cost estimates within the overall rating process. It will always be a controversial area and we suggest that:

- if your estimating skills are underdeveloped, build them up by estimating the costs of many different types of repairs until your familiarity with repair costs to residential property improves; and
- where the cost of a repair is likely to be marginal and important in the rating process, calculate the costs as precisely as you can even if you have good estimating skills.

In both of the above cases, you should document the process as follows:

- always use the *BCIS Guide to House Rebuilding Costs* to establish as many 'core' costs as you can;
- where you adjust these core costs, make a note of how and why; and
- document this process in your site notes and keep them on file.

This approach will not stop third parties challenging you, but it will give you a record of why you came to a decision and provide evidence regarding your competence.

ADDITIONAL POINTS FOR REINSTATEMENT COST CALCULATIONS

There are a number of other issues that you might need to consider when calculating reinstatement costs.

Adjustments for fixtures and fittings

The guide will accommodate a range of specifications – 'Basic', 'Good' and 'Excellent'. This allows for some variation, but may not be sufficient. The cost of installing sanitary fittings may be similar, but the specification may vary. Such features as hydrotherapy showers or baths are unlikely to be accommodated in the standard figures and allowances would need to be made.

The specifications used in the guides are clearly set out in elemental tables.

Treatment of fees and VAT

Guidance is taken on the VAT element from HM Customs and Excise. There is currently no requirement for VAT on a building started from scratch, which was designed as a dwelling. So, the tables that apply to a total rebuild do not require VAT to be included. However, professional fees do have VAT applied and so that element is included in the tables.

Scale fees are used for architects and quantity surveyors, together with any planning or building regulation fees. However, some building work may require more specialist input compared to similar properties. Only the standard fees have been included within the guides, meaning complex reconstruction costs may need to be factored into the calculations to cover additional fees.

Outbuildings, boundaries and leisure facilities

Guidance is given on certain standard features, such as woven wood panels and softwood posts, at certain heights with the costs expressed in £ per metre run. Clearly, adjustments would have to be made if hardwood posts were used.

Various designs are given for outbuildings, principally sheds and greenhouses of specific sizes. However, if a property included a stable block then it may be possible to adjust the reinstatement cost using the elemental breakdown, especially if the stable block is constructed in brick.

No provision is made in the guide for buildings housing swimming pools because these involve pumping, heating and filtration plants. In such cases it would be useful to give a figure for the property excluding the pool. The customer would be best advised to speak with a/the pool supplier and get a cost that is acceptable to the insurers.

Adjustments for different materials

The guides give some information on stone built property, particularly modern stone faced building instead of facing bricks. However, where an older property is concerned, figures are quoted with the proviso that they may vary in different locations. A supplement would need to be added to the elemental tables so that this could be used in future calculations. It would be important to clarify this in the Home Condition Report for the benefit of the insurer. Therefore, if the Home Inspector does not possess the local knowledge for such costing, specialist help would have to be sought.

No guidance is given on concrete properties or other non-traditional designs such as steel framed British Iron and Steel Federation (BISF) properties. The assumption would be made in respect of concrete property that it would be reconstructed in modern blockwork and then rendered to match adjoining property. In some areas, PRC (prefabricated reinforced concrete) dwellings have been reconstructed using brick faced main walls and so adjustments would have to be made.

Property constructed under BISF could be treated in the same way if acceptable to planners. If not, it would be subject to specialist design and construction for a one-off building and would therefore fall outside the guide.

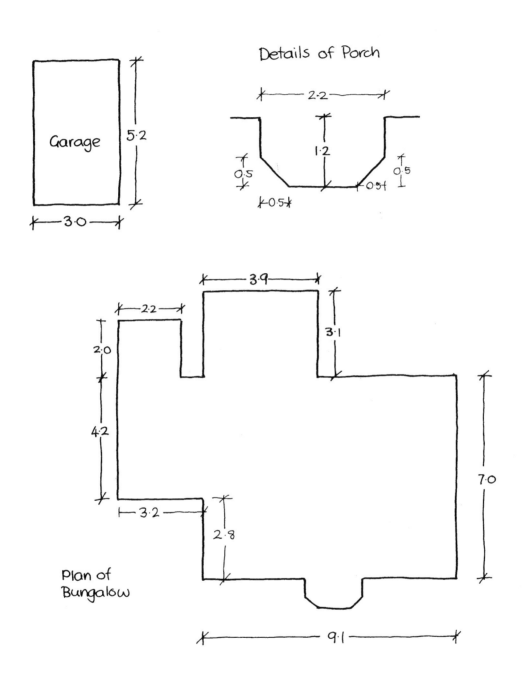

Figure 6.1: Dimensions of case study property

7 Case study property: A Home Inspection and Home Condition Report

INTRODUCTION

To illustrate how the new home inspection and reporting procedures apply in reality, this section includes a complete case study of a three-bedroom bungalow that has recently been placed on the market. It has not been selected to suit any particular purpose, but was randomly chosen from a list of empty properties that were available for viewing at the time of inspection.

Following the Guidance Notes, a home condition inspection was carried out and several photographs taken. The information was used to produce the six different parts of this case study.

PART ONE – DESCRIPTION OF THE PROPERTY

This section includes a description of the construction, accommodation and amenities of the property, along with a site plan and a floor plan.

PART TWO – ELEMENTAL DATA SHEETS

A number of the individual building elements have been described in greater detail and include:

- a description of the element's condition;
- an analysis of the element's condition, outlining the thought process behind our condition rating decisions; and
- the condition rating itself with an appropriate report extract.

Not all building elements have been included in this section. Priority was given to those elements that were given a category three condition rating, those that presented interesting or difficult rating decisions, and all of the services.

PART THREE – REVIEW OF OTHER ELEMENTS

The rationale for the category rating decisions of the more straightforward and remaining elements are briefly reviewed in this section.

PART FOUR – CALCULATION OF REINSTATEMENT COSTS FOR INSURANCE PURPOSES

Using the BCIS data and methodology, the reinstatement costs for insurance purposes for this particular property are calculated and illustrated.

PART FIVE – ENERGY REPORT

Using the approach of a particular energy rating organisation, the SAP data is discussed in this section. The actual energy report is included under Section H of the Home Condition Report.

PART SIX – THE HOME CONDITION REPORT

Using all the information generated by the previous sections, a complete Home Condition Report has been produced and is included here.

USING THIS CASE STUDY

To get the most from this case study, we suggest that you:

- familiarise yourself with the layout, details and general photographs of the property (Parts one and two);
- review each element data sheet and accompanying information so that you understand how we arrived at our rating decisions (Parts two and three);
- read the entire Home Condition Report as a whole (Part six).

Do you agree with our views? Producing Home Condition Reports is not a precise science, but a series of decisions about a range of building elements using incomplete information. There is little wonder that outcomes can vary so much between different practitioners. However, we think that our ratings and report are appropriate for the case study property. The descriptions, analysis and decisions outlined in this chapter will help you to accurately apply these new and developing approaches in your day-to-day work.

PART ONE: DESCRIPTION OF THE PROPERTY

The case study property is a three-bedroom bungalow constructed in approximately 1946. It is located in the south-east of England and has a timber-framed pitched roof over the main part of the property. There are flat roofs over the property's three extensions, which consist of:

- a porch constructed around the front entrance door, built several decades ago;
- a lounge extension to the rear elevation, approximately fifteen to twenty years old; and
- a rear extension, which is more recent than the lounge extension.

The property's construction

The property is constructed as follows:

- main roof structure – traditional cut roof with ridge-board, rafters and hip rafters, purlins and struts;

- roof covering – older style plain concrete roof tiles with half round ridge and hip tiles;
- walls – brick faced (assumed to be a cavity wall with either bricks or blocks internally);
- floors – all the floors throughout the property are solid concrete;
- internal walls (solid and 100mm thick, assumed to be either brick or block);
- windows – mainly double glazed PVC windows, except those in the porch that are single glazed and metal-framed; and
- ceilings – timber ceiling joists with plasterboard ceilings.

Services

The property's services comprise of the following:

- water – company supply pipes rises in rear entrance extension;
- gas – the property is connected to mains gas and has central heating to all spaces apart from the front porch and rear extension;
- electricity – there is an electrical supply and the utility company fuse and consumer unit is at a high level just inside the main entrance door; and

Front view of property

Site plan of property

Rear view of property

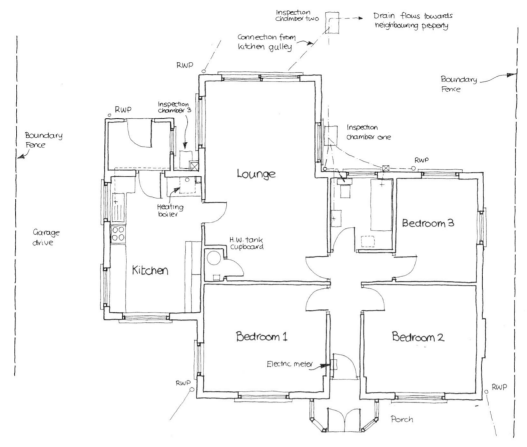

Floor plan of the property

- drainage – it is assumed that the property is connected to the public sewer through the neighbouring property.

At the time of inspection, the property had been unoccupied for approximately six months. The owner could not be contacted and the selling agent knew very little about the property. The property is located in the middle of a large and well-established plot that has vehicular access from the road to the front, running along the side of the house to the detached single garage at the rear of the plot. There are a number of well-established shrubs and small trees in the rear garden.

PART TWO – ELEMENT DATA SHEETS

ELEMENT D1 (CHIMNEY STACKS)

Description

There are two chimney stacks in the property. These are serving:

- The front right-hand bedroom that was formerly the lounge. The chimney stack has been taken down in the past and the roof covering extended over. The remainder of the stack is external to the wall and the fireplace has been taken out.

Chimney stack serving the boiler in the kitchen

Former chimney to bedroom two

Boiler in the kitchen

- The open flue boiler of the central heating in the kitchen. This chimney stack is also external and is formed by corbelling the brickwork of the external skin of the cavity wall. This extends above the roof level by approximately 1.8m.

The front chimney stack in the bedroom is in satisfactory condition, but the remaining flue has not been ventilated.

The rear chimney stack has a number of defects:

- the chimney pot is fractured and needs to be replaced;
- the flaunching and pointing are in poor condition; and
- the flashing and soakers to the base of the chimney have deteriorated, allowing water to penetrate into the kitchen below.

The lack of a metal cowl on the pot suggests that the chimney may not have a metal liner.

Analysis

The rear chimney stack

This is in a poor condition. It needs a new chimney pot, the top needs reflaunching, the whole stack needs

Chimney stack above the kitchen

repointing and the flashing needs to be renewed. The chimney stack is the cause of the dampness above the boiler in the kitchen and so needs urgent repair to prevent further damage. It is also usual for a chimney that serves a heating boiler to be lined with a flexible liner.

Although the cost of repair may get close to £1000, it is unlikely to exceed it. Despite this and because of the leak to the room below, it is more urgent than many other repairs, which in our opinion nudges this into category three.

This problem is also a classic 'widespread defect' that affects a number of other building elements, including:

- Chimney stacks (see D1);
- Roof structure (see E1);
- Ceilings (see E2);
- Internal walls, partitions and plasterwork (see E3); and
- Fireplaces, chimney breasts and exterior of flues (see E5).

It may also link with F4 (Heating) because of the flue lining. Therefore, careful cross-referencing is required.

The chimney stack serving the former lounge

The chimney stack has been removed some time ago and the roof covering satisfactorily extended over the former chimney. The only problem is that the remaining flue that is now concealed behind the blocked off fireplace is not ventilated. This could lead to a build up of moisture, so two new airbricks should be provided externally, (one at the top and bottom respectively). The airbricks should not ventilate internally because that would introduce warm moist air into a cold flue, resulting in condensation. The proposed maintenance work would give this building element a category two condition rating.

Report

Two chimneys have been included in this element, each with their own rating.

Rear Chimney – Rating three

The rear brick built chimney stack serves the open flue boiler in the kitchen. Although it is structurally sound, there are a number of defects:

- the mortar between the brick joints are deteriorating and need replacing (repointing);
- the lead water proofing at the junction of the chimney and the roof covering (flashing) is leaking and needs replacing; and
- the cement around the top of the chimney (flaunching) and the chimney pot has deteriorated and needs replacing.

A general builder or a roofing contractor should do this work.

Former Chimney – Rating two

The former chimney stack that served the front right-hand room (now used as a bedroom) has been removed above roof covering level. This has been done satisfactorily, but external ventilation bricks should be installed in the remaining flue to prevent dampness. A general builder should do this work.

ELEMENT D2 (ROOF COVERINGS)

Description

The roof is covered by plain concrete tiles laid over poor quality sarking felt and has dropped away in a number of places. The hips and ridges are covered with concrete half round tiles and many of these are in a poor condition. The valleys are formed with shaped concrete tiles laid over heavier grade roofing felt. A small number of tiles are either broken or missing and the final eaves tile course does not properly extend over the gutters. This allows water to flow down the fascia, rotting the timber in at least six locations. Most of the roof surface is overgrown with large clumps of moss and is blocking many of the gutters and downpipes. There are no roof leaks.

Typical roof slope to the property

Eaves tiles to gutters over south-west elevation

The lounge and rear entrance extensions have flat roofs that are covered with recently applied roofing felt in a satisfactory condition. The flat roofs do not have any roof space ventilation, but there is no evidence of any subsequent defects.

Analysis

Although the roof is not leaking, there are a number of defects, including:

- A small number of the roof tiles and most of the ridge and hip tiles need replacing. This is not an urgent problem, but it would be sensible to carry out the work soon because the roof will be vulnerable to possible storm damage.
- The moss on the roof will hold water and increase the rate of deterioration of the tiles. The moss is also blocking gutters and at least two of the downpipes. In usual circumstances, the moss should be removed as part of normal maintenance work, but since there is so much, it has now become a repair by itself. This is not an urgent or serious problem, but one that needs doing soon.
- Although the sarking felt is visually in a poor condition, it is not a serious problem. Although leaks are possible during high winds, it has not caused a problem yet and so is low priority at this time. The repair/replacement of the felt can wait until the whole roof is recovered. It should be mentioned in the report because the seller and buyers may notice the problem and become worried about it.
- The most serious defect is the fault with the eaves course of the roof tiles. Due to the final roof tiles and the underlying roofing felt not extending over the edge of the gutter, rainwater runs down the timber fascia board, making it rotten in a number of places. As there is a high risk of further deterioration, this should be repaired within the next six months. This affects the entire perimeter of the roof, will be expensive and therefore defined as a 'serious' defect.

We did have a debate whether we should recommend that the whole roof be recovered. Looking at this range of defects, some owners might decide that it would be economic to do the whole roof job now. However, this would not be a universal view, since the roof can be kept watertight for a further period, albeit with higher levels of maintenance. Where a choice exists, one must always be given.

Report

The roof covering element has been split into two sections:

- the pitched roof covering; and
- the flat roof coverings (the lounge and rear entrance extensions).

The flat roof covering to the front porch is included under D10 (Other) because it is in a different condition to the two other flat roofs. The flat roofs to the lounge and rear entrance extensions are dealt with together because they are very similar. This reduces the amount of subdivision.

Pitched roof covering – Rating three

The main pitched roof is covered with concrete tiles over a secondary waterproof barrier (sarking felt). Although the main roof is not leaking, there are a number of defects:

- The ridge and hip tiles are in a poor condition and need replacing.
- The roof slopes are covered with moss that may lead to the deterioration of the roof tiles. This needs removing and will result in recurring maintenance in the future.
- The rainwater does not properly discharge into the gutters from the edge roof tiles. This is rotting the timber board that supports the gutters (fascia) (see also D3 and D7). This needs repairing so that rain can properly discharge into the gutters.
- The sarking felt is damaged in a number of places and could let in water during high winds. This should be replaced when the main roof is next recovered.

A general builder should do this work.

Flat roof coverings – Rating one

The flat roofs over the lounge extension and the rear entrance extensions are covered in roofing felt and are in a satisfactory condition for their type and age. However, when compared to a pitched roof, flat roofs can leak unexpectedly. This needs to be monitored as part of normal maintenance.

ELEMENT D3 (RAINWATER PIPES & GUTTERS)

Description

All the gutters and downpipes have been recently replaced with a mixture of white and brown PVC sections. These are not leaking. The three downpipes serving the main roof connect into the original drainage connections. The downpipe from the lounge extension connects into a new drainage connection. Of all of these, only one could be traced and this discharged into the nearby combined drainage system. It is assumed that the others connect to unknown soakaways. The downpipe from the flat roof of the rear entrance extension discharges over the ground.

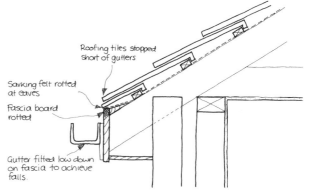

Sketch detail showing defect at eaves/gutter

Rainwater pipes to rear extension

Although the gutters have been recently cleared out, the top sections of the downpipes are solidly blocked with moss growth from the roof. Some lengths of the guttering need to be refitted at a more suitable fall.

The eaves course of the roof tiling does not discharge rainwater into the gutters properly, allowing water to run down the timber fascia, causing rot in a number of places (see D2 and D7).

Analysis

The gutters are in a satisfactory condition, but there are a number of problems:

- The downpipes need to be cleared, flushed through and left in a good working order. This goes beyond 'normal maintenance' and constitutes a repair in our view.
- The downpipe from the rear entrance extension roof should be connected into the drainage system.
- Some parts of the guttering system need to be realigned to provide a proper fall.

We have spilt the guttering into two sub-elements:

- the main house and lounge extension; and
- the rear entrance extension.

The guttering has been split up because the problems associated with it are different.

For the guttering to the main house, based on this level of repair, we think a category two condition rating is appropriate. The problems are not urgent, they are not immediately leading to further deterioration and are not serious. The guttering will have to be removed and refitted when the fascia board is renewed (see D7), but we cannot assume the owner will do this. Therefore, these two repairs have to be treated separately.

The rear entrance extension is different in its nature. The absence of formal drainage to the extension could affect the foundations, but there is no evidence of this yet. Since it is not a large flat roof, the likelihood of this is slim, but we feel it must be pointed out. The cost of a new connection will probably come to less than £1000 and we would not describe it as urgent. Consequently, we have given this element a category two condition rating.

Report

Gutters to the main house and lounge extension – Rating two

The gutters and rainwater pipes are made of PVC. Although they are in an adequate condition, there are a number of problems:

- The gutters, pipes and associated underground drains need to be cleaned out.
- The slope of the guttering needs to be altered so that it drains properly. This should be done in conjunction with the repairs to the fascia board (see D7).

A general builder should do this work.

Gutters to the rear entrance extension – Rating two

The gutters and rainwater pipe to the rear entrance extension are made of PVC. Although they are in a satisfactory condition, the rainwater pipe from the flat roof needs to be connected into the main drainage system. A general builder should do this work.

PART TWO – ELEMENT D4 (MAIN WALLS)

Mortar joint to external wall showing damage by masonry bees

Visible DPC in external wall

Description

The main walls are bricked faced with a solid but unknown inner skin. The brick bond and width of the wall suggests that it is cavity construction. This is unlikely to be insulated. The walls to the lounge extension are also brick faced and assumed cavity. The walls to the rear extension are brick, but only 102.5mm (half a brick thick).

There is no evidence of building movement. Over the recessed front entrance extension, the lintel construction is visible. It consists of brick soldier course supported by a small metal angle over the outer skin and concrete lintel over the inner skin. The lintels over the other openings are assumed to be the same. Several of these brick soldier courses have been disrupted when the windows were replaced, although none are unstable. Sloped bricks laid on edge formed the sills. A bitumen based damp-proof course can be seen in the outer skin of the wall, but this is close to the external ground levels on two sides because of the raised paths. No dampness was detected internally.

The mortar to the joints is of a sandy mix and can easily be scratched with a fingernail in several places. Around the south-west/north-west corner, masonry bees have burrowed deep into the mortar across an area of approximately 3m^2.

Analysis

This element has been divided into three sub-elements:

- the main walls;
- lounge extension walls; and
- rear entrance extension walls.

The main walls

The main walls are in a satisfactory structural condition, but there are a few problems:

- The mortar joints need to be repointed. Although some areas are worse than others, it would be sensible to do the whole property at once. In the area that has been affected by masonry bees, to avoid problems with a live colony, this work should be done in autumn. Since the walls have a cavity and there is no dampness internally, the repointing is not urgent, but clearly constitutes a repair.
- Since the brick soldier courses are partially supported by an existing metal angle, they are unlikely to become unstable, although several have been cracked when the old windows were taken out. These cracks should be raked out and repointed. This work is not urgent and can be done with the rest of the pointing as part of a planned programme of maintenance.
- The external ground levels have been raised over the years. Although these do not bridge the DPC, it comes very close in a number of locations. This has not resulted in dampness problems internally. It does not need carrying out urgently, but the report should clearly point out that it should be done in the future.

Initially we found this element difficult to rate. In cost terms, the repointing of all the main external walls will come to well over £1000, potentially placing it in category three. However, the condition of the existing pointing has not caused internal dampness, it will not deteriorate quickly, and it is unlikely to result in a serious health and safety risk. The only exception is the repair of the masonry bee damage. This should be done soon, but because of its limited extent, it still could not be described as serious. In this case, the repointing of the external wall could be described as planned maintenance, although its extent would classify it as a repair. Therefore, we have given this element a category two condition rating, albeit in the upper part. However, the eventual cost of the repointing will be high, so this should be emphasised in the report.

Lounge extension walls

The lounge extension is much younger than the main house and in a satisfactory condition, so has been given a category one condition rating.

Rear entrance extension walls

The walls to the rear entrance extension are only half a brick thick and below current standards. They will be vulnerable to rain penetration and condensation even though it is not used as a living space. This provides further evidence that the whole extension may not have building regulation approval. The cost of bringing the walls up to standard will be high and it would be economical to demolish the whole extension and reconstruct it. Therefore, this sub-element has been given a category three condition rating.

Typical window to the property

Report

Main walls – Rating two

The main walls are brick faced, assumed to be of cavity construction and have a bitumen damp-proof course. The walls are in an adequate condition, but there are a number of defects:

- The mortar between the bricks (pointing) is deteriorating, needs to be renewed and may be costly. One small area is affected by masonry bees and should be repointed in the autumn.
- Over some of the windows, the brickwork has been damaged and needs to be repaired.
- The external ground levels are too close to the damp-proof course level and may cause internal dampness in the future. These levels need to be reduced.

A general builder should do this work.

Lounge extension walls – Rating one

The main walls are brick faced, assumed to be of cavity construction, have a bitumen damp proof course and are in a satisfactory condition.

Rear entrance extension walls – Rating three

The walls are brick, are too thin and will be vulnerable to future dampness problems. The repair will be costly and so demolition and reconstruction may be an economic solution. If the walls are rebuilt, all necessary permissions should be obtained. If they are demolished and not rebuilt, then the rear entrance door will need upgrading to make it weather-tight.

ELEMENT D5 (WINDOWS)

Description

All the windows to the property have been replaced with PVC double glazed units within the last ten years, apart from the windows to the small front porch.

Patio doors to the rear lounge extension

These are the original metal single glazed windows. With the exception of the front porch, all the windows are in a satisfactory condition and work properly.

The only defect is the brick soldier course over the window openings. Most of these have been damaged when the windows were installed. These have been reported under D4 (Main Walls) and will not be mentioned in this section.

Analysis

Due to the installation date, the window replacement is unlikely to have building regulation or FENSA approval, but a check should be made to see whether any guarantees exist and are active. This information will also be needed for the RDSAP assessment.

Since the front porch has been included in D10 (Other), the condition of the metal windows has not affected the rating of this element. For these reasons, we have given this element a category one condition rating.

Report

The windows are double glazed with PVC frames and are in a satisfactory condition. The legal advisor should check whether the installation of the windows has a FENSA certificate, building regulation approval, or a manufacturer's warranty.

ELEMENT D10 (OTHER)

The front entrance porch (description)

General view of front porch

This was not built at the same time as the house, but was constructed many years ago. It consists of a felted flat roof, single glazed metal windows and double doors. The half height walls are clad externally with timber and lined internally with mineral boarding. This boarding is likely to be asbestos-based. It has a solid floor, finished with quarry tiles. The flat roof does not have any gutters or downpipes. The timber sub-frames to the metal windows have rotted in a number of areas and the felt flat roof is in poor condition.

Analysis

The front porch has been included in this section for two reasons:

- It is a distinct, self-contained part of the property that would be laborious to describe element-by-element.
- The porch has such a range of problems that they would give a false impression of the property as a whole if it was included in the main report. It would also make the report very disjointed because several elements would have to be subdivided to report on it properly.

Although the porch may have some amenity value, it is in such a poor condition that it would not be economic to repair. Additionally, the internal boarding is likely to contain asbestos. Although it does not pose an immediate risk in its present form, fibres may be released if the boards are decorated or disturbed during the repairs.

Due to these factors, we feel that it is appropriate to recommend that the porch should be removed completely and either:

- rebuilt using modern materials to current standards with all appropriate approvals; or
- affected surfaces made good and the existing front door replaced with one that is more weather resistant.

Since not all property owners would agree with this analysis, leaving the porch intact would be a specific option, so long as the inadequacies were accepted.

Report

The front porch consists of a flat roof, single glazed metal windows, timber walls and a solid floor. Internally, the walls are lined with asbestos-based boarding (see C2). The porch is in a poor condition.

The repair of these defects will be costly and so removal and reconstruction may be an economic solution. If it is rebuilt, all necessary permissions should be obtained. If the porch is demolished and not rebuilt, then the front entrance door will need replacing/upgrading to make it weather-tight. Alternatively, the porch may continue to be used as long as its inadequacy is accounted for.

Whatever the option chosen, care must be taken with the asbestos-based boarding. If this is to be disturbed in any way, a specialist will need to be appointed (see C2).

ELEMENT E1 (ROOF STRUCTURE)

Description

The pitched roof has a traditional 'cut' structure consisting of rafters supported by purlins at mid-span, with all purlins supported by strutts that are taken down to a load bearing wall. The ceiling joists are tied into the rafter feet to the north-east and south-west, but not to the north-west and south-east elevations. A smaller subsidiary pitched roof extends over the kitchen. There is no evidence of distortion in the structure and no rot or wood boring insects were found. There is no formal roof ventilation and the loft insulation is only 75mm thick. Sections of the sarking felt were hanging down where it had come loose along the hip rafters.

The structure to the flat roof over the lounge and rear entrance extension is concealed and could not be inspected. This is likely to be timber and there is no evidence of potential defects or deterioration, although neither roof is properly ventilated.

Purlin to south-west roof slope and associated strutts

View of typical hip rafter showing areas of poorly fitted sarking felt

View of rafters and ceiling joists to north-west roof slope, showing only partial restraint to the rafter feet

Analysis

The main roof structure is in a satisfactory condition. There is no evidence of any defects and although the sizes of some of the components are below current standards, they have not distorted. When the roof is recovered, additional strengthening may be required (especially to restrain the rafter feet to the hip slopes), but this does not need to be done yet.

The leak to the flashing at the base of the rear chimney may be affecting the trimming roof timbers. These could not be inspected because of the low pitch of the roof and adjacent water tanks, so will need further investigation (see B3).

The level of thermal insulation to the pitched roof will be highlighted in the energy section (Section H) of the Home Condition Report. However, where it is obviously below current levels, it should be mentioned under this element. Currently, informal roof ventilation has prevented any condensation, but if the insulation is increased and the property more consistently occupied, then water vapour levels will rise. Therefore, new roof ventilation should be provided soon. Both of these recommendations justify a category two condition rating.

This element has been divided into two: pitched roof structure and flat roof structure. The flat roof to the lounge and rear entrance extension have been combined because they are in similar condition.

As the flat roof structures are concealed, the level of insulation and roof space ventilation cannot be established. Experience suggests that both will be below current standards. There is no evidence of any deterioration, so a recommendation that these should be upgraded when the roofs are next recovered would be appropriate. This might seem to contradict the decision for the pitched roof, but it is a matter of extent and degree. The main roof space will be subjected to higher levels of moisture and the ventilation will be easily provided. For the flat roofs, the potential risk of the problem does not justify the disruption and expense of altering the construction in the short term just to provide ventilation.

As the flat roof spaces have not been inspected, the 'Not Inspected' rating has been applied.

Report

This element has been divided into two sections:

Pitched roof structure – Rating two

The main roof structure is in a satisfactory condition. The level of roof space insulation (see H3) and ventilation should be increased.

The timbers around the base of the rear chimney stack may be damp because of the leak (see D1). These need to be checked for wood rot (see B3).

Flat roof structure – Rating NI (not inspected)

The space within the flat roof structures could not be inspected. It is likely that the ventilation and thermal insulation levels do not meet current standards. These should be increased when the flat roofs are next recovered.

ELEMENT E4 (FLOORS)

Description

The floors throughout the property are solid and almost certainly made of concrete. All rooms (including the bathroom) have fitted carpets, apart from the kitchen and the entrance extension, which are covered with linoleum. Only the corners of the carpets in bedrooms two and three could be lifted. The surfaces are satisfactory, but high dampness readings were recorded. In these damp areas, there was no evidence of salt staining on the concrete and the underlay to the carpet was moist, but otherwise the floor covering was unaffected by the dampness.

Tests with a spirit level over the floor coverings showed that all floors are level, without any indication of cracking or other defects except the rear entrance extension. In this space, the floor was uneven. Externally, there is no evidence of movement at low level or slippage on the DPC that might suggest sulphate attack.

Analysis

Overall, the floors in the main house are in a satisfactory condition. They are level and free from any cracking or other defects normally associated with floors of this age. The only problem is the dampness to the surface in the two rooms where the carpets were lifted. This dampness could have been caused by:

- Rising dampness through the slab because of a defective or absent damp-proof membrane. Although solid floors are usually fitted with DPMs, they were often missed out in properties of this age.
- Condensation caused by water vapour condensing on the cold surface of the solid floor. This effect could have been made worse by the property being empty for so long. When it is occupied and properly heated, the problem may disappear.

The absence of other visual evidence of dampness supports the condensation theory, although this is not certain. Consequently, we think this needs to be investigated further, though the problem lies in selecting which type of specialist. This is not a standard dampness problem and the most appropriate type of investigation would involve carefully cutting a hole into the slab to see whether it has a DPM. A surveyor or other technical person with the right sort of knowledge and experience could do this, whereas damp proofing contractors may not be suitable. This must be carefully expressed in the report.

Even if the need for further investigations are justified, a condition rating for this element still has to be reported. There are two possible outcomes to the investigations:

1. An effective damp-proof membrane is discovered and the likely cause of the dampness is judged to be condensation, meaning no repairs will be required.
2. If there is no damp-proof membrane and the floor slab is damp throughout its thickness, the most appropriate repair will be to replace the floor with a more suitable construction or at least overlay it with a layer of asphalt or other waterproofing compound. Whatever the solution, the repair will be extensive, disruptive and considered serious. In other words, it would have a category three condition rating.

If the property was constructed more recently, we would apply our principle of 'Don't three it just because you can't see it!' For example, something built in the 1980s is more likely to have a DPM. In other words, it would be 'innocent' until proven 'guilty' and so a category one condition rating, combined with further investigations would be appropriate.

This is not the case with a property built in 1946. There is a greater probability that a DPM was not included and so it should be considered 'guilty' until the further investigations prove it 'innocent'. In this way, you should consider each case on its own merits. Consequently, we have given a category three condition rating because there is a strong possibility of problems with the floor and if this is the case, the cost of repairs could be expensive.

This emphasises the seriousness of the problem and will encourage the owner/buyers to properly evaluate the element.

This element has been split into two so that the floor to the rear extension can be reported separately. This is because the floor is more clearly defective and has been given a category three condition rating, independent of further investigations.

Report

Floors to main house and lounge extension – Rating three

The floors in all rooms are solid and probably made of concrete. They are covered with a combination of fitted carpets and linoleum. The surfaces of the floors in two rooms were inspected and this revealed high dampness readings. Either surface condensation or a lack of an effective damp-proof course may cause this.

These need to be further investigated to discover the true cause (see B3). If this reveals that the floor has no waterproof barrier within it, the repairs may be costly. Otherwise, the floors are in a satisfactory condition.

Floor to rear entrance extension – Rating three

The floor in this area is solid, probably made of concrete, and covered with linoleum. The surface of the floor is uneven, damp and unlikely to meet current standards. This will need replacing (see also comments for Rear extension walls in D4).

ELEMENT F1 (ELECTRICITY)

Consumer unit in hallway

Spur from socket in rear extension that serves the garage

Electrical fittings in garage

Description

The electrical system consists of a consumer unit with a residual current device and miniature circuit breakers. The wiring is in PVC where it can be seen and the switches, sockets and other fittings are relatively modern. The number of sockets is below current levels of provision. No supplementary bonding can be seen beneath the kitchen sink or attached to the water pipework in the bathroom. None of the visible wiring is damaged.

There is a spur connection from a double socket in the rear entrance extension and this cable runs externally. It is loosely supported on a row of small trees in the rear garden, and supplies the garage light and socket. There is no special protection for the garage system and there is no evidence of a recent test.

Analysis

The electrical system is relatively modern, but certain parts are below current standards:

- No supplementary bonding could be seen attached to any of the plumbing.
- The external electrical supply was poorly made, not properly protected and poorly supported. It was probably a 'DIY' extension.
- There is no evidence that the system has ever been tested.

Although there are no apparent defects, the external wiring to the garage could present a danger to the occupants. This factor alone raises the condition rating. If an electrician tested the system, it is likely that a number of repairs and improvements would be recommended. The cost could be in the region of £1000. For these reasons, we think that a category three condition rating would be appropriate.

Report

The electrical system has been rewired in the past, but it is now below current standards. The supply into the garage is potentially dangerous and there is no evidence that the system has been tested. A full test and report should be obtained and any repairs carried out.

ELEMENT F2 (GAS)

Description

The property has a connection to the utility company mains. The gas supply rises out of the floor in the hot water cupboard off the lounge and connects to a standard domestic gas meter. This is of a modern design, but rests on a loose brick base. The connection on the consumer's side of the meter is in a lead pipe, although this is in a satisfactory condition.

There is a gas connection to the gas heating boiler in the kitchen and the gas cooker in the same room. It is assumed that the pipework is run in the screed.

Analysis

The gas installation is in a satisfactory condition and the gas meter has probably been replaced recently. However, there are two concerns:

1. The loose brick base is not secure. It could easily be dislodged accidentally and would result in the meter hanging off its own pipework. This could put a strain on the lead pipework and cause a leak.
2. At the time of inspection, the gas was switched off. Before any gas supply is switched on and the appliances used, it is advisable to have the system tested and checked by a CORGI registered contractor.

As a result of these issues, the element should be given a category two condition rating because of the repair to the base, with a recommendation that the system is tested before it is used.

(Note: We prefer to report on ventilation to gas appliances under the Heating section.)

Report

The gas meter is situated in the cupboard in the main lounge and is supported on a loose brick base. This should be replaced by a permanently fixed support.

As the gas has been switched off for some time, the system should be tested before it is switched on.

ELEMENT F3 (WATER)

Description

The property is supplied from the water company mains. This enters the property in the rear entrance extension and passes into the kitchen where the main stopcock is located. The supply pipe is in black plastic material that is not properly insulated. This connects into copper pipework that runs through the rest of the house. The water was turned on at the time of inspection.

The property has a cold water storage system with a modern plastic storage tank in the roof space. This is

Water main in the rear entrance extension

Hot water tank cupboard

Cold water tank to the property

only partially insulated and the supporting framework is not adequate. The feed and expansion tank to the heating system is not insulated at all and has no lid. Adjacent to the cold water storage tank is the old asbestos-based tank that is used as a base for the F&E tank. The hot and cold water supplies to the bathroom fittings are run in the solid floor and there is no evidence of defects.

The hot water storage tank is in the cupboard off the lounge. The tank is insulated, but the primary pipework is not. There is no evidence of leaks and the system is appropriately controlled. An external water tap in the garden is not insulated.

Analysis

The overall impression of the water system in the property is a positive one. The hot and cold water storage tanks have been renewed in the past and the copper distribution pipework is in a satisfactory condition. Much of the plumbing system will not conform to current water regulations, but none of these contraventions are serious or urgent. The repairs include:

1. Provision of insulation to the rising main, the tanks and associated pipework in the loft, the primary pipework to the hot water heating system and the external water tap and pipework.
2. Additional support to the cold water storage tank in the loft.

Although the asbestos tank in the loft poses very little risk to health, a warning should be given that this should not be disturbed.

The scale of these repairs is relatively small, but exceed those that could be described as 'normal maintenance'. Therefore, we think a low category two condition rating would be appropriate.

Report

The water supply comes from the water company mains and enters the property in the rear entrance extension. This is in an unheated area and the pipe needs to be properly insulated.

There is a modern storage tank in the loft and the hot water tank is in the cupboard off the main lounge. The plumbing system is in an adequate condition, but the following repairs are required:

- several of the pipes and part of the tanks in unheated areas need extra insulation to prevent freezing; and
- the support to the cold water storage tank needs to be strengthened.

The disused water tank in the loft is likely to contain asbestos. This poses little risk unless it is disturbed (see C2).

ELEMENT F4 (HEATING)

Description

An open flue floor mounted gas boiler provides central heating and hot water to the property. This was not operating at the time of inspection. The boiler is

Heating boiler to the property

115

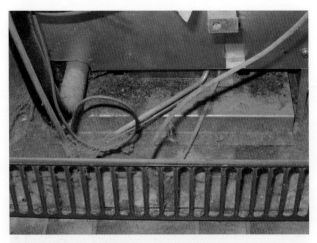

Closer internal view of boiler after removing front panel

Typical radiator to the property

an older model with a metal flue that discharges into the chimney above the kitchen. This terminates in a standard terra cotta chimney pot and it is unlikely that the chimney is lined. The front panel was easily removed and there is no evidence that the boiler has been serviced regularly. This was confirmed by the large amount of dust and fluff around the combustion chamber. Apart from the trickle vents on the two windows in the kitchen, there is no other fixed form of ventilation to the room.

Each room has a radiator controlled with a thermostatic radiator valve and there is a room thermostat in the hallway. The radiator in the bathroom is missing, presumably removed by a previous occupant and the rear entrance extension is not heated. The hot water tank is in the cupboard off the lounge and is in an adequate condition. It is insulated and has a cylinder thermostat. A digital programmer controls both the heating and hot water.

Analysis

The heating system is in an adequate condition. Although the boiler is an older model that is not as efficient as more modern ones, the system has

satisfactory heating controls. There are a number of issues to consider when applying a rating to this element:

- The high levels of dust within the boiler casing suggest that the boiler has not been serviced regularly. Not only will this potentially reduce the useful life of the boiler, but additionally, the safety of the system could not be confirmed. As a result of the system being switched off for some time, it will be necessary for the boiler to be inspected and serviced before it is used again.
- The lack of fixed ventilation is a concern. Open flue gas boilers require a lot of air to operate safely and this could be a problem in a kitchen. The use of a gas cooker may well affect the operation of the boiler and this will need checking by an engineer.
- The radiator in the bathroom will need replacing and would constitute a repair.
- The life of the boiler may be limited. The usual life cycle of a boiler is ten to fifteen years and this boiler is likely to be older.

Adding these factors together, it is our view that although the system has a limited life from a condition point of view, it still cannot be described as either urgent or serious. However, due to concern about ventilation to the kitchen, a category three condition rating is appropriate from a health and safety perspective. The replacement of the radiator in the bathroom is seen as a repair.

Report

The property has a gas fired central heating system, with radiators in every room apart from the bathroom. The heating was not switched on at the time of inspection. It is unlikely that the boiler in the kitchen has been serviced regularly and there may not be sufficient ventilation to the kitchen. As a safety precaution, a qualified contractor should test and service the whole of the heating system before it is used (see B3). The radiator in the bathroom needs to be replaced.

ELEMENT F5 (DRAINAGE)

Description

It is assumed that the property is connected to the public sewer in the road, but this could not be confirmed during the inspection. Checks included turning on the taps of the various bathroom fittings and the kitchen sink, flushing the WC and observing the flow of water in the inspection chambers.

The drainage consists of the following features and components:

Rear gulley serving the bath waste and rear rainwater pipes

Inspection chamber one

Internal view of inspection chamber one

Inspection chamber three and the gulley serving the kitchen waste

- The WC discharges into the soil and vent pipe outside the bathroom. This connects to the lower channel of the nearest inspection chamber (inspection chamber one).
- The basin in the bathroom connects directly to the inspection chamber (inspection chamber one).
- The bath discharges over the open gulley adjacent to the bathroom window and this gulley connects to inspection chamber one.
- The kitchen sink waste runs underneath the rear entrance door step and discharges over the gulley adjacent to the rear entrance extension.
- The kitchen waste gulley connects to inspection chamber two through a connection beneath the lounge extension.
- The kerb of the gulley serving the kitchen waste is partially built over another inspection chamber (inspection chamber three), preventing it from being lifted. The purpose of this chamber is unknown.
- Inspection chamber one connects to inspection chamber two.

In inspection chamber two, the main drain from the property turns by ninety degrees and heads towards the neighbouring property.

It is assumed that this then becomes a shared common drain. A few problems were noted:

- although the drains are free flowing, there is a slight build up of sediment in some channels, suggesting sluggish flow from some connections;

Inspection chamber two

- some of the connections to inspection chamber one have not been properly made; and
- the covers and frames to the inspection chambers and some of the benching are beginning to deteriorate, although this is of a minor nature.

Analysis

The underground drainage to this property was in working order at the time of inspection, but a number of faults and deficiencies need to be considered:

- There are a number of non-standard connections to the inspection chambers around the lounge extension. It is unlikely that the local building inspector would allow work like this. This raises the question whether the lounge extension has had building regulation approval. This should be picked up in Section C3 of the report.
- The function of inspection chamber three is unknown.
- The drains need to be cleared out and flushed through to make sure they work effectively. It is likely that this will be a recurring maintenance activity.
- Minor repairs to the inspection chambers and their covers need to be carried out.
- The kitchen sink waste is too long, leaving it vulnerable to self-siphonage. Ideally, this should be taken to its own gulley and connected into the main drainage system.
- If the drain connects to the neighbour's system, it becomes a common drain or private sewer and will impose an obligation on the owner of this property. Legal checks need to be carried out to establish maintenance liabilities.
- The final destination of the surface water drainage connections (apart from one downpipe) could not be traced and so the effectiveness of the (presumed) soakaways could not be evaluated. Since there are no signs of a problem, no action is required at this stage.

Some of these items could be classed as 'normal maintenance' activities whereas others clearly constitute repairs. None of the problems are urgent or serious. Therefore, we would rate this as a category two, but make it clear that future maintenance requirements might be higher than other similar systems.

Report

The drains from the property connect into an underground system to the rear. It is assumed that this joins with the drains from the neighbouring property and connects to the public sewer in the street. Legal checks are required to confirm this and establish the resulting legal obligations (see C1).

The drainage system is in an adequate condition, but there are a number of problems:

- The inspection chambers are beginning to deteriorate and some minor repairs are required.
- There is some sediment in the drains. This should be cleaned out and the drains flushed through.
- The kitchen waste pipe is too long and should have its own drainage connection.

The drainage system will have to be checked and cleaned out regularly as part of normal maintenance programmes.

PART THREE – REVIEW OF REMAINING ELEMENTS

D6 (External doors)

Both the front and rear entrance doors are original and now enclosed by the front porch and rear entrance extension respectively. The front door is fully glazed with ordinary patterned glass and so will present a safety hazard (see C2). The rear door is timber panelled and more robust with only the top half glazed. Both have the original locks that do not match current insurance company requirements. The lounge has been fitted with sliding patio doors. For ease of reference, this element has been split into three so that each door can be clearly identified and rated.

Elsewhere in the report (D10), it is recommended that the front porch is removed. If it is not rebuilt, the door would be exposed to the weather. Therefore, a comment has been included in D10 that the door will need to be upgraded, but because this does not have to be done, no mention of this has been made in D6.

One of the issues raised by the Guidance Notes is the problem of reporting on the security of properties. This is based on the concern that criminals could use Home Condition Reports to identify vulnerable dwellings. This is a dilemma for Home Inspectors and we suggest that you should avoid specific mention of individual security problems completely.

Due to the associated safety issues, the work to the front entrance door is urgent, so a category three condition rating is appropriate. The rear entrance door has been given a category two condition rating because the work is not urgent.

The lounge patio doors have been given a category one condition rating because they are in a satisfactory condition. However, it was not clear whether the doors were glazed with safety glass and because of the potential health and safety risk, further investigations are recommended.

D7 (All other woodwork)

Rotten fascia board

The only external timber element is the fascia board. This has rotted in a number of areas due to water running off the roof (see D2). These sections can be repaired, with approximately 25–30% of the total length needing replacement. This is not an urgent repair and as long as the gutter and roof repairs are not included, is likely to cost less than £1000. Therefore, a category two condition rating has been applied.

In reality, most owners might choose to replace the whole of the fascia, possibly using a PVC alternative. Since that is not necessary at this stage, the option not to have to completely replace a building element should always be given.

D9 (External decorations)

The only external element that needs to be repainted is the fascia and soffitt boards. This can only be completed once the other repairs to the fascia have been carried out. Although the fascia is relatively long, it is unlikely to cost more than £1000, which would suggest a category two condition rating. However, because the decorations are at the end of their life cycle and the timbers could begin to deteriorate if they are not repainted soon, a category three condition rating is appropriate.

E2 (Ceilings)

The property has plasterboard ceilings throughout and these are in good condition. The only minor problem is in the kitchen where the leak around the chimney has stained a small area of plasterboard. In our opinion, this needs to be sealed before it is next decorated and does not constitute a repair.

E3 (Internal walls, partitions and plasterwork)

All the internal walls are solid and assumed to be masonry. These are plastered and in satisfactory condition apart from a small area (max. 0.3m^2) that has been stained by the chimney leak. The plaster surface has been disrupted and this should be replastered to stop any 'drying out' moisture from affecting the new decorations. This constitutes a repair, giving this element a category two condition rating. This contrasts with the decision in E2 and illustrates that assessments and condition rating decisions depend on the extent of the defect.

E5 (Fireplaces, chimney breasts and exterior of flues)

Since both of the chimney breasts are external to the main wall they have been assessed under D1 and only described here. If they were internal, they would have been described and assessed under this element.

E6 (Built-in fitments)

Typical kitchen units to the property

The kitchen units were installed several years ago and now appear to be dated. However, they all work appropriately and no repairs are required. Subjective judgments are avoided and the comment, 'The kitchen units are an older design…' is factual.

E7 (Internal woodwork)

All the skirtings, architraves, etc. are in a satisfactory condition, so there is little to report here. The only potential problem is the flimsy nature of the hollow core internal doors. Although they all work, they will be vulnerable to accidental damage and misuse. This can be flagged up in an advisory way, but should not affect the ratings.

E8 (Bathroom fittings)

Bathroom fittings

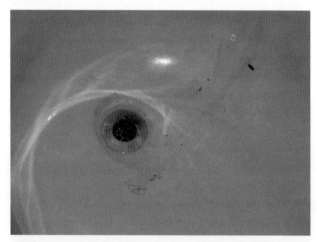

Detail of damage to bath

A pink bathroom suite is not to everyone's taste and it might not help in selling the property, but because this is a condition survey, the most important considerations are whether the fittings work and whether they need repairing. The answer is yes on both accounts and so a category two condition rating is appropriate.

E10 (Dampness)

In comparison to many properties of this age, this property does not have serious dampness problems

(apart from the potential problems of the solid floor). However, the purpose of this section is to emphasise these problems and to offer the opportunity of linking them together.

The dampness related issues are listed in this section and cross-referenced to those elements where more information can be found.

Section G

Grounds

Part of the north-west boundary

This section is mainly descriptive, but points out a number of potential problems:

- Garage drive – in its current state it is functional, but will require increasing amounts of repair in the future because continued use will result in the occasional 'pot hole'. Heavy weed growth will also need resolving from time to time.
- Other paths – there are a number of established paths of varying quality and condition. The front garden path is specifically mentioned because the loose brick edgings could present a health and safety risk.
- Shrubs and trees – these have been mentioned in other parts of the report in relation to possible future subsidence issues (see B4).

Garages

The structure of the garage is in an adequate condition although there are a small amount of brickwork repairs required. The two most important issues are the risks posed by the electrical system and the asbestos roof. These are emphasised and cross-referenced to the appropriate sections.

Permanent sheds

Although the condition of the greenhouse is in a bad state of disrepair and the inclusion of a photograph in the overall schedule of photographs would speak for itself, it is still important to state the obvious and report accordingly on its condition.

Garage at rear of plot

Boundary walls

The cost of boundary fence replacement can be very high, so it is important to identify any problems. Like many similar properties, it is impossible to deduce the ownership of the boundaries. As this could have serious maintenance implications, it is important to cross-reference this with Section C1 of the report.

PART FOUR – CALCULATION OF REINSTATEMENT COSTS FOR INSURANCE PURPOSES

The reinstatement costs for insurance purposes have been calculated using the methodology described in Chapter Six and described in detail by the Building Cost Information Service (BCIS). The dimensions are based on the measurements shown in the floor plan in Chapter Six and an explanation of how the costs have been calculated is given here. The full calculations are shown in Table 7.1.

Calculation of the external floor area of the main building

Floor areas are calculated by splitting the property down into blocks of rectangles, with the exception of the porch, which is divided into a rectangle and a trapezium. There are separate calculations for bays in the BCIS Guide, but as the porch is a little more substantial, it has been included under the standard price per square metre. In essence, you have to consider reinstatement and because it has a door, it is quite expensive in relation to brick work – rather like a mini conservatory.

External floor area calculation

Main house	Porch
$3.9 \times 3.1 = 12.09m^2$	$2.2 \times 0.7 = 1.54m^2$
$2.0 \times 2.2 = 4.4m^2$	$2.2 + 1.2/2 \times 0.5 = 0.85m^2$
$4.2 \times 3.2 = 13.44m^2$	
$9.1 \times 7.0 = 63.7m^2$	
TOTAL: 96.02 m2	

The property comes within the 1946–1979 age range, is a bungalow, and we have considered it is of good quality. Its size comes within the 84–111 m² band (see Table R25 in the *BCIS Regional Guide*).

The standard specification for 'Good' quality relates to a rectangular building, but this property is L-shaped with extensions and a hipped roof (see the specification and design notes in the *BCIS Guide to House Rebuilding Costs*). The standard would allow for two living rooms, but we have compensated because there are extensions.

We have allowed for 2.5m high ceilings.

Garage

The garage is built from brick, with a flat roof. In Table 4.12 of the *BCIS Guide to House Rebuilding Costs* the precise details regarding the construction of the garage are not included, other than brick or prefabricated. The costs (as would be expected), differ greatly. It is assumed that the typical garage would have a pitched roof with a covering of tiles. Therefore in this case, a reduction has been made to allow for rebuilding with a flat roof.

Dealing with a substandard extension

After studying D10 of the case study, you will be aware that one of the extensions is substandard and it could be argued that this should have a reduced rebuild cost. However, if there was a total loss there would be a requirement to rebuild in accordance with current building regulations. This would be stated in the report and a typical example might be:

'The rear extension is considered substandard, but if it is to be retained then it needs to be insured and provision made for rebuilding in accordance with current building regulations. This has been accounted for in our calculations.'

If you are transparent in the assumptions you have made, then whoever uses the report for whatever purpose will be aware of the circumstances and can make their own allowances/exclusions.

Boundaries

The side and rear garden are fenced in by softwood woven fencing and this matches the guidance given in Table 4.13 (External works) of the *BCIS Guide to House Rebuilding Costs.* There are also two low retaining walls to the front garden and both are less than one metre in height. There is no requirement for these to have specific reinforcement, merely weep holes and so the cost provision within the guide can be applied (Table 4.13 External works). If the retaining wall required reinforcement, then more complex calculations would be required.

Drainage

The drainage provision in this example fits the guide specifications, so the standard figures can be used.

Building up your knowledge

The *BCIS Guide to House Rebuilding Costs* sets down a basic specification for the various property types, by age and quality. If you are a new entrant to this area, there are no shortcuts other than reviewing the guide frequently and checking the specifications until it is firmly fixed in your memory. However, even if you have been calculating these costs for some time, because the guide changes annually you will need to keep checking the criteria.

PART FIVE – ENERGY REPORT

The energy report has been included as part of the Home Condition Report. It is produced in a standard format and the Home Inspector has no choice regarding most of the content, with the only option being the omission of some of the improvement recommendations. The final version of the RDSAP may vary slightly to the one included in this case study, although the component parts will largely remain the same.

The energy rating

As expected with a property of this age and type, the rating of forty is quite low, placing the property in Band E. Most owners and buyers would be concerned about this, with most buyers likely to take action. The energy rating software generates a number of energy improvements, which are discussed further in Chapter Five.

Links with the Home Condition Report

While there is no opportunity to include a commentary on the improvement recommendations in Section H of the Home Condition Report, there is potential to include a reference to energy improvement measures under relevant elements. For example, in our case study Home Condition Report, because it is obvious that the roof insulation needs upgrading, we have mentioned it accordingly in E1 (Roof structure). Similar comments could have been added under the respective elements for wall insulation and replacement of the boiler. However, since the Guidance Notes do not mention this approach to reporting on energy related matters, we have allowed Section H to speak for itself. Energy reporting is a rapidly developing area that you should review regularly.

Table 7.1: Calculation of reinstatement costs for insurance purposes

Area	Rate and notes	Cost
Floor area	Total External floor area: 96.02m² @ £907/m²	£87,253
Cellars	m²@£	Nil
Upper floors	m²@£	Nil
Garage	5.2 × 3.0 = 15.6m² (Flat roof, single brick walls, up and over door)	£8000
Conservatory	Not applicable	Nil
Outbuildings	Not applicable	Nil
Boundaries	Woven wood panels with softwood posts. 117m × 1500mm high @ £32/m run	£3,744
	Small retaining walls with maximum height of 0.9m No special structural significance 24m runs @ £149/m run	£3,576
Drainage	28m run, 1000mm depth, 100mm diameter @ £52/m	£1,456
	3 manholes: 900 × 600, 1000mm depth (£1031 each)	£3,093
	TOTAL: £107,122 (say £107,500)	

PART SIX – THE HOME CONDITION REPORT

Address of Property Inspected

HOME CONDITION REPORT

Home Inspector's Name & Qualifications	Phil Parnham, BSc, MRICS
Home Inspector's Licence Number	007
Company Name	Sheffield Home Inspectors Training Enterprises
Company Address	Howard Street Sheffield S1 1WB
Company Email	HITS@shu.ac.uk
Company Telephone	0114 225 4267
Company Fax	
Date of the Inspection	01.04.05
Report Reference Number	URRN 00001
Number of Previous Home Condition Reports in the last 12 Months	0
Related Parties Disclosure	

SECTION A

INTRODUCTION

This is a report on the condition of (address (B2 – B5). It is in a standard format and has been prepared by a Home Inspector licensed under the Home Inspectors Certification Scheme (please refer to the Appendix for more details about the licensing of Home Inspectors). The Home Inspector has a duty to provide an opinion about the condition of the property that can be used and relied upon by prospective buyers, the seller and the buyer's mortgage lender.

TERMS OF ENGAGEMENT

The report has been commissioned on the basis of these Terms of Engagement by, or on behalf of, the seller of the property, and describes the condition of the property on the date of inspection. Those parts of the property that have been inspected and those parts where an inspection has not taken place are set out in the Appendix to this report and form part of these terms.

Neither you nor the Home Inspector can amend these Terms of Engagement. Any services the Home Inspector may agree to provide in addition to preparing this Home Condition Report must be set out in a separate, written contract.

PAYMENT

The terms of payment and fees payable for the Home Condition Report are as separately agreed between the Home Inspector and the Seller (or on the Seller's behalf).

WHAT THIS REPORT TELLS YOU

This report tells you about the construction and condition of the property on the date when it was inspected, which is shown in the report. It also tells you whether and where further enquiries are needed.

It tells you about matters that are considered serious or in need of urgent attention. It also tells you about matters that require further investigation to prevent damage to the fabric of the building.

WHAT THIS REPORT DOES NOT TELL YOU

This report does not tell you the value of the property. You should commission independent advice if you require a valuation.

It does not tell you about any minor matters that would not ordinarily have any effect on a buyer's decision to purchase.

This report does not warn you about any health and safety risks to occupiers or visitors to the property except where the risks are such that repairs or building works are required.

WHAT WAS INSPECTED

The main building and all permanent outbuildings were inspected externally and internally and an inspection was made of the visible parts of the services. Full details about the inspection and the limitations on it are given in the Appendix. These details form part of the Terms of Engagement and should be read carefully.

Each part of the structure of the main building is given a Condition Rating, to make the report easy to follow. The Condition Ratings are:

CONDITION RATING	DEFINITION
Not Inspected	Not inspected.
1	No repair is presently required. Normal maintenance must be undertaken.
2	Repairs are required but the Home Inspector does not consider these to be either serious or urgent.
3	Defects of a serious nature or defects requiring urgent repair.

COMPLAINTS

Should you have any complaint about this Home Condition Report or the Home Inspector who prepared it, please follow the steps set out in the Appendix to these Terms of Engagement, to be found at the back of the report.

SECTION B

SUMMARY OF GENERAL INFORMATION ABOUT THE PROPERTY

Date of Inspection	01.04.05
Full Address	137 Shelbourne Road Grange Park Borcestershire
Postcode	AR1 3XG
Weather conditions	Cloudy, warm and dry
Was the property furnished or unfurnished	Partly furnished with fitted carpets throughout
Date of original construction	Approximately 1946
Date of construction of additions/extensions	The property has two extensions (see below)
Lounge extension	The rear living room has been extended to form the main lounge. This is approximately 15 years old. The original lounge to the front of the property has been converted into a bedroom.
Front porch	A timber porch has been added to the front entrance. This is over 30 years old.
If property is formed by conversion, state dates of original construction and conversion	
Type of property	Detached Bungalow
Are there any signs of tenancy occupation in the property?	No
Is the property of a type or located in an area where tenancy occupation is predominant?	No
Is the property in a conservation area or likely to be listed?	No
Listing Grade (if known)	

For flats and maisonettes

Flats – which floor and how many floors in the block

Number of flats in the block

Is the property purpose built or converted?

Is there a lift serving the block?

Are there any commercial uses within the block?

Approximate % of commercial use

State the current commercial use

Where in the building is the commercial use situated?

Accommodation

Storey	Living Room	Bed-rooms	Bath and/ or shower	Separate WC	Kitchen	Utility Room	Conser-vatory	Other	Name of 'Other'
Basement Lower G F									
Ground floor	1	3	1		1			1	Rear entrance extension
1st floor									
2nd and other floors									
Total number of rooms	1	3	1		1				

Gross external floor area (in m^2) | 96.02 |

Gross internal floor area for flats (in m^2) | |

Reinstatement Cost | £107,500 |

(Note: This figure is for insurance purposes only, and is not the market value of the property. It excludes leisure facilities such as swimming pools/tennis courts)

Construction

A short general description of the construction	ROOF – The pitched roof is covered with concrete tiles, the flat roofs over the extensions are covered with felt
	WALLS – The walls are brick faced and assumed to be cavity walls
	WINDOWS – Most of the windows are PVC double glazed windows apart from in the porch where they are metal
	FLOORS – All the floors are solid concrete

Is the property of system built construction?	No
If system built, state system name	

Mains Services

Drainage	Gas	Electricity	Water
X	X	X	X

Where no mains drainage or mains water is provided, state alternative type of facility	

Central Heating

Does the property have central heating?	Yes
Fuel type	Gas
Full or partial system	Full central heating

External Facilities

Is a garage provided?	Yes
Is the garage on or off site?	On site
Is the garage integral?	No
Is the garage a single, double or more?	Single
Is there a carport?	No
Number of allocated parking spaces	
Are these on or off site?	
Are there any gardens which are part of the property?	Yes
Are the gardens to the front, side or rear?	All of these
Are there any outbuildings with the property?	Yes
Number of outbuildings	One
Use of buildings	Greenhouse
Are the roads and footpaths made up?	Yes

Summary of Condition

Overall condition of the property	Although the property is in an adequate condition for its type and age, there are a number of serious or urgent defects to the roof, chimney stack, floors and electrical system as well as a range of less serious repairs.
Widespread defects that affect multiple parts of the property	Faulty roof tiles at the edge of the roof – See D2, D3 and D7. Leak to the base of the chimney stack that is causing the dampness to the ceiling and wall surfaces below – see D1, E2 and E3.
Summary of foundation related movement	The property is not affected by foundation movement, but is in an area of clay subsoil. There are a number of mature shrubs close to the property. If not maintained at the current level, they could have an impact on the stability of the foundations.
Remarks on condition	

Further Investigation

Recommended investigation of observed defects	A Chartered Building Surveyor or other qualified professional should investigate the cause of the dampness to the solid floors in the property and produce a report with recommendations. This may involve forming a hole through the floor slab to see if there is a waterproof barrier (DPM).
	A Chartered Building Surveyor or other qualified timber treatment specialist should check the roof timbers around the base of the rear chimney for signs of dampness and wood rot. Enquiries should be made of the original contractors who installed the patio doors to confirm that safety glass was used. If this is not conclusive, then an appropriate window specialist should test the glass.
Remarks on investigations	
Precautionary testing (gas)	The gas installation and the heating system by a contractor registered with CORGI before the system is used.
Precautionary testing (electricity)	The electrical system by a contractor registered with the NICEIC.

Summary of Ratings

Section of the Report	Part Number	Part Name	Identifier (where more than one entry in the table)	Rating
D: External	D1	Chimney stacks	Rear chimney	3
			Former lounge chimney	2
	D2	Roof coverings	Pitched roof covering	3
			Flat roof covering	1
	D3	Rainwater pipes & gutters	Gutters to main house and lounge extension	2
			Gutters to rear entrance extension	2
	D4	Main walls	Main house walls	2
			Lounge walls	1
			Rear extension	3
	D5	Windows		1
	D6	External doors	Front entrance door	3
			Rear entrance door	2
			Lounge patio door	1
	D7	All other woodwork		2
	D8	Claddings		
	D9	External decoration		3
	D10	Other external detail	Front porch	3
E: Internal	E1	Roof structure	Pitched roof covering	2
			Flat roof covering	NI
	E2	Ceilings		1
	E3	Internal walls		2
	E4	Floors	Main house and lounge floor	3
			Rear entrance extension floor	3
	E5	Fireplaces & chimney breasts		1
	E6	Built-in fitments		1
	E7	Internal woodwork		1
	E8	Bathroom fittings		2
	E9	Dampness		
	E10	Other internal detail		
F: Services	F1	Electricity		3
	F2	Gas		2
	F3	Water		2
	F4	Heating		3
	F5	Drainage		2

SECTION C

OTHER MATTERS

C1: LEGAL MATTERS

Legal matters identified by the Home Inspector which need to be investigated by a legal advisor/conveyancer (including, but not limited to such matters as highway adoption, sewers and drains, rights of way, covenants, easements, planning and statutory consents, environmental concerns, mining, etc.).

- The ownership of the main drain at the rear of the house should be determined, as this is likely to join up with the drain belonging to the neighbouring owner.
- The ownership of the boundaries should be established, especially the one to the rear of the property that is in poor condition.
- Building Regulation consents (including the final completion certificates) for the rear lounge extension and rear entrance lobby need to be verified.
- The existence of any guarantees or approvals for the PVC windows and rear patio doors should be determined.
- The presence of recent and historic local landfill sites should be investigated and further advice given.

C2: HEALTH AND SAFETY RISKS CONCERNING THE PROPERTY

Properties of this age may include asbestos-based materials. The following features that may contain asbestos fibres were noted in this property: internal wall panels in the front porch, roof sheets to the garage and a disused water tank in the loft. The presence of asbestos cannot be fully established without further tests. Although these features present a low risk, the risk to health may increase if they are disturbed or worked on in any way. For further advice, see the latest guidance from the Health and Safety Executive (www.hse.gov.uk).

Low level glass panels can present a health and safety risk. The glass panels to the original front door and the porch doors and windows are unlikely to be safety glass. The glass to the lounge patio doors is modern, but still needs to be checked.

C3: OTHER RISKS ASSOCIATED WITH THE PROPERTY

(including subsidence, flooding, etc. that the Home Inspector considers are a risk to this property).

Although there is no damage to the building, the property is in an area known for clay subsoil (see also B4).

Although no local evidence was noted, internet based information sources suggest that a current or historic landfill site exists within 500 metres of the property. The legal advisor should verify this and give further advice.

SECTION D

EXTERIOR CONDITION

Roofs, chimneys and other external surfaces of the building were examined from ground level and where necessary from adjoining public property with the help of binoculars. Flat roofs to single storey additions were inspected if accessible from a three metre ladder. The efficiency of rainwater fittings (gutters and down pipes) can only be assessed if there was heavy rain at the time of inspection.

Definition of ratings

NI Not inspected.
1   No repair is presently required. Normal maintenance must be undertaken.
2   Repairs are required but the Home Inspector does not consider these to be either serious or urgent.
3   Defects of a serious nature or defects requiring urgent repair.

The Home Inspector has not been able to inspect the following parts of the exterior of the property for the reasons stated here.

The rear five metres of the garden was very overgrown with vegetation and could not be fully inspected.

D.1. CHIMNEY STACKS

Rear Chimney

Condition Rating   **3**

Justification for Rating and Comments

The rear brick built chimney stack serves the open flue boiler in the kitchen. Although it is structurally sound, there are a number of defects:

- the mortar between the brick joints are deteriorating and need replacing (repointing);
- the lead waterproofing at the junction of the chimney and the roof covering (flashing) is leaking and needs replacing; and
- the cement around the top of the chimney (flaunching) and the chimney pot has deteriorated and needs replacing.

A general builder or a roofing contractor should do this work as soon as possible because water is leaking into the kitchen below.

Former Lounge Chimney

Condition Rating   **2**

Justification for Rating and Comments

The former chimney stack that served the front right-hand room (now used as a bedroom) has been removed above roof covering level. This has been done satisfactorily, but external ventilation bricks should be installed in the remaining flue to prevent dampness. A general builder should do this work.

SECTION D (continued)

D.2. ROOF COVERINGS

Pitched roof covering

Condition Rating **3**

Justification for Rating and Comments

The main pitched roof is covered with concrete tiles over a secondary waterproof barrier (sarking felt). Although the main roof is not leaking, there are a number of defects:

- The ridge and hip tiles are in a poor condition and need replacing.
- The roof slopes are covered with moss that may lead to the deterioration of the roof tiles. This needs removing and will result in recurring maintenance in the future.
- The rainwater does not properly discharge into the gutters from the edge roof tiles. This is rotting the timber board that supports the gutters (fascia) (see also D3 and D7). This needs repairing so that rain can properly discharge into the gutters.
- The sarking felt is damaged in a number of places and could let in water during high winds. This should be replaced when the main roof is next recovered.

A general builder should do this work.

Flat roof coverings

Condition Rating **1**

Justification for Rating and Comments

The flat roofs over the lounge extension and the rear entrance extensions are covered in roofing felt and are in a satisfactory condition for their type and age. However, when compared to a pitched roof, flat roofs can leak unexpectedly. This needs to be monitored as part of normal maintenance.

D.3. RAIN WATER PIPES & GUTTERS

Gutters to the main house and lounge extension

Condition Rating **2**

Justification for Rating and Comments

The gutters and rainwater pipes are made of PVC. Although they are in an adequate condition, there are a number of problems:

- The gutters, pipes and associated underground drains need to be cleaned out.
- The slope of the guttering needs to be altered so that it drains properly. This should be done in conjunction with the repairs to the fascia board (see D7).

A general builder should do this work.

Gutters to the rear entrance extension

Condition Rating **2**

Justification for Rating and Comments

The gutters and rainwater pipe to the rear entrance extension are made of PVC. Although they are in a satisfactory condition, the rainwater pipe from the flat roof needs to be connected into the main drainage system. A general builder should do this work.

SECTION D (continued)

D.4. MAIN WALLS

Main house walls

Condition Rating **2**

Justification for Rating and Comments

The main walls are brick faced, assumed to be of cavity construction and have a bitumen damp-proof course. The walls are in an adequate condition, but there are a number of defects:

- The mortar between the bricks (pointing) is deteriorating, needs to be renewed and may be costly. One small area is affected by masonry bees and should be repointed in the autumn.
- Over some of the windows, the brickwork has been damaged and needs to be repaired.
- The external ground levels are too close to the damp-proof course level and may cause internal dampness in the future. These levels need to be reduced.

A general builder should do this work.

Lounge extension walls

Condition Rating **1**

Justification for Rating and Comments

The main walls are brick faced, assumed to be of cavity construction, have a bitumen damp-proof course and are in a satisfactory condition.

Rear entrance extension walls

Condition Rating **3**

Justification for Rating and Comments

The walls are brick, are too thin and will be vulnerable to future dampness problems. The repair will be costly and so demolition and reconstruction may be an economic solution. If the walls are rebuilt, all necessary permissions should be obtained. If they are demolished and not rebuilt, then the rear entrance door will need upgrading to make it weather-tight.

D.5. WINDOWS

Condition Rating **1**

Justification for Rating and Comments

The windows are double glazed with PVC frames and are in a satisfactory condition. The legal advisor should check whether the installation of the windows has a FENSA certificate, or Building Regulation approval, or a manufacturer's warranty.

SECTION D (continued)

D.6. EXTERNAL DOORS (INCLUDING PATIO DOORS)

Front entrance door

Condition Rating **3**

Justification for Rating and Comments

The original front entrance door is fully glazed with non-safety glass and could pose a health and safety risk. This should either be replaced or protected.

Rear entrance door

Condition Rating **2**

Justification for Rating and Comments

The original rear external door is in an adequate condition although repairs are required.

Lounge patio doors

Condition Rating **1**

Justification for Rating and Comments

The doors are in a satisfactory condition. However, the glass to the patio doors may not be safety glass and could pose a health and safety risk. Enquiries should be made of the original contractors and if this is not conclusive, then an appropriate window specialist should test the glass. A check should be made for any guarantees that cover the original work.

D.7. ALL OTHER WOODWORK

Condition Rating **2**

Justification for Rating and Comments

The timber boarding that supports the guttering (fascia board) is rotten in a number of places because of a fault with the roof covering (see D3). The rotten sections need to be replaced by a general builder.

D.8. CLADDINGS e.g. boarding to the external walls

Condition Rating Not applicable

Justification for Rating and Comments

Not applicable

SECTION D (continued)

D.9. EXTERNAL DECORATION

Condition Rating **3**

Justification for Rating and Comments

The timber fascia board is in a poor decorative condition and needs to be redecorated (see also D7).

D.10. OTHER EXTERNAL DETAIL

Front Porch

Condition Rating **3**

Justification for Rating and Comments

The front porch consists of a flat roof, single glazed metal windows, timber walls and a solid floor. Internally, the walls are lined with asbestos-based boarding (see C2). The porch is in a poor condition.

The repair of these defects will be costly and so removal and reconstruction may be an economic solution. If it is rebuilt, all necessary permissions should be obtained. If the porch is demolished and not rebuilt, then the front entrance door will need replacing/upgrading to make it weather-tight. Alternatively, the porch may continue to be used as long as its inadequacy is accounted for.

Whatever the option chosen, care must be taken with the asbestos-based boarding. If this is to be disturbed in any way, a specialist will need to be appointed (see C2).

SECTION E

INTERNAL CONDITION

Floor surfaces and underfloor spaces were examined as far as they were accessible (furniture, floor coverings and other contents were not moved or lifted). The roof structure was examined from inside the roof space where accessible (insulation material, stored goods and other contents were not moved or lifted).

Definition of ratings

NI Not inspected.
1 No repair is presently required. Normal maintenance must be undertaken.
2 Repairs are required but the Home Inspector does not consider these to be either serious or urgent.
3 Defects of a serious nature or defects requiring urgent repair.

The Home Inspector has not been able to inspect the following parts of the interior of the property for the reasons stated here.

- The space within the flat roof because there was no access hatch.
- The timbers at the base of the rear chimney could not be inspected due to lack of access.
- The floor surfaces in all but the front left and rear bedrooms because of fitted carpets.

E.1. ROOF STRUCTURE

Pitched roof structure

Condition Rating **2**

Justification for Rating and Comments

The main roof structure is in a satisfactory condition. The level of roof space insulation (see H3) and ventilation should be increased.

The timbers around the base of the rear chimney stack may be damp because of the leak (see D1). These need to be checked for wood rot (see B3).

Flat roof structure

Condition Rating **NI**

Justification for Rating and Comments

The space within the flat roof structures could not be inspected. It is likely that the ventilation and thermal insulation levels do not meet current standards. These should be increased when the flat roofs are next recovered.

SECTION E (continued)

E.2. CEILINGS

Condition Rating **1**

Justification for Rating and Comments

All the ceilings are made of plasterboard and are in a satisfactory condition.

Once the roof leak to the rear chimney has been repaired, the area of stained ceiling in the kitchen will need to be sealed to prevent any new decorations from becoming disfigured. This can be done as part of normal maintenance activities.

E.3. INTERNAL WALLS & PARTITIONS & PLASTERWORK

Condition Rating **2**

Justification for Rating and Comments

The internal partitions are solid masonry and are plastered. Several of these walls are load bearing and provide support to the roof. These are in a satisfactory condition apart from the plaster that has been stained by the water leak from the chimney in the kitchen (see D1). A small area will need to be replastered once the leak has been repaired.

E.4. FLOORS

Floors to main house and lounge extension

Condition Rating **3**

Justification for Rating and Comments

The floors in all rooms are solid and probably made of concrete. They are covered with a combination of fitted carpets and linoleum. The surfaces of the floors in two rooms were inspected and this revealed high dampness readings. Either surface condensation or a lack of an effective damp-proof course may cause this. These need to be further investigated to discover the true cause (see B3). If this reveals that the floor has no waterproof barrier within it, the repairs may be costly. Otherwise, the floors are in a satisfactory condition.

Floor to rear entrance extension

Condition Rating **3**

Justification for Rating and Comments

The floor in this area is solid, probably made of concrete, and covered with linoleum. The surface of the floor is uneven, damp and unlikely to meet current standards. This will need replacing (see also comments for Rear extension walls in D4).

SECTION E (continued)

E.5. FIREPLACES & CHIMNEYS BREASTS & EXTERIOR OF FLUES

Condition Rating **1**

Justification for Rating and Comments

There is only one chimney breast in the former front lounge that is now used as a bedroom and this is in the external part of the wall. The former chimney stack above roof level has been satisfactorily removed and the fireplace has been blocked up internally (see D1).

The chimney serving the boiler in the kitchen is external to the property and has been included under D1 (Chimney stacks).

E.6. BUILT-IN FITMENTS (built-in kitchen and other fittings excluding appliances)

Condition Rating **1**

Justification for Rating and Comments

The kitchen units are an older design, but are in a serviceable condition. The fixed cupboard containing the hot water tank is in a satisfactory condition.

E.7. INTERNAL WOODWORK (STAIRCASE, JOINERY, ETC.)

Condition Rating **1**

Justification for Rating and Comments

The internal joinery is in a satisfactory condition, although some of the internal doors are of lightweight construction and will be vulnerable to damage.

E.8. BATHROOM FITTINGS

Condition Rating **2**

Justification for Rating and Comments

The bathroom fittings are in an adequate condition but there are a few problems:

- The waterproof sealant at the junction of the splash back tiles and the basin and the bath needs to be renewed.
- The surface of the bath is chipped in a number of areas and the metal beneath is beginning to rust. These will need sealing.

SECTION E (continued)

E.9. OTHER

Condition Rating

Justification for Rating and Comments

E.10. DAMPNESS

The property has been affected by dampness in two different areas:

- To the wall/ceiling junction above the boiler in the kitchen. This has been caused by a leak at the base of the chimney and needs repairing (see D1).
- To the surface of the solid floors in at least two of the rooms. The precise cause of the problem could not be determined and so further investigations need to be carried out (see E4 and B3).

SECTION F

Services are difficult to inspect as these are generally hidden within the construction of the property, for example pipes beneath the floors and wiring within the walls. Only the visible parts of the available services have been inspected. Specialist tests have not been carried out. The visual inspection did not assess the efficiency, operational, effectiveness or compliance with modern standards.

Definition of ratings

NI Not inspected.
1 No repair is presently required. Normal maintenance must be undertaken.
2 Repairs are required but the Home Inspector does not consider these to be either serious or urgent.
3 Defects of a serious nature or defects requiring urgent repair.

SERVICES

The home inspector has not been able to inspect the following parts of the interior of the property for the reasons stated here.

The inspection chamber cover adjacent to the rear entrance lobby could not be lifted.

F.1. ELECTRICITY

Condition Rating **3**

Justification for Rating and Comments

The electrical system has been rewired in the past, but it is now below current standards. The supply into the garage is potentially dangerous and there is no evidence that the system has been tested. A full test and report should be obtained and any repairs carried out.

F.2. GAS

General advice to be included here once received from CORGI

Condition Rating **2**

Justification for Rating and Comments

The gas meter is situated in the cupboard in the main lounge and is supported on a loose brick base. This should be replaced by a permanently fixed support.

As the gas has been switched off for some time, the system should be tested before it is switched on.

SECTION F (continued)

F.3. WATER

Condition Rating **2**

Justification for Rating and Comments

The water supply comes from the water company mains and enters the property in the rear entrance extension. This is in an unheated area and the pipe needs to be properly insulated.

There is a modern storage tank in the loft and the hot water tank is in the cupboard off the main lounge. The plumbing system is in an adequate condition, but the following repairs are required:

- several of the pipes and part of the tanks in unheated areas need extra insulation to prevent freezing; and
- the support to the cold water storage tank needs to be strengthened.

The disused water tank in the loft is likely to contain asbestos. This poses little risk unless it is disturbed (see C2).

F.4. HEATING

Condition Rating **3**

Justification for Rating and Comments

The property has a gas fired central heating system, with radiators in every room apart from the bathroom. The heating was not switched on at the time of inspection. It is unlikely that the boiler in the kitchen has been serviced regularly and there may not be sufficient ventilation to the kitchen. As a safety precaution, a qualified contractor should test and service the whole of the heating system before it is used (see B3). The radiator in the bathroom needs to be replaced.

F.5. DRAINAGE

Condition Rating **2**

Justification for Rating and Comments

The drains from the property connect into an underground system to the rear. It is assumed that this joins with the drains from the neighbouring property and connects to the public sewer in the street. Legal checks are required to confirm this and establish the resulting legal obligations (see C1).

The drainage system is in an adequate condition, but there are a number of problems:

- The inspection chambers are beginning to deteriorate and some minor repairs are required.
- There is some sediment in the drains. This should be cleaned out and the drains flushed through.
- The kitchen waste pipe is too long and should have its own drainage connection.

The drainage system will have to be checked and cleaned out regularly as part of normal maintenance programmes.

SECTION G

GROUNDS, BOUNDARY WALLS, OUTBUILDINGS AND COMMON FACILITIES

Outbuildings include conservatories and other attachments that are not part of the main structure. Leisure facilities, landscaping and other amenities, including swimming pools and tennis courts, and non-permanent outbuildings were not inspected and are not reported on.

HOME INSPECTOR'S COMMENTS

Grounds

The grounds of the property consist of equally sized front and rear gardens with the garage drive along the south-east boundary and a narrow access pathway along the north-west boundary. The garage drive provides ample off-street parking (approximately five cars in a row) and is surfaced with loose gravel. This is uneven and will require occasional repair.

There are a number of paths around the property and grounds. The brick edgings along each side of the front garden path are loose and need resetting.

Most of the front and rear garden consists of lawn, but there are a number of well established large shrubs and small trees. Many are overgrown and require pruning and/or removal to make sure boundary fences and external walls are not damaged (see B4).

Garages

The garage is located towards the rear of the plot at the end of a long drive. It is brick built with an asbestos cement roof. Although the garage is in an adequate condition, some brickwork repairs are required. Care should be taken if work has to be done on the asbestos roof in the future (see C2).

The electrical supply to the garage does not meet current standards and could be potentially dangerous. An electrical contractor should check this as soon as possible (see F1).

Permanent outbuildings

There is one timber greenhouse in a very poor condition. This is beyond economic repair and should be demolished.

Other permanent buildings

Not applicable.

Boundary walls

A mixture of timber panel fencing and rows of large shrubs and small trees define the boundaries of the property. The timber fence along the rear boundary is in a poor condition and several of the fence panels need replacing. The ownership of the boundaries could not be established during the inspection and should be checked by the legal advisor (see C1).

Retaining walls

There are a number of dwarf retaining walls running along the side of the garage drive in the front garden. The top few courses of brickwork are loose and need repairing.

Common facilities

There are no shared facilities.

SECTION H

How to save money on your fuel bills, improve the comfort of your home and help the environment.

Home Energy Report

Certificate / RefNo: 1

Date of Issue:

For

This property has an Energy rating of: **E**

An Energy Rating gives a measure of the overall energy efficiency of a home, based on energy consumption for space and water heating. The rating is based on the SAP scale of 1 to 120: the higher the number, the more energy efficient the property and the less your fuel bill for space and water heating. This scale is further subdivided into energy rating bands A-G which is similar to the energy labelling found commonly on household appliances.

ENERGY RATING AND TYPICAL RUNNING COSTS OF THIS HOME

Energy Rating	E
SAP Rating	40
Estimated annual Heating Cost (£ per annum)	£466
Carbon dioxide emissions (tonnes per annum)	6.2

Delivered energy and typical running costs shown above are for space and water heating assuming a standard occupancy pattern.

Rating method: UK Standard Assessment Procedure

Energy Certificate

Building Energy Performanc		Average new build rating	Current rating	Potential rating
Certificate Type — FULL				
Building Type — Home				
Whole or Part of Building — Whole				

Very energy efficient - lower running costs

(100-120) **A**

(85-99) **B** — — — — 95

(70-84) **C** — — — — — — — 70

(55-69) **D**

(40-54) **E** — — — — 40

(25-39) **F**

(1-24) **G**

Not energy efficient - higher running costs

GB 2004

Directive 2002/91/EC

Please see page 2 for details of good energy efficiency measures already installed and details of further possible improvements that have been used to calculate the potential for this property.

How to save money on your fuel bills, improve the comfort of your home and help the environment.

Good Energy Efficiency measures already installed

Hot water tank insulation

Draughtproofing doors and windows

Heating system programmer, roomstat and thermostatic radiator valves

Possible Energy Efficiency improvements

Improvement Options	Annual Savings	Estimated Cost	Payback Years
Increase roof insulation thickness to 250mm (10 inches)	£39	£337	8.6
Install cavity wall insulation	£82	£274	3.3
Replace boiler with fully controlled gas condensing boiler for heating and hot water	£101	£1440	14.3

The potential property figures are calculated assuming all the Improvement Options as listed in the table above and the fuel switch if suggested has been carried out. The installation costs, except where indicated, are based on a contractor carrying out the work but a cheaper alternative may be DIY where appropriate.

Excluded from the above figures further possible improvement options are:

Green Electricity - electric generated from a renewable source such as hydro, wind or wave. While the cost of green electric may not be less than normal electricity production it does however produce no CO_2 which means it is extremely good for the environment.

Low energy light bulbs - these may cost as little as £1 but each may save up to £10 a year.

Energy efficient appliances - the cost of running A rated appliances such as fridges and washing machines is considerably less than an equivalent D rated appliance.

How to save money on your fuel bills, improve the comfort of your home and help the environment.

MEASURES TO REDUCE THE RUNNING COSTS AND IMPROVE COMFORT

Lower Cost Measures (up to £500)

These improvements are relatively cheap to install and will be worth tackling first.

Measure 1
CAVITY WALL INSULATION
The external walls of your home are built with a gap, called a cavity, between the inside and outside layers of the wall. Cavity Wall insulation fills this gap with an insulating material. The material is pumped into the gap through small holes, which are drilled into the outside layer of the walls (the small holes are sealed up afterwards). Because this involves using specialist machinery, a professional installation company must carry out the work. The contractor will thoroughly survey your walls before commencing work to be sure that this type of insulation is right for your home.

Measure 2
TOPPING UP LOFT INSULATION
This cost is based upon a contractor installing an additional 100mm of glass fibre or mineral wool insulation in your loft, but a capable DIY enthusiast can install it. If you choose a DIY installation then take care not to block ventilation at the edge of the loft pace as this may cause condensation. When handling the insulation wear gloves and a mask.

Measure 3
HOT WATER TANK AND PIPE INSULATION
By improving the insulation of your hot water tank using a jacket of at least 80mm thickness and also insulating the hot water pipe connections to the cylinder for about a metre or for as far as they are accessible will help reduce your heating bills.

Higher Cost Measures (up to £3000)

Measure 4
CONDENSING BOILER
This improvement is most appropriate when your existing central heating boiler requires repair or replacement. A condensing boiler is capable of much higher efficiencies than other types of boiler, meaning it will burn less fuel to heat your property. Since condensing boilers require an additional drain to be connected, only a qualified heating engineer should carry out the installation.

Measure 5
INSTALLATION OF FULL HEATING CONTROLS PACKAGE
Thermostatic radiator valves (TRVs) allow you to control the temperature of each room to suit your needs (e.g. warmer in your living room and bathroom than in your bedrooms) adding to comfort and reducing your bills. You will need a plumber to fit them to every radiator except one - the radiator in the same room as your room thermostat.

Measure 6
DOUBLE GLAZING
Replacing the existing single glazed windows with double-glazing will improve your comfort in the home by reducing draughts. This will also help to save on your heating bills during the long winter months.

Further Improvements

You should consider these if you want to improve your home to the highest possible standard. Your new energy performance rating for your home would be D and would be the highest possible standard, for that property.

Measure 7
SOLAR WATER HEATING
Energy from the sun can be harnessed to provide domestic hot water. These systems do not generally provide space heating, and are described as 'Solar Thermal' systems. They are among the most cost effective renewable energy systems that can be installed on dwellings in urban or rural environments.

In a typical system, a panel on the roof, a heat transfer fluid travels through a series of heat conducting tubes. During its circulation through the tubes, the fluid picks up heat which is then transferred to the domestic hot water supply as it passes through a coil in an appropriate storage cylinder.

How to save money on your fuel bills, improve the comfort of your home and help the environment.

About your Energy Rating

An energy rating for a home can be compared to a "miles per gallon (mpg)" figure for your car. This energy rating has used "standard occupancy" to make assumptions about how many people live in your home, and how they use the home. This is a bit like using the "standard driving cycle" to arrive at a mpg figure for a car. Just as we would not claim that everyone drives to match the standard driving cycle, the way in which we all use our homes does differ from the assumed standard occupancy. However, the standard occupancy remains a useful tool in calculating an energy rating because it allows one house to be directly compared with another. Standard occupancy assumes that the property is heated for 9 hours a day during weekdays and 16 hours a day at weekends, with the living room heated to 21 °C, and the rest of the property is heated to 18°C.

About your Energy Survey

Energy Surveys are not new. They have been available in the UK for about 15 years. Your survey has been undertaken by a qualified inspector who has been trained to collect the correct information about the energy efficiency of your home. This information has been processed by a Government approved organisation to produce the energy rating and suggestions in the report. Both the Home Inspector and the energy report processor are regularly monitored to show that their work is up to standard.

If you would like more technical information relating to this energy report please contact the
Home Inspector   on
Home Inspector Registration Number

No Cost and Low Cost Measures

In addition to the specific measures suggested in this report, don't forget that there are many other no-cost and low-cost measures that will save money and help reduce the impact on the environment.

For example:

- Check that your heating system thermostat is not set too high (21°C in the living room is suggested)

- Make sure your hot water is not too hot (60°C is suggested)

- Fit low energy lights, particularly in rooms with a heavy lighting use (typically about 50% of rooms might be suitable)

- Turn off your lights and domestic appliances when not needed, and do not leave TVs and videos on standby

- Do not overfill kettles and saucepans, and use a lid where possible

- Buy 'A' Rated kitchen appliances

Do Your Bit for the Environment

It is now generally accepted that the world's climate is warming up due to emissions of "greenhouse gases", primarily carbon dioxide (CO_2). Homes contribute more than a quarter of CO_2 emissions. A 50% reduction in CO_2 emissions will be needed by the year 2050 if we are to avoid catastrophic consequences for the planet. The Government has set a target of a 20% reduction of CO_2 emission levels by 2010 (based on 1990 levels). These reductions can only be achieved if we all do our bit. The CO_2 in your home is generated when you burn fossil fuels - coal, oil or gas. CO_2 is also given off at the power stations that supply you with electricity, if they burn fossil fuels instead of generating the electricity from renewable sources. Planting trees helps to soak up CO_2, because they absorb it during photosynthesis - but it's better not to produce the CO_2 in the first place!

Signature of Home Inspector: ....

Accreditation Licence No: ....

Name: ....

Qualifications: ....

Address: ....

....

....

....

....

....

Telephone No: ....

Fax No: ....

Date of Report: ....

APPENDIX TO THE TERMS OF ENGAGEMENT OF A HOME INSPECTOR

These notes tell you more about the Home Inspector and the work that is done to prepare the Home Condition Report. They are important because they form part of the Terms of Engagement of a Home Inspector. You should read them carefully.

1. The Home Inspector

1.1. The Home Inspector (HI) who performed the inspection and prepared the report is licensed by [Scheme name] (See below). To obtain a licence the Home Inspector must:

- pass an assessment of skills, in accordance with National Occupational Standards; and
- have insurance that covers negligence.

1.2. The licence sets out the duties and responsibilities of the HI and a summary of these is described in a leaflet (Leaflet HCR 1), which is available from the HI on request. These duties and responsibilities do not form part of these Terms of Engagement, but if you wish to complain that the conduct of the Home Inspector falls below the standards they set, you can do so using the process outlined below.

2. The [Scheme name]

2.1 [Scheme name], which licenses HIs, operates under approval from the Government.
Only a person who is licensed by a government-approved scheme can prepare Home Condition Reports. It is the duty of the [Scheme name] to license Home Inspectors and to withdraw the licence of any HI who fails to maintain the required standards.

3. What to do if you have a complaint

3.1. Home Inspectors or companies employing Home Inspectors must operate a 'Complaints Handling Procedure', as a condition of their licence. The Home Inspector is required to give you a written copy of this Procedure, on request, and, if you are not satisfied with the service you have received, you should follow the process outlined in the Procedure document.

3.2. In the first instance, this involves making a formal complaint to the HI or the organisation/ company named on the front of the report, (excepting where the complaint includes an allegation of a criminal nature.)

3.3. If this process is unsuccessful in resolving your complaint, you may apply to the [Scheme name], which will pass the complaint to the Home Inspectors Adjudication Service (known as HIAS) (this is an independent mediation and adjudication service which considers a complaint and decides whether to take action against HIs as a result). The HIAS can order a Home Inspector to do various things, including paying compensation where it believes the HI has failed to comply with the duties and responsibilities set out in the HI's licence. The adjudicator acts entirely independently of the [Scheme name].

3.4. The decision of the adjudicator is binding on the HI unless and until it is overruled in Court. Full details are contained in the Leaflet HCR2, available from the [Scheme Name].

3.5. This process for dealing with complaints is intended to help buyers and sellers pursue legitimate complaints quickly, with minimum cost and to ensure the quality of service provided to the public by Home Inspectors. However, the existence of this process does not prevent you from pursuing a complaint through the courts.

4. Limitation of Liability under the Scheme

If you pursue a complaint under the rules of the [Scheme name], you need to know the limitations of liability.

4.1. If you are a buyer

4.1.1. Where the Home Inspector fails to report a serious or urgent defect and a repair is required, you may be entitled to compensation from the HI.

4.1.2. If the reasonable cost of carrying out the repairs would be less than £500, then no compensation will be payable at all.

4.1.3. If the cost of carrying out the repairs to individual defects is more than £500, but less than £2,500, then you may choose to be paid the actual cost of carrying out the repairs in place of the difference in value.

4.1.4. Any compensation is payable by the HI, not [Scheme name] itself.

4.2. Seller

4.2.1. If you can show that the report describes your property as being in a worse condition than it really is, you will be entitled to apply to the [Scheme name] to get a fresh report from a different Home Inspector and have the erroneous report removed from the register. Compensation is not payable by the [Scheme name] where a report is removed from the register.

4.2.2. An application form can be obtained by using any of the contact methods outlined below, quoting your own contact details and the Unique Report Reference Number given on the first page of the report.

4.2.3. Sellers are entitled to complain to [the Scheme name] in respect of errors or failings by the Home Inspector.

5. Contacting [The Scheme Name]

If you have reason to complain, you can obtain application forms from the Scheme Website www   ..org.uk or you can contact [Scheme Name] by

5.1. Email

5.2. Fax

5.3. Telephone

5.4. Letter

6. More information about the inspection

6.1. The purpose of the report is to provide reliable information on the state of condition and repair of the home to the seller, prospective buyers and mortgage lenders.

6.2. The main objective of the report is to tell you about problems that require urgent attention, are of a serious nature, or both. The report gives 'Condition Ratings' to the major parts of the main building (it does not give 'Condition Ratings' to outbuildings). The report will not highlight minor defects.

6.3. **The report does not contain a valuation and the inspection does not include matters that are more specifically considered when a valuation is provided, such as the location of the home or the availability of public transport or amenities. A seller, buyer or lender requiring a valuation must arrange for one to be separately prepared.**

6.4. The Home Inspector (HI) carries out a 'non-invasive' inspection. That means that the HI does not take up carpets or floor coverings, move furniture or remove the contents of cupboards. Nor, for example, does the HI lift floorboards, remove secured panels or undo electrical fittings. The HI will state at the start of sections D, E and F of the report if it was not possible to inspect any parts of the home that are normally reported on. Where the HI has reason to be concerned about these parts, the report will tell you about any further investigations that are needed.

6.5. The report does not contain advice on the cost of any remedial work or the methods of repair that should be employed. A seller, buyer or lender requiring advice on these subjects must arrange for it to be provided separately.

6.6. The report is not an Asbestos Inspection within the meaning of the Control of Asbestos at Work Regulations 2002.

The following sections give more detailed information on the extent of the inspection.

7. The exterior of the property (Section D)

7.1. The HI carries out a non-invasive inspection of the outside of the main building and permanent outbuildings, from various vantage points within the boundaries of the property and from public areas such as footpaths and open spaces, using binoculars where necessary. The HI does not stand on walls or enter adjacent private property. The HI has a ladder for viewing flat roofs and other features that are up to 3 metres (10 feet) above the adjoining ground level. Features above this level that cannot be seen from any vantage point are not inspected. Because of the risk of causing damage, the HI does not walk on flat roofs.

7.2. The HI looks at the overall condition and the state of repair of the exterior parts of the property. The report does not reflect every minor blemish, and by way of example, it does not point out each individual minor defect in the external walls. Where however, there are so many minor defects that taken together they are serious, then the report states this.

8. The interior of the property (Section E)

8.1. The HI carries out a non-invasive inspection of all the parts of the home that can be seen without causing damage. In the event, however, that the HI cannot see a part of the home without the risk of damage, and suspicion exists that there could be a defect, the report states this and includes recommendations on the need for further investigation.

8.2. The HI checks for damp penetration in vulnerable locations with the use of a moisture-measuring meter.

8.3. The HI opens a selection of the windows and all the doors, where possible. The HI enters the roof space, so long as there is safe access. In properties where there are obstructions, for example, where there is a deep thickness of insulation over the ceiling joists, the HI does not walk around the space because of the risk to safety, but views the roof from the access point.

The HI does not comment on the condition or adequacy of chimney flues.

9. Services (Section F)

9.1. The HI is not required to hold the qualifications of a 'services' engineer and therefore does not give a comprehensive test report on any of the services. The HI reports on those parts of the services that can be seen and no formal tests are undertaken. If any services such as the boiler or mains water are turned off, the HI will state that in the report and will not turn them on.

9.2. Otherwise, the HI turns on a selection of water taps to sanitary appliances and lifts the covers on the drainage inspection chambers where it is safe and practical to do so.

9.3. The HI reports only on the services expressly covered in Section F – Electricity, Gas, Water, Heating and Drainage. All other services and appliances are excluded from the report, e.g. security and door answering systems, television, cable, wireless and satellite communication systems, cookers, hobs, washing machines and fridges (even where built-in).

10. Flats

10.1. It is frequently difficult to see the entire exterior of the property or block, and its maintenance is seldom the responsibility of a single flat occupier. The HI will only carry out a non-invasive inspection to the level of detail referred to above (the main walls, windows and roof over the flat). The remainder of the block will not be inspected to this detail. The HI will form an opinion based on a general inspection of the remainder of the block that is accessed by the entrance to the flat or common parts serving the flat, as to the standard of maintenance and management. Information given about the exterior and common parts is provided so that the conveyancer can check whether the maintenance provisions within the lease or other title documents are adequate.

10.2. The Home Inspector inspects the common access way to the flat, where such exist, and the area where car parking and garaging for the flat are located, together with the access thereto. Other common parts, such as separate halls, stairs and access ways to other flats in the block, the lift motor room and cleaning cupboards are not inspected.

10.3. The interior of the flat is inspected in the same manner as is described under 'The interior of the property' above. However, the roof space is only inspected where access can be safely made from within the flat itself. Access to the roof space is not undertaken where it is only possible from the common parts or from within another flat.

11. Grounds

11.1. The Home Inspector walks round the grounds and the report provides an overview of the general condition of any garden (but not the way it is stocked), retaining and other walls, fences, and permanent outbuildings. Conservatories, with translucent or clear roofs, attached to the main buildings are treated as outbuildings in the main report (but not for the energy performance report), as are garages and permanent store sheds. Buildings containing swimming pools and sports facilities are treated as outbuildings, but the Home Inspector does not report on the leisure facilities, such as the pool itself and its equipment.

12. Reinstatement Cost

12.1. **THIS IS NOT A VALUATION OF THE HOME**

12.2. The report includes a reinstatement cost (except where the property has special features which mean that the services of a specialist are required to assess the cost, in which event the report states that a specialist is required). This figure represents the sum at which the home should be insured against fire and other risks. It is based on building and other related costs and does not include the value of the land on which the home is built. The figure should be reviewed regularly as building costs change.

13. Hazardous materials and contaminated land

The Home Inspector assumes that the home is not built with, nor does it contain hazardous materials, and that it is not built on contaminated land. If, however, any such materials are found during the inspection, or the Home Inspector finds evidence to suspect that the land may be contaminated, this is stated within the report along with recommendations on the need for further investigation.

14. Health & safety and other risks

14.1. The Home Inspector draws attention to health and safety issues where, to ensure a safe environment, the homeowner will need to expend money as part of the improvement of the condition of the home.

14.2. The HI is not required to identify hazards which are inherent, by reason of the age of the property, and which cannot reasonably be changed. By way of example, the HI will not draw attention to uneven floor surfaces that have existed for decades.

15. Matters that need to be investigated by conveyancers

15.1. It is not the role of the HI to act as 'the conveyancer'. If however, during the Home Inspection, the HI identifies matters that may require further investigation by the conveyancers who are advising the parties on the transaction (frequently a Solicitor or Licensed Conveyancer), then the HI will make reference to these in the report. The purpose of this is to draw the matters to the attention of others to improve the quality of the information in the Home Information Pack.

15.2. The HI will not have seen the legal and other documents within the Home Information Pack.

Appendix A – Glossary

ABBE – Awarding Body for the Built Environment
ABE – Association of Building Engineers
ABI – Association of British Insurers
ACE – Association of Consulting Engineers
ACES – Association of Chief Estate Surveyors and Property Managers in Local Government
acm – asbestos containing material
ASI – Architecture and Surveying Institute
BBA – British Board of Agrément
BCIS – Building Cost Information Service
BGS – British Geological Survey
BIAT – British Institute of Architectural Technologists
BISF – British Iron and Steel Federation (now the UK Steel Association)
BRE – Building Research Establishment
BSI – British Standards Institution
BSRIA – Building Services Research and Information Association
BWPDA – British Wood Preserving and Damp Proofing Association
CDM – Construction (Design and Management)
CIBSE – Chartered Institution of Building Services Engineers
CIEH – Chartered Institute of Environmental Health
CIH – Chartered Institute of Housing
CIOB – Chartered Institute of Building
CORGI – Council for Registered Gas Installers
CPD – Continuing Professional Development
dpc – damp-proof course
dpm – damp-proof membrane
EA – The Environment Agency
EMF – Electromagnetic fields
EPR – Experienced Practitioner Route
FAERO – Federation of Authorised Energy Rating Organisations
FENSA – Fenestration Self-Assessment Scheme (set up by the GGF)
FTA – Forestry and Timber Association
GGF – Glass and Glazing Federation
HCR – Home Condition Report
HI – Home Inspector
HICB – Home Inspector Certification Board
HIP – Home Information Pack

HSE – Health and Safety Executive
HSV – Homebuyer Survey and Valuation
IEE – Institution of Electrical Engineers
IMBM – Institute of Maintenance and Building Management
ICE – Institution of Civil Engineers
ICES – Institution of Civil Engineering Surveyors
ICW – Institute of Clerks of Works
IRTS – Institute of Remedial Treatment Surveyors
ISA – Independent Surveyors Association
IStructE – Institution of Structural Engineers
LDAI – Lead Development Association International
LLL – life-long learning
MCB – miniature circuit breaker
NAEA – National Association of Estate Agents
NER – New Entrant Route
NHBC – National House-Building Council
NICEIC – National Inspection Council for Electrical Installation Contracting
NOS – National Occupational Standards
NQF – National Qualification Framework
NRPB – The National Radiological Protection Board
NVQ – National Vocational Qualification
ODPM – Office of the Deputy Prime Minister
prc – prefabricated reinforced concrete
PSNTO – Property Services National Training Organisation
RCD – residual current device
RDS – Remedial Treatment Surveys
RDSAP – Reduced Data Standard Assessment Procedure
RIBA – Royal Institute of British Architects
RICS – Royal Institution of Chartered Surveyors
SAP – Standard Assessment Procedure
SAVA – Surveyors and Valuers Accreditation
SPAB – Society for the Protection of Ancient Buildings
SEDBUK – Seasonal Efficiency of Domestic Boilers in the UK
SPI – Structured Professional Interview
TCPA – Town and Country Planning Association
VRQ – Vocationally Related Qualification

Appendix B – Extract from the National Occupational Standards (NOS) for Home Inspectors

This appendix provides a summary of the different units and elements that make up the NOS for Home Inspectors, and the skills and knowledge required to qualify. The scope of the NOS identify areas such as best practice and competence. A complete copy can be downloaded from www.assetskills.org.

Unit number	Competency	Elements (scope) of unit
1	Work in an effective and professional manner	**1.1:** Develop and maintain effective working relationships **1.2:** Manage your own time and resources **1.3:** Develop yourself to improve your performance **1.4:** Conduct work in a professional and ethical manner
2	Contribute to the safety and security of people and property	**2.1:** Contribute to the maintenance of health and safety at work **2.2:** Contribute to the security of self, colleagues and others **2.3:** Contribute to the security of property **2.4:** Contribute to the security of information
3	Prepare for Home Inspections	**3.1:** Agree and confirm instructions to carry out a Home Inspection **3.2:** Investigate relevant matters relating to the property
4	Undertake Home Inspections	**4.1:** Inspect property for condition **4.2:** Make complete and comprehensive records of findings **4.3:** Interpret evidence to determine condition ratings **4.4:** Collate information for the assessment of energy efficiency
5	Prepare and disseminate Home Condition Reports	**5.1:** Produce complete and comprehensive Home Condition Reports **5.2:** Make completed Home Condition Reports available and maintain own records

Appendix C – Self assessment profiling tool for Home Inspectors

INSTRUCTIONS

This self assessment profiling tool is based on a series of competencies taken from the different units and elements within the National Occupational Standards for Home Inspectors. For each one, you should reflect on your level of knowledge, skills and experience in that area. Do not be too restrictive because many of the elements can be partially satisfied by experience gained in other related areas of work. For example, consider unit 4 (Undertake Home Inspections) and its element 4.1(Inspect property for condition). Although this is obviously set in context with the Home Inspection and report process, some of this element can be satisfied by inspections of other types. Examples could include:

- condition inspections for social landlords;
- homebuyer surveys;
- building surveys;
- specialist defect inspections;
- inspections of dangerous structures; and
- environmental health inspections of tenanted properties.

Depending on the circumstances, these activities may be able to show an assessment centre that you are competent in inspecting residential properties and all that you may need is the specific knowledge of how to carry out a Home Condition Report. The same approach will be appropriate for the 'soft' skills included in units one to three. Many experienced practitioners will be competent in these elements, although they might have worked in diverse environments.

Carefully consider each element and tick one of the three boxes using the following criteria.

Column 1

You have little direct experience or knowledge in this area. Although you might be able to describe what is involved, you would not be able to produce specific evidence that supports your competency. You have not been on any relevant training courses or CPD seminars.

Column 2

You have some experience in this area. You will be familiar with this topic and you would be able to produce evidence to support your experience. It will not be your main area of activity, but occasionally you will do this type of work. You might have attended a few CPD seminars, but this was a passive experience with little evidence of learning.

Column 3

Your core business and the majority of your working day is associated with this role in one way or another. You have attended a number of training seminars and other courses that produced clear evidence of learning such as credit bearing courses or courses involving a process of formative assessment and feedback.

INDICATIVE SCORES

This simplistic approach to your skill assessment must always be treated with caution. It does not follow a rigorous methodology and self-assessment is always dogged by subjectivity. The methods used by assessment centres will be more sophisticated and reliable, although this approach may give you an early indication of your strengths and weaknesses. The following banding may be helpful in this appraisal.

Score of 16–24

You are well off the mark. You will probably have to improve your underpinning knowledge and theory by taking a course of study that is relevant to the role of the Home Inspector. It will take you some time before you are ready to obtain your licence.

Unit 1: Work in an effective and professional manner

Ref.	Description	1	2	3
1.1	Develop and maintain effective working relationships			
1.2	Manage your own time and resources			
1.3	Develop yourself to improve your performance			
1.4	Conduct work in a professional and ethical manner			
	Totals			

Unit 2: Contribute to the safety and security of people and property

Ref.	Description	1	2	3
2.1	Contribute to the maintenance of health and safety at work			
2.2	Contribute to the security of self, colleagues and others			
2.3	Contribute to the security of property			
2.4	Contribute to the security of information			
	Totals			

Unit 3: Prepare for Home Inspections

Ref.	Description	1	2	3
3.1	Agree and confirm instructions to carry out a Home Inspection			
3.2	Investigate relevant matters relating to the property			
	Totals			

Unit 4: Undertake Home Inspections

Ref.	Description	1	2	3
4.1	Inspect property for condition			
4.2	Make complete and comprehensive records of findings			
4.3	Determine condition ratings			
4.4	Collate information for the assessment of energy efficiency			
	Totals			

Unit 5: Prepare and disseminate Home Condition Reports

Ref.	Description	1	2	3
5.1	Produce complete and comprehensive Home Condition Reports			
5.2	Make completed Home Condition Reports available and maintain own records			
	Totals			

OVERALL SCORE

Enter your scores in the following table:

	Number of occurrences	Numerical total
Total Number of 1s		
Total Number of 2s		
Total Number of 3s		
Grand total		

Score 25–32

You have some relevant knowledge and experience although this is lacking in several areas. You will have some significant gaps that can be filled with carefully selected modules and training courses.

Score 33–40

A significant proportion of your knowledge and experience is relevant to the role of the Home Inspector. You will need to fill some gaps, but this would be achieved by a series of good quality short courses.

Score 41–48

You are not exactly a Home Inspector yet, but not far off. A lot of your knowledge is very relevant and it is likely that you will only need top-up training. This will usually involve short courses and modules focused specifically on the Home Inspection and reporting methodologies.

Appendix D – Indicative syllabus for courses that may provide underpinning knowledge for the Diploma in Home Inspection

The topic areas included in this table are based on an indicative list produced by ABBE and our own interpretation of the knowledge required to be a Home Inspector. To assess your own underpinning knowledge, work through the list and identify those areas where you do not have a good working knowledge or familiarity with the latest developments in the topic. For example, assume that you took your original qualification fifteen years ago and this included the study of wood rot and wood boring insects. Since then, you have not been on any CPD seminars or other training events dealing with these topics and your job role means that you do not come across these problems in your day-to-day work. This is likely to be identified by the assessment centre as a gap in your knowledge.

This kind of self assessment can help you begin to identify other similar gaps and establish an action plan for your personal development. Ironically, by working through this process you can show that you have started to 'Develop yourself to improve your performance' (unit 1, element 1.3 of the NOS). This will be useful evidence to show an assessor in the future.

General topics	Construction of residential properties
• communication skills including interpersonal skills and report writing • research skills • time management • reflective skills and personal development • ethics • general health & safety legislation • *Health & Safety at Work Act 1974* • CDM Regulations • health & safety and personal safety during surveys and inspections • safety of colleagues • property security • data protection legislation and guidelines • Home Inspector guidelines	• residential building construction • common materials, composition and performance • foundations and relation to ground conditions/geology, groundworks, basements • ground and first floor construction • external and internal walls • roof construction and covering, including flat roofs • rainwater goods and drainage • windows, stairs and doors • finishes and decoration • external works and features **Services** • including electricity, gas, water, heating, sewerage

Building pathology/Defects in residential property	Related matters
• performance of common building materials • causes of building movement and analysis of building damage • causes and remedies of all forms of dampness and timber defects, including wet and dry rot and wood boring insects • deterioration of roofs and their coverings • external joinery and decorations • internal defects including problems with walls, partitions, fireplaces, floors, joinery, decorations and basements • problems with building services • external and environmental issues including general site problems, contaminated land, radon and deleterious materials • non-traditional housing	• maintenance considerations for domestic buildings • planning permission, listed buildings and conservation areas • building regulation approval • SAP ratings • flooding risk • trees • basic land law including legal estates, easements and covenants • law of contract including Terms of Engagement • NHBC Standards and other related standards • knowledge of BRE guidance material

Appendix E – Condition descriptors

INTRODUCTION

This appendix presents descriptions of condition associated with the different condition ratings for each building element. We have tried to identify typical visual indicators associated with each element so that you develop a feel for the rating process, but it is important to consider that these are not exhaustive and do not suit all types of property construction. They relate to traditional domestic construction and you will have to adapt these descriptions for different buildings.

To match the descriptions of the various ratings, the element does not have to display all the characteristics described. For example, an element may generally be in a satisfactory condition, but a defect may make part of it a serious health and safety risk, thus placing it in a higher category than its condition might otherwise suggest.

The paragraphs are designed to describe a situation – they are not standard paragraphs designed for the Home Condition Report. In other words, the following tables provide a guide that may help you to allocate correct ratings in a consistent and objective way. Take care – it is not a precise science!

Definition of terms used

To distinguish between the different categories, three adjectives have been used. Although these can be misinterpreted, we think that they do help to describe the condition associated with each rating. They are included below along with their definitions, and then described in a building context against a technical benchmark.

Condition descriptors in relation to technical benchmarks

Adjective	Definition	Technical benchmark
Satisfactory	• suitable, acceptable • describes a situation that makes you feel satisfied because it is what you are hoping for • sufficient to meet a demand or requirement	The element meets the technical benchmark current at the time of construction. No known defects have occurred since then or were apparent at the time of inspection.
Adequate	• an amount of something that is just enough for a particular purpose • sufficient without being abundant or outstanding • barely satisfactory or sufficient	The element could have met an appropriate technical benchmark at the time of construction or installation, but is now showing signs of wear and tear. Despite this, it will still be fulfilling its function. Alternatively, it may not have met an appropriate technical benchmark, but with increased levels of maintenance it will continue to perform its intended function.
Poor	• inferior, inadequate, inefficient	The element probably never met an appropriate technical benchmark and there are clear indicators why this element does not meet the standard now.

Technical benchmark

When allocating a condition rating to a building element, it is important to compare it to an 'acceptable' standard. This is difficult to define because residential properties come in all shapes, sizes, ages and conditions, and will meet standards of acceptability in a range of different ways. Although this rating allocation should bear some relationship with current standards, you should not expect them to conform exactly.

We have called this 'acceptable' standard a 'technical benchmark'. It applies to a broad range of construction and is related to:

• standards at the time of construction;
• current building regulations, British Standards, agreement certificates, NHBC Guidelines, views of professional institutions and codes of practice issued by reputable trade associations; and
• good practice standards in the construction industry.

This definition has been kept broad so that it does not become prescriptive.

SECTION D – EXTERNAL CONDITION

D1 – *Chimney stacks*

Condition category	Typical description of condition
One	The chimney is in a satisfactory condition. It is vertical and not excessively high in relation to its width (height less than 4.5 times its width). The pointing, flaunching and pots all look satisfactory and do not require any repair in the short or medium term. The flashings are not loose and there is no evidence of leaks in the roof space below. The stack is adequately supported.
Two	The chimney is in an adequate condition. It is vertical and not excessively high in relation to its width (height less than 4.5 times its width). The pointing, flaunching and pots are adequate although some repairs will be required. Some smaller sections of the flashings have come loose, but the majority is securely fixed. There is no evidence of persistent leaks in the roof space below. The stack is adequately supported. Minor repairs are required as part of programmed maintenance work.
Three	The chimney is in a poor condition. It could be out of vertical and there is a risk that it might collapse during stormy weather (especially tall and slender ones). The pointing and flaunching are in a poor condition and the top courses of masonry may be unstable and need rebuilding. The pots appear loose and are deteriorating. Large plants/shrubs can be seen growing out of the flaunching masonry. The flashings are loose or partly absent and there is evidence of leaks in the roof space below that may be affecting the rafters/ceilings. The stack may not be properly supported from below, adding to its instability. The cost of repairs will be more than £1000. The stack needs repairing within the next six months for safety reasons.

D2 – *Roof coverings*

Condition category	Typical description of condition
One	The roof covering is in a satisfactory condition. The roof slopes are even and there is little or no evidence of previous repair work. There is no water getting through the covering and the flashings to the neighbouring property(s) are in a satisfactory condition. There is a satisfactory level of ventilation to the roof space. Hip and ridge tiles are adequately bedded. Internally, sarking felt provides a secondary protection against water penetration. Where there is no sarking, the tiles/slates are adequately laid or pointed to prevent water penetration. Any minor repairs can wait until the next programmed maintenance work.
Two	The roof covering is in an adequate condition. The roof slopes are generally even and there is little evidence of previous repair work. There may be one or two small leaks, but this does not have a significant impact internally. The flashings to the neighbouring property(s) are in an adequate condition although small sections may have started to come loose. There is some ventilation to the roof space. Hip and ridge tiles are adequately bedded, but a few are loose. Internally, sarking felt provides a secondary protection against water penetration. Where there is no sarking, the tiles/slates are adequately laid or pointed to prevent all but a few minor leaks. Repairs are needed, but these can be included in the next programmed maintenance work and will be less than £1000.
Three	The roof covering is in a poor condition. The roof slopes are uneven and there is considerable evidence of previous repair work (say 20% of surface area repaired). There are a number of slates/tiles missing or defective. Water is getting through the covering and beginning to affect the construction below. The flashings to the neighbouring property(s) are in a poor condition and have come loose in some areas. There is no (or very little) formal ventilation to the roof space. Hip and ridge tiles are poorly bedded and some have come loose or are missing. Internally, sarking felt may be present but has a number of holes in it. Where there is no sarking, daylight can be seen in a number of places. The covering needs to be repaired as soon as possible to prevent further damage to other parts of the building and will cost more than £1000. This needs to be done within the next six months.

D3 – Rainwater pipes and gutters

Condition category	Typical description of condition
One	The rainwater system is in a satisfactory condition. The gutters are properly aligned, well supported and there is no evidence of leaks or blockages. The downpipes are adequately fixed and there are enough for the roof area to drain. Most are well decorated with little or no sign of deterioration. The downpipes discharge into well maintained clear gullies. Where visible, the valley and parapet gutters are free of defects and obstructions. Any minor repairs can wait until the next programmed maintenance work.
Two	The rainwater system is in an adequate condition. Most of the gutters are properly aligned and well supported, but there is evidence of minor leaks or blockages. The downpipes are adequately fixed and there are enough for the roof area to drain. Most are well decorated with little or no sign of deterioration. The downpipes discharge into adequately maintained gullies, although some may need clearing out. Where visible, the valley and parapet gutters are generally free of defects and obstructions. Any repairs can wait until the next programmed maintenance work.
Three	The rainwater system is in a poor condition. Some of the gutters are poorly aligned and supported. There are a number of leaks and blockages. Plant growth may be seen in a number of locations. The downpipes are poorly fixed and leaking, which may result in damp penetration through the wall. The decorations are poor and there are a number of deteriorated gutters and downpipes. The system discharges into poorly maintained gullies that may be blocked with missing grates. Where visible, the valley and parapet gutters are poor, with a number of splits or other defects and obstructions that may have caused leaks to the spaces below. The guttering needs to be repaired as soon as possible to prevent further damage to other parts of the building. This could cost more than £1000 and needs to be done within the next six months.

D4 – Main walls

Condition category	Typical description of condition
One	The main walls are in a satisfactory condition. They are vertically aligned without any signs of recent or active movement that might suggest a problem with the foundations. The pointing or external finish (e.g. render) is satisfactory. The lintels and masonry sills are generally defect free. Any minor repairs can wait until the next programmed maintenance work.
Two	The main walls are in an adequate condition. They are generally vertically aligned, but there may be signs of recent movement. This could suggest a previous problem with the foundations. The pointing or external finish (e.g. render) is beginning to deteriorate and a small amount of repointing/repair will be required. The lintels and masonry sills are generally defect free, although replacement/rebedding may occasionally be required. Although repairs are required, they can usually wait until the next programmed maintenance work.
Three	The main walls are in a poor condition. Typical defects will include: • some walls are not vertical and may need securing or possibly rebuilding; • recent damage to the masonry suggests possible foundation movement; • the pointing or external finish have deteriorated to the point where more than a substantial portion needs to be renewed, and could soon result in dampness internally; and • some of the lintels and sills need replacing. The repairs are likely to cost considerably more than £1000 and will need to be done within the next six months.

D5 – Windows

Condition category	Typical description of condition
One	The windows are in a satisfactory condition. There is little evidence of rotten timber, corrosion or distortion in the frames. The glazing putties/beads are satisfactory, most of the opening casements operate easily and the frames are satisfactorily bedded with appropriate sealant. There is little evidence of condensation internally and any minor repairs can wait until the next programmed maintenance work.
Two	The windows are in an adequate condition, but a few have developed minor defects. These would typically include small areas of rotten timber, cracked or missing glazing putties and a number of open joints. A few casements may be difficult to open and there is some evidence of condensation internally. Some of the sealants at the junction with the wall may need renewing and there may have been previous timber repairs. None of the defects are allowing water to enter the building and the repairs can usually wait until the next programmed maintenance work.
Three	Most of the windows are in a poor condition with a number (say 55–60%) showing significant defects. These might include several rotten areas of timber, cracked and missing glazing putties, many sprung and open joints, or a number of casements that are impossible or difficult to open. The sealants to frame/wall junctions are usually in a poor condition and there may be some evidence of rainwater penetration internally as well as serious condensation problems. One or two windows may be insecure and there is evidence of previous timber repairs to the casements and frames. The repairs are likely to cost considerably more than £1000 and will need to be done within the next six months.

D6 – External doors (including patio doors)

Condition category	Typical description of condition
One	The doors are in a satisfactory condition. There is little evidence of rotten timber, corrosion or distortion in the frames. They open and close easily, and latches, locks and bolts all work properly. The level of security meets current expectations. The frames are satisfactorily sealed with the appropriate sealant. If the doors are partially glazed, then safety glass is used where required. The doors are satisfactorily draft stripped and the threshold waterproof. Any minor repairs can wait until the next programmed maintenance work.
Two	The doors are in an adequate condition with only a few minor defects. They open and close adequately, and latches, locks and bolts all work. The level of security just meets current minimum standards. The frames are adequately sealed with the appropriate sealant. If the doors are partially glazed and safety glass is not used, the position of the opening poses little danger to the users. The doors have some draft stripping, but this could be improved. The threshold is not allowing water to enter the building. Any repairs can usually wait until the next programmed maintenance work.
Three	The doors are in a poor condition with several defects including rotten areas of timber, open joints and cracked or missing glazing putties/beads. It may be difficult to open and close them, and latches, locks and bolts may not work properly. The level of security will often be well below current minimum standards. The frames may not be properly sealed, and doors may have large areas of non-safety glass that presents a danger to the users. The doors are draughty and the threshold may be allowing water to enter the building and wet the floor. The repairs are likely to cost considerably more than £1000 and will need to be done within the next six months. These condition descriptors should be used to support your assessment decision. Although the security of the doors will contribute to the rating decision, no mention should be made in your report.

D7 – All other woodwork

Condition category	Typical description of condition
One	The external woodwork is in a satisfactory condition. There is little evidence of rotten timber or distortion of the individual sections. All the joints and junctions look satisfactory, and any minor repairs can wait until the next programmed maintenance work.
Two	The external woodwork is in an adequate condition. There is some evidence of rotten timber and possibly slight distortion of individual sections. There may be a few open/poorly made joints and any repairs can usually wait until the next programmed maintenance work.
Three	Much of the external woodwork is in a poor condition with visible wood rot in many different sections. Many of the joints are either open or poorly made, leaving them vulnerable to further deterioration. Some parts may be close to falling away. The repairs are likely to cost more than £1000 and will need to be done within the next six months.

D8 – Claddings (e.g. boarding) to the external walls

Condition category	Typical description of condition
One	The cladding is in a satisfactory condition. There is little evidence of rotten timber, distortion of panels, or slipped, missing or loose tiles. All the joints/junctions with adjacent walling look satisfactory, and any minor repairs can wait until the next programmed maintenance work.
Two	The cladding is in an adequate condition. There are a few areas of rotten timber, some of the panels may be slightly distorted and there are a few slipped, missing or loose tiles. All the joints/junctions with adjacent walling appear adequate and there is no evidence of water penetration internally. Any minor repairs can wait until the next programmed maintenance work.
Three	Much of the cladding is in a poor condition with visible wood rot in many different sections. A number of cladding panels are distorted and a few are in danger of falling off. There are many tiles that are missing, slipped or have lost their backing. Many of the joints/junctions with adjacent walling are either open or poorly made, leaving them vulnerable to moisture penetration. There may be evidence of water penetrating internally. The repairs are likely to cost more than £1000 and will need doing within the next six months.

D9 – External decoration

Condition category	Typical description of condition
One	The external painted surfaces are in a satisfactory condition. There are only a few areas of loose and flaking paint or loose glazing beads/putties. The decorations look like they have been recently renewed.
Two	Although much of the external decorations are in an adequate condition, a number of areas are developing defects. These typically include small areas of blistering, flaking, peeling or powdering paintwork, and a few cracked glazing putties, but the decorations can wait until the next planned programme of maintenance (within a maximum of two years).
Three	Most of the external decorations are in a poor condition with the majority showing defects. These might include cracked and missing glazing putties, and large areas of missing, peeling, flaking or powdering paint and varnish. These will need to be renewed within the next six months to prevent the underlying material from further deteriorating.

D10 – Other

This element refers to other external building elements that do not fit in the categories listed previously, such as balconies, roof terraces, fire escapes and large dormer constructions.

SECTION E – INTERNAL CONDITION

E1 – Roof structure

Condition category	Typical description of condition
One	The roof structure is in a satisfactory condition. The roof slopes are even and there is little or no evidence of distorted sections. Most structural members are correctly sized. The ceiling joists are connected to the base of the rafters and any struts and other supports are taken to load bearing walls. There is no evidence of wood boring insects or wood rot. Any minor repairs can wait until the next programmed maintenance work.
Two	The roof structure is in an adequate condition. The roof slopes are generally even. Where they are undulating, this is on a small scale and there is no evidence to suggest the distortion will get worse. Most of the structural members are correctly sized. The ceiling joists are adequately connected to the base of the rafters and where they are not, roof spread is not a problem. Any struts and other supports are taken to load bearing walls. There may be some wood boring insects, but this is limited, of a less harmful species and can easily be contained.
	Repairs are needed, but these can be included in the next programmed maintenance work and will be less than £1000.
Three	The roof structure is in a poor condition. The roof slopes are uneven, with the distortion likely to get worse. Many of the structural members are under sized and the ceiling joists are not well connected to the base of the rafters. In some cases, roof spread will be a problem. Some struts and other supports may not be taken down to load bearing walls. There may be active wood boring insects of a more harmful species that is very widespread. Repairs are required within the next six months and are likely to cost more than £1000.

E2 – Ceilings

Condition category	Typical description of condition
One	The ceilings are in a satisfactory condition. They are even with few (if any) cracks and no evidence of previous roof leaks. Any plaster cornices, mouldings, roses, etc. are securely fixed and any minor repairs can wait until the next time the ceilings are decorated.
Two	The ceilings are in an adequate condition. They are generally even and where there are cracks, these appear stable. There may have been one or two previous leaks that have stained the ceiling, but these are no longer active and only require sealing and redecorating. The plaster cornices, mouldings, roses, etc. are adequately fixed and do not pose a threat to the occupiers. Any minor repairs are small, will cost less than £1000 and can wait until the next time the ceilings are decorated.
Three	The ceilings are in a poor condition. Several are uneven with a number of cracks that could threaten their stability. There may be a number of previous leaks that have damaged the plaster, with some still active. The plaster cornices, mouldings, roses, etc. are adequately fixed, but some areas are coming away. Some parts of the ceilings may be a threat to the safety of the occupiers. Repairs are required within the next six months and are likely to cost more than £1000.

E3 – Internal walls, partitions and plasterwork

Condition category	Typical description of condition
One	The internal walls, partitions and plasterwork are in a satisfactory condition. All the internal walls are properly supported and robust enough for shelves and other fittings. Plaster finishes are sound, damp free and there are no signs of building movement.
Two	The internal walls, partitions and plasterwork are in an adequate condition. Most of the internal walls are properly supported and where they are not, there is no evidence of building movement. Most of the partitions are robust enough for shelves and other fittings. Plaster finishes are adequate, but a few small areas are loose and will need repairing when the room is next decorated. There are only small areas that are damp.
Three	The internal walls, partitions and plasterwork are in a poor condition. Some of the internal walls are poorly supported and this has led to distortion in the adjacent partitions. Several partitions are not robust enough for shelves and other fittings, and large areas of plaster finishes have lost their backing. Some patches may be close to falling away. Several walls are affected by dampness and will need repairing within the next six months.

E4 – *Floors*

Condition category	Typical description of condition
One	Suspended timber floors are in a satisfactory condition. The floors are level and do not deflect too much during the 'drop heel' test. The floorboards/panels are not damp and there is no evidence of wood rot or wood boring insects. There is sufficient under floor ventilation and where visible, the under floor thermal insulation appears to meet modern standards. Fixed floor coverings are in a satisfactory condition.
	Solid floors are even and generally level. The edge of the floor is not damp and there are no gaps below the skirtings. Fixed floor coverings are in satisfactory condition. Any minor repairs can wait until the next programmed maintenance work.
Two	Suspended timber floors are in an adequate condition. The floors are generally level and do not suffer from excess deflection during the 'drop heel' test. The floorboards/panels are not damp and where there is evidence of wood rot or wood boring insects, this is very limited and easily treated. There is sufficient under floor ventilation although it may not exactly match current standards and there is some under floor thermal insulation. Fixed floor coverings are in an adequate condition.
	Solids floors are generally even and level. Where they are not, sulphate attack is NOT suspected. Most of the floor is not damp and where it is, this is very isolated and easily treated. Any fixed floor coverings are in an adequate condition with some small areas needing repair.
	Minor repairs in either type of floor can wait until the next programmed maintenance and will cost less than £1000.
Three	Suspended timber floors are in a poor condition. The floors are sloping and deflect excessively during the 'drop heel' test. The floorboards/panels are damp in places and there is clear evidence of wood rot or wood boring insects. In some cases, this is widespread and requires further investigation. There is insufficient under floor ventilation and there is no under floor thermal insulation. Fixed floor coverings are in a poor condition.
	Solids floors are uneven and sloping. Sulphate attack is suspected. Some areas of the floor are affected by dampness that may be difficult to repair. Any fixed floor coverings are in a poor condition and would be more economic to replace.
	For both types of floor, repairs are required within the next six months and are likely to cost more than £1000.

E5 – *Fireplaces, chimney breasts and exterior of flues*

Condition category	Typical description of condition
One	All the fireplaces and chimney breasts are properly supporting the chimney above. Where chimney breasts have been removed, there is clear evidence that the structure is properly supported. There are no stains on the chimney breasts and the fireplaces are in working order. Where blocked, the flues are properly ventilated. External flues are in a satisfactory condition and appropriately positioned.
Two	All the fireplaces and chimney breasts are properly supporting the chimney above. Where chimney breasts have been removed, there is clear evidence that the structure is properly supported. There may be a few minor stains on the chimney breasts, but these can be easily repaired. The fireplaces are in working order and where some are blocked, the flues may not be properly ventilated. External flues are in an adequate condition and appropriately positioned.
Three	Some of the fireplaces and chimney breasts have been removed and there is clear evidence that the structure is NOT properly supported. There are several large stains on the chimney breasts that need to be replastered. Some of the fireplaces may be defective and several have been blocked up without proper ventilation. External flues are in a poor condition and inappropriately positioned.

E6 – Built-in fitments (including kitchen and other fittings, but excluding appliances)

Condition category	Typical description of condition
One	The kitchen cupboards, worktops and sink(s) are in a satisfactory condition. The doors and drawers operate properly. There is no dampness under the sink.
Two	The kitchen cupboards, worktops and sink(s) are in an adequate condition although they are an older design. On the whole, the doors and drawers operate properly, but a few may need minor repairs/small scale replacement. Although there might be a little dampness beneath the sink, it is not considered a serious problem. Although repairs are required, these are not urgent and they do not spoil the use of the kitchen.
Three	The kitchen cupboards, worktops and sink(s) are in a poor condition and may be of some age. Many doors and drawers do not work properly, requiring considerable repair or replacement. It may be more economic to replace the units. There may be evidence of dampness beneath the sink. Repairs and replacements are required that prevent the kitchen from being properly used and are likely to cost more than £1000.

E7 – Internal woodwork

Condition category	Typical description of condition
One	The internal woodwork is in a satisfactory condition. The internal doors open and close properly, and the handrails and balusters are secure and safe. Picture rails and dado panels are securely fixed and free from rot. The staircases are in a satisfactory condition, with all treads and risers securely fixed. Skirtings are straight and free from distortion.
Two	The internal woodwork is in an adequate condition. Most of the internal doors open and close properly, but a few may need adjusting. The handrails and balusters are mostly secure and safe, but a few balusters may need some repair. Picture rails and dado panels appear adequate and free from rot. The staircases are in an adequate condition, with only a few treads and risers needing minor repair. Skirtings are generally straight and free from distortion. Although repairs are required, these are not urgent and can wait until the next programmed maintenance.
Three	The internal woodwork is in a poor condition. A number of the internal doors need replacing and several do not operate properly. The handrails and balusters may be insecure, presenting a safety risk to the users. Picture rails and dado panels may be poorly fixed, with some possibly affected by wood rot. Several of the treads and risers to the staircase need repairing, the design may present a danger to users and there may be signs of active woodworm. Some of the skirtings may be distorted, damp and affected by rot. Some of the repairs are serious, need doing as soon as possible and are likely to cost more than £1000.

E8 – Bathroom fittings

Condition category	Typical description of condition
One	The bathroom fittings and appliances are in a satisfactory condition. All fittings work properly, are well secured, and all splashbacks are properly water-proofed with appropriate sealant.
Two	The bathroom fittings and appliances are in an adequate condition. They may be an older design and in need of minor repair, but are generally fit for their purpose. Some fittings may be loose and a few splashbacks may need to be water-proofed with appropriate sealant.
Three	The bathroom fittings and appliances are in a poor condition. They may be an older design and require a number of repairs. A few may not be working at all. Many fittings may be loose, unstable or cracked, and most splashbacks may need to be water-proofed with appropriate sealant.

E9 – Other

This element refers to other parts of the internal structure that do not fall into the previous eight elements, such as cellars. If relevant, notes should be made concerning ventilation, drainage or inappropriate use by sellers.

E10 – Dampness

This element does not require a condition rating and so no descriptors are required.

SECTION F – SERVICES

F1 – Electricity

Condition category	Typical description of condition
One	The electrical system appears satisfactory. There are no obvious defects or deficiencies. The fittings and wiring are modern and there is evidence of supplementary bonding (green and yellow earth wires), MCBs and RCDs in appropriate locations. There is evidence of an electrical test carried out within the last five years and there are no signs of DIY or other alteration work since that test.
Two	The electrical system appears adequate although there are a small number of defects and deficiencies. Although most of the wiring and fittings are of a modern design, it is unlikely that the electrical system will fully comply with current regulations. There is some supplementary bonding, but few (if any) MCBs and RCDs. Although there might be evidence of a test, this might have been some time ago and there is evidence of alteration work since then. Although the whole installation needs to be tested and some repair work will be required, it is unlikely to result in complete rewiring.
Three	The electrical system is in a poor condition. There are considerable defects and deficiencies indicating that extensive repair or complete replacement will be required. It is an older system with a number of out-of-date fittings and wiring circuits. There is little supplementary bonding and no MCBs or RCDs. Some parts may be damaged and present a threat to the building and/or to the occupants. There have been a number of DIY alterations. Further inspection and testing by an appropriately qualified specialist is required. Although the true extent of the problems will not be known until the report is received, it is likely that the electrical system will require significant investment to render it safe and efficient to use.

F2 – Gas

Condition category	Typical description of condition
One	There are no obvious defects or deficiencies indicating problems with the service system. There is a current Gas Completion Certificate and there is no evidence that the gas system has been altered or developed defects since it was issued. All of the gas appliances are included in the Gas Completion Certificate.
Two	Although there is a Gas Completion Certificate, this does not cover all the appliances in the property. There may also be some defects and deficiencies of a minor nature, including gas meters not properly supported and gas pipes vulnerable to accidental damage. It is unlikely that the service system will fully comply with modern regulations and the whole installation needs to be tested and checked as soon as possible. Some repair work may be required, but is unlikely to result in complete replacement.
Three	There is no evidence of a Gas Completion Certificate and if there is one, it does not cover any of the current gas appliances. There will also be several defects and deficiencies, some of a serious nature including poorly installed gas meters, damaged gas pipes and evidence of unauthorised DIY alterations. The gas system will not comply with modern regulations and the whole installation needs to be tested and checked as soon as possible. The system needs to be repaired and may require complete replacement.

F3 – Water

Condition category	Typical description of condition
One	There are no obvious defects or deficiencies that indicate there might be problems with the water system. The rising main is insulated and the storage tanks are plastic, insulated and well supported, with overflows. Hot water cylinders are insulated and appear properly ventilated. Where the hot water tanks are unvented, there is evidence that the whole system has been properly maintained. The pipework is modern, made of compatible materials and there is no evidence of leaks.
Two	The water system is adequate. There are no apparent serious or urgent repairs required, although some upgrading may be needed. The rising main may be partially insulated and often made of lead. The storage tanks are usually plastic, but may need updating, including additional insulation and better support from beneath with more suitable overflows. Hot water cylinders are generally insulated and appear properly ventilated. Where the hot water tanks are unvented, there is evidence that the whole system has been maintained in the past. The pipework is mostly modern, but there are some incompatible materials that do not seem to have caused a problem. There is no evidence of leaks.
Three	There are a considerable number of defects and deficiencies indicating that the water system will require extensive repair or complete replacement. These could include an uninsulated lead rising main (both externally and internally), galvanised steel or asbestos water tanks without lids, or a variety of DIY type plumbing and hot water tanks that are not properly vented or maintained. The system may be leaking, in some cases requiring urgent attention.

Further inspection and testing is required by an appropriately qualified contractor as soon as possible. Although the true extent of the problems will not be known until the report is received, it is likely that the water system will require significant investment to render it safe and efficient to use. |

F4 – Heating

Condition category	Typical description of condition
One	There are no obvious defects or deficiencies that indicate there might be problems with the heating system. The boiler will usually be less than ten years old and have a Benchmark Certificate issued by a CORGI-registered contractor. If not, there should be clear evidence that the system has been adequately and regularly maintained.
Two	There are a small number of defects and deficiencies with the heating system. The boiler might be an older model (say more than ten years old), some of the radiator valves may be stuck and there might be loose and poorly fitted pipework. The feed and expansion tank may not have a lid and some pipes may not be insulated in unheated areas. Although there may be some evidence of maintenance work being carried out on the system, this has not been on a regular basis.

It is unlikely that the service system will fully comply with modern regulations and it needs to be tested and checked as soon as possible. Some repair work will be required, but it is unlikely to result in complete replacement. |
| Three | There are a considerable number of defects and deficiencies indicating that the system will require extensive repair or complete replacement. The defects could include an older boiler (say fifteen to twenty years) with signs of escaping combustion products, poor DIY alterations and installations, and current leaks. Some of these may be an actual or developing threat to the fabric of the building or to personal safety.

Further inspection and testing by an appropriately qualified specialist should be arranged urgently. Although the true extent of the problems will not be known until the report is received, it is likely that the service system will require significant investment to render it safe and efficient to use. |

F5 – Drainage

Condition category	Typical description of condition
One	There are no obvious defects or deficiencies that indicate there might be problems with the drainage system. Most inspection chamber covers have been lifted and the benching and channels were in a satisfactory condition. There is no vehicular access or large shrubs/trees over the line of the drains and all the gullies are working satisfactorily.
	Where the property has a private drainage system (e.g. septic tanks), there is evidence that this has been properly installed and maintained.
Two	There are a small number of defects and deficiencies with the drainage system. Some of the inspection chamber covers have been lifted and were in an adequate condition, although a few channels may be slightly cracked and benching beginning to deteriorate. There may be some light vehicular access (e.g. car hardstanding) or large shrubs/trees over the line of the drains, but these do not appear to have caused a problem. Some of the gullies may need clearing.
	Where the property has a private drainage system, although there might not be evidence to show that this has been properly installed and maintained, it appears to be working adequately (e.g. no smells, no flowing sewerage, etc.) and there is no evidence that it is polluting local water courses.
	Some repair work will be required, but it is unlikely to result in complete replacement. Due to the specialist nature of some parts of the installation (especially private drainage systems), a precautionary test by an appropriate specialist should be arranged in the short term.
Three	There are a considerable number of defects and deficiencies indicating that the drainage system will require extensive repair or complete replacement. Where the inspection chambers have been lifted, they were in poor condition with much of the benching broken down, channels cracked and roots visible where there are shrubs/trees close by. The drains may run close to the building that has been damaged by building movement. The channels will usually be full of sediment, suggesting sluggish flow.
	Where the property has a private drainage system, this will be an older system with no evidence that proper maintenance work has been carried out. There are signs that it is not working properly (e.g. bad smells, signs of flowing sewerage, etc.) and there are local water courses close by that may become polluted.
	Some of the faults may present a developing threat to the fabric of the building or to personal safety. Further inspection and testing by an appropriately qualified specialist should be arranged as soon as possible. Although the true extent of the problems will not be known until the report is received, it is likely that the drainage system will require significant investment to render it safe and efficient to use.

Appendix F – Seller's questionnaire

The following sets of questions help outline the range of information that will be very helpful to the Home Inspector. Apart from helping you to evaluate whether you have the skills and knowledge to complete an inspection of the seller's type of property, it will also help you prepare for the inspection and identify some of the potential problems even before you arrive.

The questionnaire should be sent to the seller before the inspection and ideally returned to you, fully completed before you get there. The questions below help towards identifying the most important

issues in relation to information you need **before** an inspection. If you choose to base a pre-inspection questionnaire on what is included here, make sure you express the questions in an unambiguous and 'customer-friendly' manner. If you do not send a pre-inspection questionnaire to the seller, then you should spend five or ten minutes going through the questions at the beginning of the inspection, completing it on their behalf. The questions are in no particular order as many different inspectors will want to organise their information in different ways.

Questions to ask a seller prior to inspection	
About the property	• What date was the house built? • What type of property is it (terrace/semi/detached/flat/bungalow)? • Do you know the name of the builder who constructed the house? • What is the tenure – freehold or leasehold? ○ If leasehold, how many years until expiry? • What is the ground rent? What is the service charge? • How long have you owned/leased the property? • Is the property constructed using any particular system or using non-traditional materials (e.g. concrete or steel framed, etc.)? • Is the property liable to flooding? • What chattels/possessions are going to remain? • What fixtures are going to be removed?
Legal issues	• Are there any rights of way over the property? • Is there any shared access? • Do you know which boundaries you are responsible for maintaining? • Is your property currently affected by boundary disputes? • Are there any outstanding party wall issues? • Has the road to the property been adopted? • Is the property listed or is it in a conservation area? • Are there any tree preservation orders on trees within the grounds? • Are there any flying freeholds? (i.e. Do any parts of your property protrude over your neighbour's?) • Do you know if there are any bats in the property?
Access for inspection	• Does the property have any concealed access hatches or doorways that can be opened? • Are there any parts of the property that cannot be inspected because of stored possessions, etc?

Repairs and defects	• Have you carried out any structural alteration work or added an extension?
	  ○ If yes, what date did you do this?
	  ○ Do you have building regulation approval and planning permission?
	  ○ Do you have the appropriate documentation?
	• Have you had other structural repairs carried out (e.g. underpinning)?
	• Do you have any guarantees/warranties for any of the repairs carried out?
	• Is the property affected by any known current defects or other problems?
	• Have you improved the energy efficiency of the property?

Services	• What type of service systems does the property have (electricity/mains water supply/private water supply/mains drainage/private sewerage system/gas/LPG/oil/solid fuel, etc.) and how old are they?
	• When was the property last rewired?
	• How old is the main boiler/source of heating?
	• Do you have maintenance records for the service systems?
	• Do you have a private drainage system?
	  ○ If yes, is it a cess pit or septic tank?
	  ○ How often is it emptied?

Appendix G – HCR inspection checklist & site notes

Home Inspector name		Licence number	
Inspection date		Report reference number	
Address of property inspected		Post code	
Time of appointment:		Viewing arrangements:	
Arrival time :		Departure time:	

Circumstances of inspection:_____ Seller's questionnaire: Yes/No

Weather	Fine ☐ Windy ☐ Sunny ☐ Showers ☐ Heavy rain ☐ Frost ☐ Snow ☐	Comments on limitations/weather:	
Occupation	Owner ☐ Tenanted ☐ Vacant ☐		
Furnished	Yes ☐ No ☐ Part-furnished ☐	Date of construction	
Floor coverings	Full ☐ None ☐ Part ☐ Carpeted ☐ Other:	Alterations and date	
		Tenure	

PROPERTY TYPE HOUSE ☐ BUNGALOW ☐ CHALET ☐ FLAT ☐ MAISONETTE ☐ SHOP ☐

DETACHMENT DETACHED ☐ SEMI-DETACHED ☐ TERRACED ☐ END-TERRACED ☐ PURPOSE BUILT ☐ CONVERTED ☐

Accommodation

Number of rooms	Living rooms	Beds	Bath and/ or shower	Separate WC	Kitchen	Others
Basement/Lower ground floor						
Ground floor						
1st Floor						
2nd and other floors						
Total number of rooms						
Traditional construction:	Roof:					
	Walls:					
	Windows:					
	Floors:					

Non-traditional construction:	Material:								
	System name:								
Services:	Drainage		Gas		Electricity		Water		
Garage: Yes/No	Single/ Double		Integral		Off/on site		Parking space		

Gardens Are there any gardens? Front/Side/Rear?	
Roads/paths Are they made up?	
Conservation area Is the building listed or in a conservation area?	

Flats and Maisonettes	
Which floor and how many floors in the block? Number of flats in block? Purpose built or converted? Is there a lift? Are there any commercial uses? Percentage of building under commercial use? Current commercial use? Where in the building is the commercial operation situated?	
Legal/Environmental matters Highway adoption Rights of way Shared access Shared drains Flying freeholds Party wall issues Building regulations Planning permission Guarantees Conservation area/listed building Tree preservation orders Hazardous materials EMF Flooding Noise Smells	
Health and safety issues Asbestos Lead pipes Lead paint	

SITE PLAN (not to scale)

Key
Trees
Drain lines
Inspection chambers
Boundaries
Retaining walls

←⊕→ Orientation

Garden as part of site	
Front/side/rear	
Outbuildings Yes/no	
Number	
Roads made and adopted	

INSURANCE
FLOOR AREA
INTERIOR/EXTERIOR

TOTAL m²@£	£_____
CELLARS m²@£	£_____
UP. FLOORS m²@£	£_____
GARAGE	£_____
CONSERVATORY	£_____
OUTBUILDINGS	£_____
BOUNDARIES	£_____
DRAINAGE	£_____
TOTAL	£_____

Location

Established residential area ☐ Local authority ☐ Industrial ☐

Commercial ☐ Conservation area ☐ Listed building ☐ Rural ☐

OTHER:

FLOOR PLAN (not to scale)

Key

Damp

Floor covering

Wall covering

Ceiling covering

Room heights

FLOOR PLAN (not to scale)

FLOOR PLAN (not to scale)

	Key
	Damp
	Floor covering
	Wall covering
	Ceiling covering
	Room heights

Section and checklist	Movement (describe and draw sketch or refer to photographs)	Linked sections
Walls/cracks/plumbness/ bulges Floors/level/cracks Ceilings/cracks/bulges Window openings/cracks/ displacement/ binding casements Door openings/cracks/ displacement/binding doors Roof/level Skirtings/Architraves/gaps Underpinning Chimneys Heave Lintels Sills Trees Nearby drains Slopes/landslip Mining area Outbuildings/boundaries		
Section and checklist DPC External walls Internal walls Beneath flat roofs Beneath bathrooms Around bathroom fittings Chimney breasts Beneath valley gutters Staining to roof timbers Flashings Roof covering Around windows	**Dampness** (describe/note position on floor plan sketch and differentiate from condensation)	**Linked sections**
Section and checklist Subfloor vents Under stairs cupboard Around roof hatch Floors Windows Soffits and fascias Cupboards Damp affected areas Outbuildings	**Timber-related defects** (note suspect areas and timbers affected by rot/wood boring insects)	**Linked sections**

SECTION D – EXTERIOR CONDITION	
Section and checklist	**Description and condition**
D1 Chimney stacks Construction Height DPC Leaning Flues Flaunching Pointing Rendering Flashings Back gutters Sulphates Aerials, etc.	
D2 Roof coverings Construction Repairs? Recovered? Dish to slopes Roof spread Hip/ridge tiles Condition of slates/tiles Tingles Flashings to neighbouring properties Parapets Dormers Roof lights/windows Ventilation Flat roofs Falls Unseen areas	
SAP Main roof	Pitched … Flat … Other dwelling above …
SAP Extended roof	Pitched … Flat … Other dwelling above …
D3 Rainwater pipes and gutters Construction Condition Hopper heads Gullies Valley gutters Parapet gutters Unseen areas	

SECTION D – EXTERIOR CONDITION (continued)	
Section and checklist	**Description and condition**
D4 Main walls Construction *Stone/solid brick* *Cavity* *Timber frame* *System built* Thickness Movement Frame Lintels Sills Pointing Rendering Sulphate Cavity ties **Insulation** *External* *Cavity* *As built* *Unknown* *U value* Parapet DPC External ground/ internal floor levels Injection holes Efflorescence Stains **Wall SAP** Extension *Construction* *Insulation* *U value*	
D5 Windows Material Rot Rust Water leaks Usability Double glazing Secondary glazing Security fittings Sealants Guarantees **SAP**	
Area of glazing	Normal　　More than typical　　Less than typical
% double glazing	_____ %
Date of installation	pre 2002　　post/during 2002　　Don't know

SECTION D – EXTERIOR CONDITION (continued)	
Section and checklist	**Description and condition**
D6 External doors Type Condition Usability Thresholds/damp Seal to frame Draught stripping Hazardous glazing Weatherboard Ironmongery/Security Access/ramp	
D7 All other woodwork Fascias Soffits Decorative features (e.g. mock Tudor panels) Wood rot Ventilation to roof space through fascia Presence of asbestos	
D8 Claddings Material Condition Warped boarding Loose fixings Slipped tiles Loss of key	
SAP	Note material for wall assessment
D9 External decoration Type Lead paint Obscuring defects	
D10 Other Roof terraces Balconies Large dormers External stairs Fire escapes Railings	

SECTION E – INTERIOR CONDITION	
Section and checklist	**Description and condition**
E1 Roof space Inaccessible Close boarding Timber structure Lateral restraint/Roof spread Wind bracing Strengthening Alterations Loft conversion Room in roof Insulation Insulation thickness Cold water tank F&E tank Electricity Decay/infestation Chimney breasts Party/fire walls Damp penetration Birds/vermin/insects/bats **SAP**	
Main roof insulation at:	Rafters joists no access
Extension insulation at:	Rafters joists no access
Room in roof	
E2 Ceilings Distortion Key – lath and plaster Cracks Damp staining Lowered/Suspended Finishes Period features (e.g. covings, centre rose) Possible asbestos materials	

SECTION E – INTERIOR CONDITION (continued)	
Section and checklist	**Description and condition**
E3 Internal walls & partitions Settlement Subsidence Binding doors Loadbearing Non-loadbearing Non-robust partitions Through lounge Loss of key to plaster Shrinkage cracks Possible asbestos wall panels	
E4 Floors Construction Movement/binding doors Cracking Sulphate attack Slopes/hogging Ventilation to floor void Damp/DPM Rot/decay to timbers Beetle infestation Floor covering *Floor tiles* *Wood floor* *Sheet flooring*	
E5 Fireplaces & chimneys Lack of support to chimney breast Gas fires Open fires Flue liners Sealed flues Damp/condensation to chimney breast Staining to plaster Position of flues Condition of external flues	
SAP	Number of open fireplaces:

SECTION E – INTERIOR CONDITION (continued)	
Section and checklist	**Description and condition**
E6 Built-in fitments Kitchen fittings Damp fittings Wastes Bedroom fittings DIY Functionality Age	
E7 Internal woodwork Doors/binding Stairs Steep staircase Headroom Handrails & balusters H&S Under stair cupboard Skirtings Decay Beetle infestation	
E8 Bathroom fittings Bath WC Shower Bidets Age Condition Leaks Cracks Splashback/seals Dampness	
E9 Other Cellars Dampness Dry lining Tanking Services Ventilation Timber decay Infestation Habitable?	

SECTION F – SERVICES	
Section and checklist	**Description and condition**
F1 Electricity Mains entry Fuseboard Consumer unit RCD/MCB Visible wiring Sample of fittings Supplementary bonding External wiring and fittings Date of last test DIY features Old wiring Dangerous features **SAP** Electric meter type	 Single Dual Unknown
F2 Gas Mains entry Gas meter supply on/off Gas pipework Pipe ducts Fixed gas appliances Smell of gas Health & Safety issues LPG storage *Position* *Fire safety* *LPG piping*	
F3 Water Utility company stopvalve Water meter Rising main Stopcock Visible pipework External pipework and taps Hard/soft water Water softeners Cold and hot water storage tanks Insulation to tanks and pipes Overflow systems Private water supply *Water treatment system* *Date installed/inspected*	

SECTION F – SERVICES (continued)	
Section and checklist	**Description and condition**
F4 Heating Main heating source Gas/electric room heaters Heat distribution pipework Circulation pumps Motorised valves Heat emitters (radiators) Expansion vessels **HW tank** *Size* *Insulation type and thickness* **Heating controls** *Programmer* *Room thermostat* *Cylinder thermostat* *TRVs* Ventilation for open flue boilers/fires **Oil storage tanks** *Position* *Condition* *Fire safety* **SAP**	 Solar water heating? Yes/No Secondary heating? Yes/No Type and controls of secondary immersion heater system? Single/Dual
F5 Drainage Above and below ground Foul and grey water drainage Gullies Inspection chambers Rodding access points Extension over drains? Blockage? Shared? **Cess pits** *Type* *Amount emptied* **Septic tanks** *Type* *Age* *Distance from building* *Proximity to water source* *Smells* *Perm. To discharge?* **Soakaways** *Connection to?* *Distance from building*	

SECTION G – Grounds, Boundary Walls, Outbuildings, Garages and Common Facilities	
Section and checklist	**Description and condition**
Grounds Description Main paths/drives Hazards/health issues Nuisance Unauthorised use Commercial use Ponds/lakes Flooding Waterlogged areas Landslip Trees and shrubs Rights of way Shared access Radon EMF Local area/neighbouring uses Mining	
Boundaries Description of type/condition Ownership Retaining walls Moved boundaries	
Outbuildings Type Condition Hazards Asbestos Unsafe electrics Commercial use Attached to property	
Garages Type Construction Size Integral Fire proofing Attached to property SAP impact	
Conservatory Type/age Description Building regulations? Heated? Safety glass? Over drains? Open to house? Access to upper levels?	
SAP *Conservatory*	Floor area...m² Double Glazing? Yes/No Glazed perimeter...m² Room height: 1 storey 1.5 storey 2 storey 2.5 storey 3 storey

SECTION G – Grounds, Boundary Walls, Outbuildings, Garages and Common Facilities (continued)	
Section and checklist	**Description and condition**
Leisure facilities Type Description Attached to building? Condition of building	
Common facilities Staircases and associated hallways Shared garden/drying areas Bin stores Communal garages and forecourts, etc. Type Construction Condition Structural defects Usability	
Other	

PROPERTY RISK ASSESSMENT

Risk checklist	Identification of significant hazards (following brief walk around the property)	Level of risk (H/M/L)	Action required and/or taken (including special equipment needs)
Parking/road safety			
Empty property			
Access			
Animals			
Occupants			
Chemical substances/ syringes			
Vermin			
Construction			
Voids/holes			
Loft access			
Services			
Weather			
Other			

SCHEDULE OF PHOTOGRAPHS

Number	Photo description	Number	Photo description

Appendix H – Useful addresses and websites

The information contained in this appendix is correct at the time of going to press.

Awarding Body for the Built Environment (ABBE)
Edge Building
Perry Barr
Birmingham
B42 2SU
Tel: +44 (0)121 331 5174
www.uce.ac.uk/abbe

Asset Skills
6a Christchurch Road
Unit 16, Mobbs Miller House
Abington
Northampton NN1 5LL
Tel: +44 (0)1604 233336
Fax: +44 (0)1604 233573
www.assetskills.org

Association of British Insurers (ABI)
51 Gresham Street
London
EC2V 7HQ
Tel: +44 (0)20 7600 3333
Fax: +44 (0)20 7696 8999
www.abi.org.uk

Association of Building Engineers (ABE)
Lutyens House
Billing Brook Road
Weston Favell
Northampton
NN3 8NW
Tel: +44 (0)1604 404121
Fax: +44 (0)1604 784220
www.abe.org.uk

Association of Chief Estate Surveyors and Property Managers in Local Government (ACES)
23 Athol Road
Bramhall
Cheshire
SK7 1BR
Tel: +44 (0)161 439 9589
Fax: +44 (0)161 440 7383
www.aces.org.uk

Association of Consulting Engineers (ACE)
Alliance House
12 Caxton Street
London
SW1H 0QL
Tel: +44 (0)20 7222 6557
Fax: +44 (0)20 7222 0750
www.acenet.co.uk

British Board of Agrément (BBA)
PO Box 195
Bucknalls Lane
Garston
Watford
Hertfordshire
WD25 9BA
Tel: +44 (0)1923 665300
Fax: +44 (0)1923 665301
www.bbacerts.co.uk

British Geological Survey (BGS)
Kingsley Dunham Centre
Keyworth
Nottingham
NG12 5GG
Tel: +44 (0) 115 936 3100
Fax: +44 (0) 115 936 3200
www.bgs.ac.uk, www.bgs.ac.uk/geoindex, www.bgs.ac.uk/georeports

British Institute of Architectural Technologists (BIAT)
397 City Road
London
EC1V 1NH
Tel: +44 (0)20 7278 2206
Fax: +44 (0)20 7837 3194
www.biat.org.uk

British Standards Institution (BSI)
389 Chiswick High Road
London
W4 4AL
Tel: +44 (0)20 8996 9000
Fax: +44 (0)20 8996 7001
www.bsi-global.com

Building Services Research and Information Association (BSRIA)
BSRIA Ltd.
Old Bracknell Lane West
Bracknell
Berkshire
RG12 7AH
Tel: +44 (0) 1344 465600
Fax: +44 (0) 1344 465626
www.bsria.co.uk

Building Cost Information Service (BCIS)
3 Cadogan Gate
London
SW1X 0AS
Tel: +44 (0)20 7695 1500
Fax: +44 (0)20 7695 1501
www.bcis.co.uk

Building Research Establishment
Bucknalls Lane
Garston
Watford
WD25 9XX
Tel: +44 (0)1923 664000
www.bre.co.uk

British Wood Preserving and Damp Proofing Association (BWPDA)
1 Gleneagles House
Vernon Gate
Derby
DE1 1UP
Tel: +44 (0)1332 225100
Fax: +44 (0)1332 225101
www.bwpda.co.uk

Chartered Institute of Environmental Health (CIEH)
Chadwick Court
15 Hatfields,
London SE1 8DJ
Tel: +44 (0)20 7928 6006
Fax: +44 (0)20 7827 5862
www.cieh.org

Chartered Institute of Building (CIOB)
Englemere
Kings Ride
Ascot
Berks
SL5 7TB
Tel: +44 (0)1344 630700
Fax: +44 (0)1344 630777
www.ciob.org.uk

Chartered Institute of Housing (CIH)
Octavia House
Westwood Way
Coventry
CV4 8JP
Tel: +44 (0)24 7685 1700
Fax: +44 (0)24 7669 5110
www.cih.org

Chartered Institute of Building Services Engineers (CIBSE)
222 Balham High Road
London
SW12 9BS
Tel: +44 (0)20 8675 5211
Fax: +44 (0)20 8675 5449
www.cibse.org

Construction Industry Research and Information Association (CIRIA)
Classic House
174–180 Old Street
London
EC1V 9BP
Tel: +44 (0)20 7549 3300
Fax: +44 (0)20 7253 0523
www.ciria.org.uk

CORGI (The Council for Registered Gas Installers)
1 Elmwood
Chineham Park
Crockford Lane
Basingstoke
Hants
RG24 8WG
Tel: +44 (0)870 401 2200
Fax: +44 (0)870 401 2600
www.corgi-gas-safety.com

Elmhurst Energy Systems Ltd.
Elmhurst Farm
Bow Lane
Withybrook
Coventry CV7 9LQ
Tel: +44 (0)1788 833386
Fax: +44 (0)1788 832690
www.elmhurstenergy.co.uk

English Heritage
PO Box 569
Swindon
SN2 2YP
Tel: +44 (0)870 333 1181
Fax: +44 (0)1793 414926
www.english-heritage.org.uk

The Environment Agency
For information on regional offices, contact General Enquiries (+44 (0)8708 506 506) or visit www.environment-agency.gov.uk

Federation of Authorised Energy Rating Organisations (FAERO)
For information on FAERO's member organisations, see entries for Elmhurst Energy Systems Ltd., MVM Consultants Plc. and National Energy Services

Forestry and Timber Association (FTA)
5 Dublin Street Lane South
Edinburgh
EH1 3PX
Tel: +44 (0)131 538 7111
Fax: +44 (0)131 538 7222
www.forestryandtimber.org

Glass and Glazing Federation (GGF)
44–48 Borough High Street
London
SE1 1XB
Tel: +44 (0)870 042 4255
Fax: +44 (0)870 042 4266
www.ggf.co.uk

Home Inspector Certification Board (HICB)
c/o Property Industry Research Ltd.
PO Box 3546
Ferndown
Dorset
BH22 0XP
Tel: +44 (0)1202 890988
www.hicb.co.uk

Health and Safety Executive (HSE)
Magdalen House
Trinity Road
Bootle
Merseyside
L20 3QZ
Tel: +44 (0) 8701 545 500
www.hse.gov.uk

Institution of Civil Engineers (ICE)
1 Great George Street
London
SW1P 3AA
Tel: +44 (0)20 7222 7722
www.ice.org.uk

Institution of Civil Engineering Surveyors (ICES)
Dominion House
Sibson Road
Sale
Cheshire
M33 7PP
Tel: +44 (0)161 972 3100
Fax: +44 (0)161 972 3118
www.ices.org.uk

Institute of Clerks of Works of Great Britain Incorporated (ICW)
Equinox
28 Commerce Road
Lynch Wood
Peterborough
PE2 6LR
Tel: +44 (0)1733 405160
Fax: +44 (0)1733 405161
www.icwgb.org

Institution of Electrical Engineers (IEE)
Savoy Place
London
WC2R 0BL
Tel: +44 (0)20 7240 1871
Fax: +44 (0)20 7240 7735
www.iee.org

Institute of Maintenance and Building Management (IMBM)
Keets House
30 East Street
Farnham
Surrey GU9 7SW
Tel: +44 (0)1252 710994
Fax: +44 (0)1252 737741
www.imbm.org.uk

Institute of Remedial Treatment Surveyors (IRTS)
Essex House
High Street
Chipping Ongar
Essex
CM5 9EB
Tel: +44 (0)800 915 6363
Fax: +44 (0)870 755 5432
www.irts.co.uk

Independent Surveyors Association (ISA)
Broadbury
Okehampton
Devon EX20 4NH
Tel: +44 (0)1837 871700
www.surveyorsweb.co.uk

Institution of Structural Engineers (IstructE)
11 Upper Belgrave Street
London
SW1X 8BH
Tel: +44 (0)20 7235 4535
Fax: +44 (0)20 7235 4294
www.istructe.org.uk

Lead Development Association International (LDAI)
42 Weymouth Street
London W1G 6NP
Tel: +44 (0)20 7499 8422
Fax: +44 (0)20 7493 1555
www.ldaint.org

MVM Consultants
MVM House
2 Oakfield Road
Clifton
Bristol BS8 2AL
Tel: +44 (0)117 9744477
Fax: +44 (0)117 9706897
www.mvm.co.uk

National Association of Estate Agents (NAEA)
Arbon House
21 Jury Street
Warwick
CV34 4EH
Tel: +44 (0)1926 496800
www.naea.co.uk

National Energy Services Ltd.
The National Energy Centre
Davy Avenue
Knowlhill
Milton Keynes
MK5 8NA
Tel: +44 (0)1908 672787
Fax: +44 (0)1908 662296
www.nesltd.co.uk

National House Building Council (NHBC)
Buildmark House
Chiltern Avenue
Amersham
Buckinghamshire HP6 5AP
Tel: +44 (0)1494 735363
www.nhbc.co.uk

National Inspection Council for Electrical Installation Contracting (NICEIC)
Vintage House
37 Albert Embankment
London SE1 7UJ
Tel: +44 (0)20 7564 2323
Fax: +44 (0)20 7564 2370
www.niceic.org.uk

National Radiological Protection Board (NRPB)
Chilton
Didcot
Oxon
OX11 0RQ
Tel: +44 (0)1235 831600
Fax: +44 (0)1235 833891
www.nrpb.org

Office of the Deputy Prime Minister (ODPM)
26 Whitehall
London
SW1 2WH
Tel: +44 (0)20 7944 4400
www.odpm.gov.uk

Ordnance Survey
Romsey Road
Southampton
SO16 4GU
Tel: (UK) 08456 05 05 05
Fax: (UK) 023 8079 2615
www.ordnancesurvey.co.uk

Qualifications and Curriculum Authority (QCA)
83 Piccadilly
London
W1J 8QA
Tel: +44 (0)20 7509 5555
Fax: +44 (0)20 7509 6666
www.qca.org.uk

Royal Institute of British Architects (RIBA)
66 Portland Place
London
W1B 1AD
Tel: +44 (0)20 7580 5533
www.architecture.com

RICS Books
Surveyor Court
Westwood Way
Coventry
CV4 8JE
Tel: +44 (0)20 7222 7000
(or 0870 333 1600 Contact Centre)
www.ricsbooks.com

Royal Institution of Chartered Surveyors (RICS)
12 Great George Street
London
SW1P 3AD
Tel: +44 (0)20 7222 7000
(or 0870 333 1600 Contact Centre)
www.rics.org

Royal Institution of Chartered Surveyors (Scotland)
9 Manor Place
Edinburgh
EH3 7DN
Tel: +44 (0)131 225 7078
Fax: +44 (0)131 240 0830
www.rics-scotland.org.uk

Surveyors and Valuers Accreditation (SAVA)
PO Box 5603
Milton Keynes
MK5 8XR
Tel: +44 (0)870 837 6565
Fax: +44 (0)870 837 6566
www.sava.org.uk

SEDBUK (Seasonal Efficiency of Domestic Boilers in the UK)
www.sedbuk.com

Society for the Protection of Ancient Buildings (SPAB)
37 Spital Square
London
E1 6DY
Tel: +44 (0)20 7377 1644
Fax: +44 (0)20 7247 5296
www.spab.org.uk

Soil Association
Bristol House
40–56 Victoria Street
Bristol
BS1 6BY
Tel: +44 (0)117 314 5000
Fax: +44 (0)117 314 5001
www.soilassociation.org

Subsidence Claims Advisory Bureau
Charter House
43 St. Leonards Road
Bexhill-on-Sea
East Sussex
TN40 1JA
Tel: +44 (0)1424 733727
Fax: +44 (0)1424 731781
www.subsidencebureau.com

The Suzy Lamplugh Trust
PO Box 17818
London
SW14 8WW
Tel: +44 (0)20 8876 0305
Fax: +44 (0)20 8876 0891
www.suzylamplugh.org

Town and Country Planning Association (TCPA)
17 Carlton House Terrace
London
SW1Y 5AS
Tel: +44 (0)20 7930 8903
Fax: +44 (0)20 7930 3280
www.tcpa.org.uk

UK legislation
UK legislation from 1988 onward is published on the HMSO website
www.hmso.gov.uk/legislation/about_legislation.htm.
UK legislation prior to 1988 may be purchased through The Stationery Office Limited (TSO).
HMSO legislation enquiries tel: 020 7276 5210

UK Steel Association
Broadway House
Tothill Street
London
SW1H 9NQ
Tel: +44 (0)20 7222 7777
Fax: +44 (0)20 7222 2782
www.uksteel.org.uk

Further reading

Architects Journal, *Art of Construction*, AJ Information Library, 1981

Architects Journal, *Corrosion*, AJ Guide to Building Failures, 1978, Technical Study

Architects Journal, *Diagnosis principles and procedures*, AJ Guide to Building Failures, 1978, Technical Study 3

Architects Journal, *Failures in Context*, AJ Guide to Building Failures, 1978, Information Sheet

ASI, *Repair and Maintenance of Brickwork*, ASI Journal, Vol. 10, No 3, Sept. 1998

Barry, R., *The Construction of Buildings: Windows, Doors, Fires, Stairs, Finishes (volume 2)*, Blackwell Science, 1999 (ISBN 0 6320 5092 6)

BCA, *Basement Waterproofing: Design Guide*, British Cement Association, Crowthorne, 1994 (ISBN 0 7210 1475 5)

BCIS, *Housing Repair Cost Guide*, BCIS Limited, 2004 (ISBN 190482 910 4)

Biddle, P. G., *Patterns of soil drying and moisture deficit in the vicinity of trees on clay soils*, Geotechnique, 1983

Bonshor, R. B. and Bonshor, L. L. (1996), *Cracking in Buildings*, Garston, BRE Bookshop, Ref. BR 292. Available from IHS Rapidoc (BRE Bookshop), Willoughby Road, Bracknell, RG12 8DW

BRE, *Alkali-silica reaction in concrete*, BRE Digest 330: Part 1, Building Research Establishment, Watford, 1997 (ISBN 1 86081 158 2)

BRE, *Assessment of damage in low-rise buildings*, BRE Digest 251, BRE Bookshop, Watford, 1995 (ISBN 1 86081 045 4)

BRE, *Assessment of existing high alumina cement concrete construction in the UK*, BRE Digest 392, Building Research Establishment, Watford, 1994 (ISBN 0 85125 625 2)

BRE, *Cementitious renders for external walls*, BRE Digest 410, Building Research Establishment, Watford, 1995 (ISBN 1 86081 047 0)

BRE, *Common defects in low-rise traditional housing*, BRE Digest 268, Building Research Establishment, Watford, 1982 (ISBN 0 11726 844 5)

BRE, *Concrete: cracking and corrosion of reinforcement*, BRE Digest 389, Building Research Establishment, Watford, 1983 (ISBN 0 85125 619 8)

BRE, *Concrete: Part 1: materials*, BRE Digest 325, Building Research Establishment, Watford, 1987 (ISBN 0 85215 268 0)

BRE, *Concrete: Part 2: specification, design and quality control*, BRE Digest 326, Building Research Establishment, Watford, 1987 (ISBN 0 85215 269 9)

BRE, *Condensation Checklist*, (AP58), Building Research Establishment, Watford

BRE, *Connecting floors and walls: A practical guide*, BRE Good Building Guide 29: Part 1, Building Research Establishment, Watford, 1997 (ISBN 1 86081 182 5)

BRE, *Connecting floors and walls: Design and performance*, BRE Good Building Guide 29: Part 2, Building Research Establishment, Watford, 1997 (ISBN 1 86081 183 3)

BRE, *Corrosion of steel in concrete*, BRE Digest 444 (Parts 1–3), Building Research Establishment, Watford, 2000 (ISBN 1 86081 360 7) (ISBN 1 86081 361 5) (ISBN 1 86081 362 3)

BRE, *Cracks caused by foundation movement*, BRE Good Repair Guide 1, Building Research Establishment, Watford, 1996 (ISBN 1 86081 097 7)

BRE, *Damage to buildings caused by trees*, BRE Good Repair Guide 2, Building Research Establishment, Watford, 1996 (ISBN 1 86081 098 5)

BRE, *Durability of pre-cast HAC concrete in buildings*, BRE Information Paper 8/00, Building Research Establishment, Watford, 2000 (ISBN 1 86081 368 2)

BRE, *Estimation of thermal and moisture movements and stresses: Part 2*, BRE Digest 228: Part 2, Building Research Establishment, Watford, 1979 (ISBN 0 11725 037 6)

BRE, *External masonry walls: eroding mortars – repoint or build?*, BRE Defect Action Sheet (Design) DAS 70, Building Research Establishment, Watford, 1986

BRE, *External masonry walls: vertical joints for thermal and moisture movements*, BRE Defect Action Sheet (Design) DAS 18, Building Research Establishment, Watford, 1983

BRE, *Foundation for low-rise building extensions*, BRE Good Building Guide 53, Building Research Establishment, Watford, 2002 (ISBN 1 86081 589 8)

BRE, *Ground Floors: Replacing Suspended Timber with Solid Concrete dpcs & dpms, Defect Action Sheet (DAS22)*, Building Research Establishment, Watford, 1983

BRE, *Hardcore*, BRE Digest 276, Building Research Establishment, Watford, 1983 (ISBN 0 11726 853 4)

BRE, *Installing wall ties in existing construction*, BRE Digest 329, Building Research Establishment, Watford, 2000 (ISBN 1 86081 405 0)

BRE, *Low-rise buildings foundations: the influence of trees in clay soils*, BRE Digest 298, Building Research Establishment, Watford, 1999 (ISBN 1 86081 278 3)

BRE, *Low-rise buildings on shrinkable clay soils: Part 1*, BRE Digest 240, Building Research Establishment, Watford, 1980 (ISBN 0 11725 065 1)

BRE, *Low-rise buildings on shrinkable clay soils: Part 2*, BRE Digest 241, Building Research Establishment, Watford, 1980 (ISBN 0 11725 066)

BRE, *Monitoring building and ground movement by precise levelling*, BRE Digest 386, Building Research Establishment, Watford, 1993 (ISBN 0 85215 608 2)

BRE, *Repairing brick and block masonry*, BRE Digest 359, Building Research Establishment, Watford, 1991 (ISBN 0 85125 485 3)

BRE, *Repairing Brickwork*, BRE Digest 200, Building Research Establishment, Watford, 1977 (ISBN 0 11724 112 1)

BRE, *Repairing Flood Damage: Foundations and Walls* (BRE Good Repair Guide; 11 Part 3), CRC Ltd., London, 1997 (ISBN 1 86081 152 3)

BRE, *Repairing Flood Damage: Ground Floors and Basements* (BRE Good Repair Guide; 11 Part 2), CRC Ltd., London, 1997 (ISBN 1 86081 151 5)

BRE, *Repairing Flood Damage: Immediate Action* (BRE Good Repair Guide; 11 Part 1), CRC Ltd., London, 1997 (ISBN 1 86081 150 7)

BRE, *Repairing Flood Damage: Services, Secondary Elements, Finishes, Fittings* (BRE Good Repair Guide; 11 Part 4), CRC Ltd., London, 1997 (ISBN 1 86081 153 1)

BRE, *Simple measuring and monitoring of movement in low-rise buildings: Part 1: cracks*, BRE Digest 343: Part 1, Building Research Establishment, Watford, 1989 (ISBN 0 85125 380 6)

BRE, *Simple measuring and monitoring of movement in low-rise buildings: Part 2:settlement, heave and out-of-plumb*, BRE Digest 344, Building Research Establishment, Watford, 1995 (ISBN 1 86081 043 8)

BRE, *Site Investigation for Low-rise Building: Trial Pits*, BRE Digest (DG381), Building Research Establishment, Watford, 1993 (ISBN 0 895125 570 1)

BRE, *Surveying masonry chimneys for repair or rebuilding*, BRE Good Building Guide (GBG2), Building Research Establishment, Watford, 1990

BRE, *Tilt of low-rise buildings*, BRE Digest 475, Building Research Establishment, Watford, 2003 (ISBN 1 86081 613 4)

BRE, *Treating Damp in Basements* (BRE Good Repair Guide; 23), CRC Ltd., Watford, 1999 (ISBN 1 86081 277 5)

BRE, *Wall cladding defects and their diagnosis*, BRE Digest 217, Building Research Establishment, Watford, 1978 (ISBN 0 11724 145 8)

BRE, *Why do buildings crack?*, BRE Digest 361, Building Research Establishment, Watford, 1991 (ISBN 0 85125 476 4)

Brett, P, *Building Terminology*, Butterworth-Heinemann, Oxford, 1989 (ISBN 0 75063 684 X)

British Chemical Dampcourse Association , *The Use of Moisture Meters to Establish the Presence of Rising Damp*, (Technical Information 1), British Chemical Dampcourse Association, Reading, 1980

BSI, *Code of practice for Drainage of roofs and paved areas*, BS EN 12056–3:2000, British Standards Institution, London, 2000 (ISBN 0 58013 402 4)

BSI, *Code of practice for External renderings*, BS 5262: 1991, British Standards Institution, London, 1991 (ISBN 0 58014 368 6)

BSI, *Code of practice for Installation of resilient floor coverings*, BS 8203: 1996, British Standards Institution, London, 1996 (ISBN 0 58025 743 6)

BSI, *Code of Practice for Protection of Structures against Water from the Ground* (BS 8102: 1990) , British Standards Institution, London, 1990 (ISBN 0 58017 897 8)

BSI, *Code of practice for Use of masonry: Part 1: Structural use of unreinforced masonry, BS 5628: Part 1*: 1992, British Standards Institution, London, 1992 (ISBN 0 58021 113 4)

BSI, *Code of practice for Use of masonry: Part 2: Structural use of reinforced and prestressed masonry, BS 5628: Part 2*: 1985, British Standards Institution, London, 1985 (ISBN 0 58014 363 5)

BSI, *Code of practice for Use of masonry: Part 3: Materials and components, design and workmanship, BS 5628*: 1985, British Standards Institution, London, 1985 (ISBN 0 58014 368 6)

BSI, *Construction and Testing of Drains and Sewers, EN 1610*, British Standards Institution, London, 1998 (ISBN 0 580 28885 4)

BSI, *Guide to accuracy in building, BS 5606: 1990*, British Standards Institution, London, 1990 (ISBN 0 58018 657 1)

BSI, *Lead and lead alloys: Rolled lead sheet for building purposes, BS EN 12588*:1999, British Standards Institution, London, 1999 (ISBN 0 58032 668 3)

BSI, *Methods of Test for Masonry Units (Part 7 of BS EN 772–7: 1998)*, British Standards Institution, London, 1998 (ISBN 0 580 30696 8)

BSI, *Structural use of concrete: code of practice for special circumstances, BS 8110: Part 2: 1985*, British Standards Institution, London, 1985 (ISBN 0 58014 490 9)

BSI, *Structural use of concrete: design charts for singly reinforced beams and rectangular columns, BS 8110: Part 3: 1985*, British Standards Institution, London, 1985 (ISBN 0 58014 781 9)

Building Employers Federation, *Definition of Prime Cost of Daywork Carried Out Under a Building Contract* (2nd edition), RICS/BEC, 1975 (ISBN 0 85406 059 6)

Burberry, P., *Environment and Services* (8th edition), Longman Scientific and Technical, Harlow, 1997 (ISBN 0 58224 521 4)]

Burkinshaw, R., *Dampness Abounding*, SPAB News, September 2001, Society for the Protection of Ancient Buildings, 2001

Burkinshaw, R. and Parrett, M., *Diagnosing Damp*, RICS Books, 2003 (ISBN 1 84219 097 0)

Burkinshaw, R., *The Round Chapel Comes Full Circle* (Chartered Surveyor Monthly 5(5)), 1996

BWPDA, *Lime Mortar vs Cement, Preserve* (Summer 2003), British Wood Preserving and Damp-proofing Association, 2003

Chanter, B. and Swallow, P. Building Maintenance Management, Blackwell Publishing, 2000 (ISBN 0 63205 766 1)

Construction Industry Research and Information Association, *Water-resisting Basement Construction – A Guide – Safeguarding New and Existing Basements Against Water and Dampness (CIRIA Report 139)*, CIRIA, London, 1995 (ISBN 0 72772 042 2)

Crilly, M. S. and Driscoll, R. M. C., *Subsidence damage to domestic buildings: lessons learned and questions remaining*, FBE Report 1, Sept. 2000, Foundation for the Built Environment

CSM, *The case of the cracked partitions*, CSM Nov 1994

Currie, R. J. and Robery, P. G., *Repair and Maintenance of Reinforced Concrete*, BRE Report 254, Building Research Establishment, Watford, 1994 (ISBN 0 85125 623 6)

Cutler, D. F. and Richardson, I. B. K., *Tree roots and buildings* (second edition), Longman, Harlow, 1989, HMSO (ISBN 0 58203 410 8)

Department of Trade and Industry, *Rethinking Construction*, 1998.

Dickinson, P. and Thornton, N., *Cracking and Building Movement*, RICS Books, 2004 (ISBN 1 84219 156 X)

EA/CIRIA, *After a Flood – how to restore your home*, Environment Agency/CIRIA, 2001

EA/CIRIA, *Damage Limitation – how to make your home flood resistant*, Environment Agency/CIRIA, 2001

Hollis, M., *Surveying Buildings* (5th edition revised), RICS Books, Coventry, 2005 (ISBN 1 84219 192 6)

Howell, J., *Moisture Measurement in Masonry: Guidance for Surveyors COBRA '95*, RICS Construction and Building Research Conference, 1995

Institute of Measurement and Control, *A Guide to the Measurement of Humidity*, Institute of Measurement and Control, London, 1996

ISE, *Subsidence of low-rise buildings: a guide for professionals and owners*, Institution of Structural Engineers, London, 2000 (ISBN 1 87426 654 9)

Lead Sheet Association, *Rolled Lead Sheet: The Complete Manual*, Lead Sheet Association, Tunbridge Wells, 2003

Loss Prevention Council, *Property subject to structural movement: guidelines on the assessment of cracks, Loss Prevention Council Report LPR3*, Fire Protection Association, 1995

MCB UP Ltd, *The significance of cracks in low-rise buildings*, Structural Survey, vol. 20 No 5 2002

Monk, W., *External Rendering, Appearance Matters 2*, British Cement Association, Crowthorne, 1992, (ISBN 0 72101 364 3)

Murdoch, J. *Negligence in Valuations and Surveys*, RICS Books, 2002 (ISBN 1 84219 072 5)

Nanayakkara, R., *Condition Survey of Building Services*, AG 4/2000, BSRIA, 2000, (ISBN 0 86022 551 8)

NHBC, *Movement Joints Below DPC*, NHBC Technical Newsletter Dec 2002

NHBC, *NHBC Standards*, Chapter 4.2 and 4.3, July 2003

NHBC, *Precautions to take when building near trees*, Practice Note 3, National House Building Council, 1985

Nicholas, J. and Proverbs, D., *Surveying Flood Damage to Domestic Dwellings: the Present State of Knowledge* (RICS Foundation Research Paper Series: 3(8)), RICS Research Foundation, London, 2000 (ISBN 0 84219 033 4)

ODPM, English House Condition Survey, 2001 (ISBN 1 85112 686 4)

Oxley, R., *Do's and Don'ts Guide 3 – Damp and Timber Treatment*, RICS, 1997

Oxley, R., *Ignore it and it will go away!* (Building Conservation Journal 13), 1995

Parnham, P. and Rispin, C., *Residential Property Appraisal*, Spon Press, 2001 (ISBN 0 41922 570 6)

Parrett, M.J., *Managing Disrepair in Local Authority Housing: The Misdiagnosis of Rising Damp using Electrical Moisture Meters Professional paper 97009*, Institute of Maintenance and Building Management, Farnham, 1997

Paterson, B., *Dealing effectively with wall tie failure*, Preserve (Spring 2003), British Wood Preserving and Damp-proofing Association, 2003

Reville, J., *Surveying Safely – Rights and Responsibilities*, Structural Survey, 16 (4), 1998

RICS, *Code of Measuring Practice – A Guide for Surveyors and Valuers*, RICS Books, Coventry, 2001 (ISBN 1 84219 060 1)

RICS, *Surveyors Acting as Expert Witnesses* (2nd edition), Practice Statement and Guidance Note, RICS Books, Coventry, 2001 (ISBN 1 85406 960 7)

Singh, J., *The Built Environment and the Development of Fungi*, E & F.N. Spon, London, 1994

The Builder Group, *Floor Flaws*, Building, November 1992 (now published by CMP Information)

The Builder Group, *Still crazing – concrete slabs and screeds*, Building, April 1990 (now published by CMP Information)

Thomas, A. R., *The Control of Damp in Old Buildings*, Technical Pamphlet (TP/8), Society for the Protection of Ancient Buildings, London, 1986

Ward, W. H., *The effects of fast growing trees on shallow foundations*, Journal of the Institute of Landscape Architects, 1947

Williams, G.B.A., *Chimneys in Old Buildings* (3rd edition), Technical Pamphlet (TP/3), Society for the Protection of Ancient Buildings, London, 1989

Index